Method in Translation History

Anthony Pym

St. Jerome Publishing
Manchester, UK

First published 1998 by

St. Jerome Publishing
2 Maple Road West, Brooklands
Manchester, M23 9HH, United Kingdom
Telephone +44 161 973 9856
Fax +44 161 905 3498

ken@stjeromepublishing.com
http://www.stjerome.co.uk

ISBN 1-900650-12-6

Printed and bound in Great Britain by
4edge Limited, Hockley, Essex, UK

Cover: Maylis Ayats Caminade and John Pym Caminade
Photo: Cécile Caminade

Cover design by Steve Fieldhouse, Oldham, UK (+44 161 620 2263)

British Library Cataloguing in Publication Data
A catalogue record of this book is available from the British Library.

Library of Congress Cataloging in Publication Data
A catalogue record of this book is available from the Library of Congress.

Contents

Preface

The problems of carrying out research on past translators and past translations should, by rights, constitute a fairly obscure topic, of interest to no more than the occasional graduate student. Yet translation history has attracted considerable academic interest in recent years, as indeed have all aspects of translation theory and practice. As a part of the much wider problem of how cultures should interrelate, historiographical methods in this field go well beyond narrow technical skills; they are of concern to the many neighbouring disciplines that translation studies now draws on and to which, in the best of cases, it can contribute. Translation history can be a source of ideas and data for the political or sociological study of international relations; it might have more than a few words to say in the development of language policies; its models should be able to address the increasing internationalization of audiovisual culture; it has a great deal to contribute to the general history of literature and of ideas, especially given the way nationalist paradigms have traditionally excluded translators from such fields of inquiry. Any attempt to develop a method for translation history must thus be prepared to address at least two related questions: first, how to do translation history (for people who are going to do some); second, why it should be done one way rather than another (for people who want to relate translation history to wider concerns in the humanities). This book tries to ask both these questions, addressing them with both potential readerships in mind.

My main concerns in the first six or so chapters are with practical aspects like how to identify a problem to be solved, how to make a list of translations, how to plot translations and translators on a map, and what it actually means to arrange elements in a system. Readers in search of more purely theoretical ideas might find some of this material cook-bookish, although I do not believe that technical discussions are only for technicians.

A few largish ideas nevertheless start to stir from about chapter seven, where the dominant concepts of descriptive translation studies are reviewed in terms of international relations, the allusiveness of causation, the identity of translators, a search for interculturality, and a few laments about the current lack of any strong interdisciplinary framework adequate to the task. If you like, the second half of this book is for those more interested in the theory than the practice of translation history. Yet my overall aim is to explore the relations between the two sides, hopefully encouraging each potential readership to consider seriously the perspectives of the other.

Given that this general aim requires me to position myself rather explicitly,

I have sought to discuss problems in a fairly personal way, on the basis of my own experience. This has meant writing in search of a method, not in defence of one; I am interested in postulates, not axioms. The result involves only brief discussions about what history is or what translations could be. Nor have I been overly worried about inventing names for things. In fact, despite my desire to focus on methodology, I often find myself trying to deflate the more theoretical aspects of translation history, insisting that the real knowledge comes from the study of history itself. A good deal of this book is based on the argument that historians should grapple quite directly with their material, getting their hands dirty before elaborating any grand principles concerning the methodology of their task. In keeping with this stance, the ideas have been at every stage elaborated while I was working on the history of past translators.

So why should I now present the ideas more or less by themselves?

One of the answers is that I like to keep my actual translation history relatively free of theoretical reflections. If I am writing about the twelfth-century School of Toledo, for example, I believe the results of my research should speak for themselves, regardless of what methods I use to reach them. This is in accordance with a certain separation of discourses proposed in the first chapter of this book.

A slightly better response is to insist that theorization is not some alien element accidentally embedded in the historian's descriptive practice. It is itself a practice, with its own narrative qualities. The idea of theorization-as-practice can be appreciated on several levels: as the legitimate and necessary activity of arguing against other theories, as a way of making someone think about how to do translation history, as a confessional peek into the laboratory behind the scenes, or simply as a process of self-reflection for the perplexed. In the case of this book, despite any pedagogical virtues in an ostensibly step-by-step approach, my theorization has its origins awash in the last-mentioned waters, those of perplexity. Most of my reflections on method have actually evolved from very practical methodological mistakes. You only have to navigate when you feel lost; I have only sought a method in moments when I felt I had none. The resulting kind of theorization is very much a part of practice, no matter how silent its workings.

Here is my first mistake: During much of 1992-93 I found myself carrying out two research projects at virtually the same time. One was on twelfth-century Hispania; the other was on translation flows between French and German poetry at the end of the nineteenth century. The fields were so different that they seemed not to belong to the same discipline. There was little information on twelfth-century translations; there was too much on nineteenth-century work.

One project required careful attention to manuscript traditions; the other needed publishers' statistics. Medievalists were arguing about commas; modernists were busy defending social classes, genders and various ideas of progress or non-progress. Given the very different objects, the two projects involved quite different problematics, approaches and methods. However, since both studies concerned the history of translation, I felt in some way obliged to apply the same concepts and procedures. When something gave interesting results in the nineteenth century, I tried to make it work in the twelfth, and vice versa. This was good fun. But my research was very quickly in a mess.

This book has its origins in the notes I took to sort out the mess. The notes were essentially logbook reflections, founded not on pride but on personal questioning. True, I have done a lot of rearranging to make the result look reasonably coherent and consequential, going from fundamental issues to the more complex concepts. Yet no one should feel obliged to follow the steps one after the other. The various chapters are best read as fragmentary sketches for procedures that are not yet in place. I do not claim to have cleaned up all the mess. This also means my examples are rather more than examples; they are not mere illustrations that placidly confirm any grand theory. They are instead part and parcel of the theoretical reflections, since they have played their role in transforming, falsifying and occasionally confirming my ideas about translation history.

Despite this tentative spirit, I am prepared to formulate four principles that gradually emerged from the research process, although not all on the same level or with the same potential use to other researchers:

1. The first principle says that translation history should explain *why* translations were produced in a particular social time and place. In other words, translation history should address problems of social causation. This seems straightforward until you realize that narrowly empirical methods – the kind we find in many systemic descriptive approaches – are fundamentally unable to model social causation.
2. The second principle is that the central object of historical knowledge should not be the text of the translation, nor its contextual system, nor even its linguistic features. The central object should be the human translator, since only humans have the kind of responsibility appropriate to social causation. Only through translators and their social entourage (clients, patrons, readers) can we try to understand why translations were produced in a particular historical time and place. To understand why translations happened, we have to look at the people involved. True, a focus on people should not condemn us to random anecdotes and details: this book will take some nine chapters to construct a field of socially conditioned subjectivity as a preliminary to

the history of translators. Yet the ultimate focus of attention must remain human rather than textual, almost in spite of the constraints of method.

3. The third principle follows on from the above. If translation history is to focus on translators, it must organize its world around the social contexts where translators live and work. These contexts are nowadays commonly assumed to be target cultures. If I translate into English, I am somehow supposed to belong to English-language culture (which one?); I am perhaps even supposed to be dominated by English-language clients and patrons. Yet here I am, a professional translator born in Australia and living in Spain, selling translations and teaching translation in a situation I consider neither exotic nor atypical. In this professional context I cannot help but fix part of my attention on at least one culture beyond my native English, notably the Spanish/Catalan culture of my clients, source texts and students. So how can I be identified with any supposed monoculture? More important, if monocultural identifications are not consistently possible, many more translators than just myself stand a good chance of finding themselves in the intersections or overlaps of cultures, in what I would like to call 'intercultures'. Of course, the hypothetical interculturality of translators could be shared by all kinds of intermediaries, from diplomats and traders through to spies and smugglers. Such people might even form intercultural social groups. As chance would have it, this is a suggestive and sometimes successful idea for the particular periods and places I have been working on. It has become a principle of the way I organize translation history. As a general working hypothesis, then, translators tend to be intercultural, although far more research must be done before we can hope to give this term 'intercultural' a precise programmatic meaning.

4. The fourth principle concerns the reasons why anyone would want to do translation history in the first place. It basically states that the reasons – and my own reasons will be explained somewhere near the end of chapter one – exist in the present. We do translation history in order to express, address and try to solve problems affecting our own situation. This does not mean we blatantly project ourselves onto the past. On the contrary, the past is an object that must be made to respond to our questions, indicating categories and potential solutions that we had not previously thought of. Yet our initial point of departure is always the here and now. There should be no illusions on this point. The priority of the present is not only unavoidable but also highly desirable; I am in favour of serious subjective involvement in translation history. If humans are to stand at the centre of our object, then our historiographical subjectivity must also be humanized.

Here again are my four general principles for a particular kind of translation history: attention to causation, a focus on the human translator, a hypothesis projecting intercultural belonging, and the priority of the present. None of these ideas are radically new; they all float in the intellectual air of our age. What might be new, though, is that I have sought to make them talk, together, in terms of the actual practice of translation history.

If any of the above principles find favour, all well and good. If not, let them at least suggest a soft transformation of our studies. I believe translation history will eventually have to become something else, something wider, and not necessarily part of a revitalized comparative literature (there are more things in the world than literature) nor a facet of cultural studies (a concept that remains in dire need of definition). If we learn to focus on human translators, and if translators can be seen as members of intercultural groups, a logical extension of our discipline could be to study all kinds of intercultural groups, in the sense of intersections of cultures. Translation studies could become intercultural studies; translation history could be an essential part of intercultural history. And the world, currently regressing to scenes of competing cultural specificities, might one day be a little better as a result. Translation history need not point only to the past.

Acknowledgements

I would like to express my sincere appreciation of the translation scholars who have helped me in recent years, particularly Gideon Toury, José Lambert and Armin Paul Frank, professors all. As dialectics might justify, my occasional dissent from the pioneer scholars of our age involves serious recognition of their importance, at the great risk of appearing ungrateful for their generous advice and encouragement. I am also extremely grateful to Harald Kittel and the Göttingen Research Centre in Literary Translation, where I held a Humboldt fellowship in 1992-94. Many useful critical comments have also been received from Judith Woodsworth, Theo Hermans, Mona Baker and Olivier Giménez López.

Since much of this text is based on previous research, I offer the following compilation of sources and complementary studies. The first three chapters include material used in my 1996 CETRA lectures in Leuven. Chapters 4 and 5 refer to research first presented as 'The Importance of Salomé: Approaches to a *fin de siècle* theme', published in *French Forum* 14/3 (1989): 311-322, and to unpublished work on late-nineteenth-century French-German translations, carried out in Göttingen thanks to a grant from the Humboldt Foundation. Some of the diagrams in chapter 5 have been published in 'Catalogues and Corpora in Translation History', in *The Knowledges of the Translator: From Literary Interpretation to Machine Translation*, ed. Malcolm Coulthard and Pat Odber de Baubeta (Lewiston, Queenston, Lampeter: Edwin Mellen Press, 1996), 167-190, as have longer versions of the comments on German bibliographies. The 'fin de siècle' map (figure 11) was first published in 'Les notions de "réseau" et de "régime" en relations littéraires internationales' in *L'Internationalité littéraire*, ed. Anthony Pym (Paris-Barcelona: Noésis, 1988), 5-18; the 'Toledo' map (figure 12) is due to appear in 'Alternatives to Borders in Translation Theory' in *Koinè*. Chapter 7 draws partly on 'Why translation conventions should be intercultural rather than culture-specific: An alternative basic-link model', published in *Parallèles* 15 (1993): 60-68. Chapter 8, on regimes, summarizes the following longer analyses: 'Twelfth-Century Toledo and Strategies of the Literalist Trojan Horse', *Target* 6/1 (1994): 43-66; 'Negotiation theory as an approach to translation history: An inductive lesson from fifteenth-century Castile', in *Translation and Knowledge,* ed. Yves Gambier and Jorma Tommola (Turku: University of Turku Centre for Translation and Interpreting, 1993), 27-39; and 'Translational and Non-Translational Regimes Informing Poetry Anthologies. Lessons on Authorship from Fernando Maristany and Enrique Díez-Canedo,' in *International Anthologies of Literature in Translation*, ed. Harald Kittel (Berlin: Erich Schmidt, 1995), 251-270. The theory of transaction costs mentioned at the end of chapter 8 is more fully developed in 'Translation as a Transaction Cost' in *Meta* 40/4 (1995): 594-605, and, like the chapter on causes, is a reworking of part of *Pour une éthique du traducteur* (Artois Presses Universitaires, 1997), first presented in a seminar given at the Collège International de Philosophie in Paris in 1994. Chapter 10, on translators, includes several paragraphs and examples taken from my contributions to *Translators through History*, ed. Jean Delisle and Judith Woodsworth (Benjamins, 1995), pp. 152-3, 193, 195-7; the story of Henri Albert is more fully contextualized in 'Lives of Henri Albert, Nietzschean Translator', due to be published in *Translation and Creativity* (Benjamins). Chapter 11, on intercultures, draws on 'Coming to terms with and against nationalist cultural specificity: notes for an ethos of translation studies', published in *Folia Translatologica* (Prague: Charles University, 1993), 49-69. Finally, a longer version of Chapter 12 has been accepted for publication as 'Why Translation Studies should be Homeless', in *Translation and Multidisciplinarity*, ed. Marcia A.P. Martins and Heloisa G. Barbosa, Rio de Janeiro: PUC, UFRJ. Needless to say, I contradict this last title by seeking to give these dispersed studies some kind of unified home in this book.

Our thanks to John Benjamins Publishing for permission to reproduce the Holmes map (page 2) in the version taken from Gideon Toury's *Discriptive Translation Studies and beyond* (1995), and to Routledge for permission to reproduce Figure 3 (page 73), taken from Lawrence Venuti's *The Translator's Invisibility* (1995).

1. History

This chapter will outline the general nature of translation history, particularly its parts, its background, and a few reasons for its existence. These are all fundamental aspects of the approach to be elaborated in greater detail in the following chapters.

History within translation studies

James S Holmes' seminal lecture 'The Name and Nature of Translation Studies' (1972) set out to orient the scholarly study of translation. It put forward a conceptual scheme that identified and interrelated many of the things that can be done in translation studies, envisaging an entire future discipline and effectively stimulating work aimed at establishing that discipline. Historically, this was a major step forward, none the least because it involved a frontal attack on the hazy but self-assured categories that had long been used to judge translations. Holmes' categories were simple, scientifically framed, and hierarchically arranged: 'Applied' was opposed to 'Pure', the latter was broken down into 'Theoretical' and 'Descriptive', then 'Descriptive' divided in turn into 'Product Oriented', 'Process Oriented' and 'Function Oriented', and so on. Figure 1 shows the apocryphal graphic form these categories received later from scholars who saw it as a legitimate point of departure. Many wonderful things found a place in this map; a few more have benefited from the modifications and variants proposed since (notably Lambert 1991a, Snell-Hornby 1991, Toury 1991). Of course, translation studies cannot be reduced to this one map, and the map itself has been evolving dynamically, along with the lands it purports to represent. Yet the curious fact remains that neither Holmes nor his commentators – at least those subscribing to the map and its variants – explicitly named a unified area for the *historical* study of translation. This merits some thought.

It could be that everything Holmes called 'descriptive' is automatically historical. But is this a fair reading of what we have on the map? Holmes certainly allowed that the translations of the past could be studied under his 'product-oriented descriptive' branch, and there is no reason why the historical functions of translations might not also be studied under 'function-oriented description'. Yet here we run into a series of problems. Does the Holmes map mean history is just a matter of describing objects? Is there no history in apparently non-descriptive slots like 'Translation Criticism'? Do 'Theoretical Studies' somehow stand

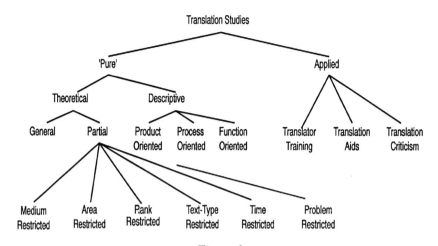

Figure 1
Holmes' conception of translation studies (from Toury 1991:181)

outside of history? And why does Holmes' theoretical branch only explicitly include history as a possibility for 'time-restricted theories' (specifically the subset dealing with 'the translation of texts from an older period') as well as its obvious role in a general 'history of translation studies' (1972:72, 76, 79)? Whatever the reasons behind these categories, the field of history is strangely fragmented on both sides of the descriptive/theoretical divide.

A facile way to overcome this fragmentation is to claim that all the categories are interrelated dialectically. You are supposed to add or imagine little arrows all over the place. Is this a real solution? If arrows really do go from all points to all other points, who would need the map in the first place? Maps name consecrated plots and the easiest routes between them. The Holmes map suggests translation history has no consecrated plot within translation studies. Translation historians of any but the narrowest variety would seem condemned to jump from one patch to another, describing products here, analyzing functions there, and finding themselves marginally implicated in a metadescription of the whole lot. The Holmes map also omits a few areas of possible interest: it delineates no ground for any specific theory of translation history, nor for historiography as a way of applying and testing theories (although this is certainly what Holmes wanted us to do). Despite its many virtues in its day, I suggest the map is no longer a wholly reliable guide.

I sow these few doubts because some scholars, notably Gideon Toury (1995:10), see the Holmes map as mandatory orientation for any work in translation history, and indeed for translation studies as a whole. Whatever we do now, it seems, should be located somewhere within the schemata inherited from the past. To do otherwise, claims Toury, would be to risk compromising the "controlled evolution" of translation studies. Yet is there any reason to suppose that the Holmes map is automatically suited to what we want to do in translation studies now? Does the map infallibly locate places for the particular hypotheses we want to test or the specific problems we are trying to solve? If not, what kind of price are we being asked to pay for the 'controlled evolution' of a scholarly discipline? Exactly who is doing the controlling, and to what end? Indeed, aren't the problems to be solved of more importance than the maintenance of an academic discipline? No matter how pretty the maps, if a branch of scholarship fails to address socially important issues, it may deserve to disappear or to be relegated to academic museums, like the first navigation charts of Terra Australis.

Maps are peculiar instruments of power. They tend to make you look in certain directions; they make you overlook other directions. Consider, for instance, the general orientation of the Holmes map in its consecrated graphic form (Figure 1). Look at the form, not the labels. Now compare that modern map with Figure 2, which is Lawrence Humphrey's much earlier attempt to envisage a global translation studies (first published in 1559). I suggest there are two main differences.

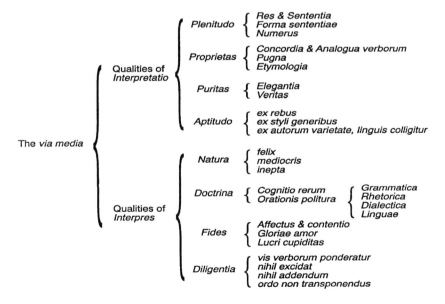

Figure 2

Diagramma from Lawrence Humphrey's Interpretatio linguarum (Basle 1559)
(from Norton 1984:12)

First, Humphrey's map breaks down the categories horizontally, from left to right, whereas the Holmes map is vertical, going from top to bottom, like company organization charts. Thanks to the modern verticality, the most general theoretical categories find a presidential space well away from empirical details. Ungenerous minds might suspect the modern maps represent a kind of professorial power, allocating the top to an all-seeing eye able to place the more specific subjects ranged along the bottom. Yet this would be unfair: translation studies is still far too small for such a radical division of labour; a good deal of the spadework at the bottom is actually being done by the same names that are looking out from the top. But if everyone can be everywhere, what real good is the map?

Second, the major division in the sixteenth-century map is between translation (*interpretatio*) and the translator (*interpres*), the process-product and the agent, whereas the modern map calmly divides up the products – translations – without offering so much as a glance at any translator, living or dead. Where did all the people go? If the modern maps provide images of organizational domination, then the people most effectively dominated must surely be researchers and translators, especially the ones with flesh, blood, mobility and subjectivity. These people seem to have been excluded from the world of 'pure research'. Perhaps they deserve to be put back in.

One of my aims in this book is to bring together a few of these fragmented or overlooked aspects of maps. I would like to see translation history as a unified area for the humanistic study of human translators and their social actions, both within and beyond their material translations. Of course, in the process of presenting my arguments, I will be drawing many maps of my own. Maps are instruments of power. They name and control. A displacement of power in this field might thus be intimated by a certain remapping.

The parts of translation history

There is nothing particularly new or revolutionary in wanting to write about the history of translation. Yet tradition provides a rather indefinite vocabulary for the undertaking. As the Holmes map suggests, there are some doubts as to how the historical object should be named, what the general field is called, and what kinds of subdivisions are to be allowed for. Not all these doubts can be dispelled here. A few internal conventions might nevertheless be proposed, if only to describe the words I'll be using.[1]

---

[1] While we're busy attacking the terminology, note that I use 'translative' to refer to translating or translation as a process, and 'translational' for aspects of translations as texts. The variants 'translatory' and 'translatorial' (I hope there are no others!) have been buried.

Translation history ('historiography' is a less pretty term for the same thing) is a set of discourses predicating the changes that have occurred or have actively been prevented in the field of translation. Its field includes actions and agents leading to translations (or non-translations), the effects of translations (or non-translations), theories about translation, and a long etcetera of causally related phenomena.

Thus conventionalized, translation history can be subdivided into at least three areas: 'archaeology', 'criticism' and something that, for want of a better word, I shall call 'explanation':

- *Translation archaeology* is a set of discourses concerned with answering all or part of the complex question 'who translated what, how, where, when, for whom and with what effect?'. It can include anything from the compiling of catalogues to the carrying out of biographical research on translators. The term 'archaeology' is not meant to be pejorative here, nor does it imply any particularly Foucauldian revelations. It simply denotes a fascinating field that often involves complex detective work, great self-sacrifice and very real service to other areas of translation history.
- *Historical criticism* would be the set of discourses that assess the way translations help or hinder progress. This is an unfashionable and perilous exercise, not least because we would first have to say what progress looks like. In traditional terms historical criticism might broadly cover the philological part of historiography, if and when philology conjugates notions of progress as moral value (and the best of it used to). Yet the resulting criticism cannot apply contemporary values directly to past translations. Rather than decide whether a translation is progressive for us here and now, properly historical criticism must determine the value of a past translator's work in relation to the effects achieved in the past. This would be the difference between historical and non-historical criticism. Perhaps happily, neither historical nor non-historical criticism will be of great concern to us in this book, since they both require degrees of ideological certitude for which I await revelation. A few of the following pages (35-36, 168-169) will nevertheless suggest, for example, that a certain French translator of Nietzsche could have contributed to highly non-progressive cultural conflict. Those pages, tenuous and tentative as they are, should count as historical criticism, or at least as a bookmark for where criticism is required. Clearly, I would welcome rather than shun any critical minds brave enough to say where we should be going and how translations can help get us there. Their activity should also be part of our endeavour. In the meantime, our translation history has many

very practical questions to answer before progressive moral values can be distributed with any degree of confidence.

- *Explanation* is the part of translation history that tries to say *why* archaeological artefacts occurred when and where they did, and how they were related to change. Archaeology and historical criticism are mostly concerned with individual facts and texts. Explanation must be concerned with the causation of such data, particularly the causation that passes through power relationships; this is the field where translators can be discovered as effective social actors. Other levels of explanation, perhaps dealing with technological change or power relations between social groups, can equally privilege large-scale hypotheses concerning whole periods or networks. 'Why?' might seem a very small question for a project that should properly encompass all the other parts of translation history. Yet it is by far the most important question. It is the only one that properly addresses processes of change; it is the only one seriously absent from the Holmes map. A history that ignored causation would perhaps be able to describe actions and effects, it might even have a one-dimensional idea of progress, but it would not recognize the properly human dimension of documents and actions as processes of change.

The interdependence and separateness of the parts

All translation history comprises or assumes discourses from all the above categories. The discourses are not really 'parts' in the sense that they can be detached from the whole. They might be thought of as parts that individuals or individual groups can sing in order to make up full harmonies as they go along. The parts can be sung by themselves. There can even be a few star soloists. Yet each individual part assumes a relation to the wider whole. It is impossible to write an archaeological catalogue or even locate items for catalogues unless one has some general idea of the change process framing those values (explanation), and there is little reason to do this unless one at least hopes the past can lead to a positive future (criticism). Similarly, there can be no criticism or explanation without archaeological evidence, and no explanation of change without some idea of the values involved in change. In short, none of these three parts can assume epistemological independence from the others. Anyone doing translation history is to some extent involved in all three activities (there is no purely 'informative' or 'descriptive' discourse, just as there is no abstract speculation without at least some archaeological grounding). However, since the superficial modes of presentation are quite different, there are good practical reasons why each individual part should be considered in relative isolation.

Why maintain the above distinctions? First, they are a way of organizing a book on the subject. The following chapters will go from archaeology to questions of causation, with just a few passing comments on criticism. This structure is useful to the extent that any signpost is better than none, and a communicative virtue is a very serious virtue. Although unwritten research can and should wander from one set of questions to another, doing history is also a matter of communicating the results of research. This is important because archaeology, criticism and explanation tend to mix quite badly on the more practical levels of translation history. Each discourse has its optimal mode of presentation. Archaeology is suited to lists; criticism is suited to analysis and argument; explanation is often best when close to good storytelling. If archaeological lists weigh down explanatory storytelling, the result is immediate boredom, just as apparent flippancy could result from good storytelling in the midst of archaeology or detailed evaluation. Keeping the parts relatively separate could be a way of keeping them relatively interesting.

A brief example might illustrate the point. Valentín García Yebra's potted history of translation in Spain (1983) is both explanatory and critical with respect to the twelfth and thirteenth centuries, where a reasonable amount of archaeological work had been done before him. But since little archaeology had been done for the following centuries, García Yebra's translation history quickly becomes a list of dates and texts, written in prose but reducing narrativity to repeated claims that the whole catalogue would take up far more than the available space ('to list all the great translations of this period would require several books...', and so on). The result is not particularly fruitful, since a straight list would have been more readable. Yet the problem doesn't stop there. A university textbook based on García Yebra (Pascua and Peñate 1991:2-4) gives a basically narrative summary of the twelfth and thirteenth centuries (mixed together as the 'School of Toledo') then crashes into a wonderfully reductive sentence: "After the seventeenth century, translations went parallel with literature" (1991:4). This sentence reflects a certain understanding of García Yebra's lists for the period in question, but it is not helpful history: it shows nothing and it explains nothing; it is neither archaeological nor explanatory. The initial solution should have been for García Yebra to keep the lists and the stories in separate paddocks. Lists are for archaeology; century-spanning prose belongs to explanatory discourse.

The division of translation history into separate but related parts could also prove useful for the actual organization of research. Although history requires the three parts, no one is obliged to engage in all of them in an equal way or at the same time. It is impossible to insist that everyone should have read everything, and mostly unprofitable to ask exacting archaeologists to defend a philosophical position in the history of ideas. Balanced and vital history should instead come from the constitution of research teams able to integrate expertise from the various disciplines bearing on a particular field, not just from the philological perspective but also paying attention to insights from social and economic history. The divisions could become guidelines for exchange, collaboration and teamwork.

Examples of the need for teamwork are not difficult to find in studies of Iberian translation history. Explanatory historians have traditionally rushed ahead of everyone and everything, advancing global hypotheses and not infrequently making mistakes. The archaeologists often come up behind, building castles stone by stone and mistrusting large-scale conceptual conclusions. A classic case is the French historian Amable Jourdain, who claimed to have discovered the Toledan 'college of translators' as a result of very hard work: "We confess, with a joy that all men of letters will appreciate, that the discovery of this college of translators has made up for the innumerable thorns that have covered our path" (1873:108). What was he so proud of? Jourdain had actually found two manuscripts in which different translations seemed to name a certain Raimundus, archbishop of Toledo, as their patron. The historian had struggled to locate these manuscripts, so he thought a discovery would be just compensation. Monsieur Jourdain found what he wanted to find, and was no doubt doubly pleased because Archbishop Raimundus of Toledo, the patron, just happened to be every bit as French as Jourdain himself. However, work by Marie-Thérèse d'Alverny (1964), a French translation archaeologist who deserves real praise, compared 45 manuscripts from right across Europe and discovered that one of the two texts where the archbishop was named actually had quite a different meaning: Jourdain had read a comma that had little reason to be there and he had been misled by a proper name ('Johannes' instead of 'Johanni'). The wider manuscript tradition made it clear that the sponsor of one of the translations was not Archbishop Raimundus but his successor Johannes. The careful archaeology of a syntactically implied comma thus pulled down an entire explanatory edifice. The French archbishop became the patron of just one translation, with no firm connection with anything like a college or school of translators. Archaeology undid hasty explanation. Yet both approaches were surely necessary. If Jourdain had not formulated his large-scale concept, d'Alverny's alternative comma would not have been important as an object of research. The comma may well have been lost among many thousands of manuscript variants. The big idea had to exist first so that it could be corrected by some small but significant words.

Archaeology requires explanation.

This same example also illustrates the need for teamwork. Research on twelfth-century translations in the Iberian peninsula requires competence in Arabic, Latin, Romance, Hebrew, astronomy, mathematics, theology, social history and the history of ideas, for starters. Remarkably few researchers have been expert in all these fields. Yet no extensive research teams seem to have been formed for this particular area (although there has been rather more collaboration for studies on the thirteenth-century Alfonsine translators). Individual researchers are still supposed to know everything about many different fields, limiting collaboration to occasional consultation on points of detail. This is despite the message glaringly inscribed in the historical object itself: just as teams were required to carry out the twelfth-century translations, teams are required for their analysis.

The distinctions between the parts of translation history are thus epistemologically useful in that they allow us to identify and appreciate each discourse on its own terms, without assuming that any one of them holds all the answers. This is not always done. When Mary Snell-Hornby takes descriptive translation histories to task for not using "that hermeneutic component which relates past writings to modern thinking and hence makes them live" (1988:26), she is regretting the fact that a certain kind of translation history is not the same thing as non-historical criticism. This is like criticizing sociologists for not being politicians. The comment is short-sighted in that, just as the work done by sociologists can be of political value precisely to the extent that it can appear to be apolitical, the work done by descriptive historians can do much to orient and improve criticism, both historical and non-historical. Even the most apparently non-evaluative descriptive discourses are founded on evaluative premises.

So much for the parts of our history. We should use them to accept a certain division of labour, yet we should also recognize that the divisions themselves are by no means absolute. Our distinctions are only useful for as long as we can jump over them when necessary.

A too-brief history of translation history

Generalist research in translation history might vaguely be dated from the 1960s, particularly the overviews of Cary (1963), Mounin (1965) and Kloepfer (1967), backed up by Störig's seminal editing of some of the major theoretical texts of the past (1963). Publications have been fairly regular ever since. Discussions and surveys have been provided by George Steiner(1975), Kelly (1979), Berman (1984), Norton (1984), Van Hoof (1986, 1991), Rener (1989), Ballard (1992), and Vermeer (1992, 1996), while the editing of historical translation theory has been carried out by T. R. Steiner (1975), Lefevere (1977), Horguelin (1981), Santoyo (1987), D'hulst (1990), Copeland (1991), Lefevere again (1992b), Robinson (1997), and others I may not yet have sighted.

Note that most of the texts just referred to deal with the history of translation *theory*; they are not particularly interested in the past of translating translators. Worse, although old theories must certainly be accounted for in translation history, when isolated and strung together they very often form a field of unbearable repetition and unprofitable generalization. For example, George Steiner's attention to theories allows him to reduce the history of translation to a meandering search for fidelity (1975:261-262); Mary Snell-Hornby consequently describes centuries of serious thought about fidelity as a "heated debate" of little import for the present (1988:22, 26); and deconstructionists like Rosemary Arrojo may further relegate the same centuries to the level of a benighted 'logocentricity' that must be surpassed (1993:92). The focus on theory can thus become a way of producing explanations so powerful that they effectively obscure the complexity defensive roles played by theorization. No one writes a theory to state the obvious; many translators have theorized in order to justify and sometimes conceal their far more interesting translation practices. Awareness of the calculated or even misleading role of theory means that translation history cannot be based exclusively on what has been said about translation. Better historiography requires awareness of what translators have actually done. And the best historiography must surely come from relating the two, investigating the complex relationships between past theories and past practices.

If we insist that strict translation history should deal with what translators do – with translation as a practice and a theorizing in itself rather than with pure external theories of the practice and theorizing – it is rather more difficult to locate authoritative historians matching the definition. How many histories have truly placed translators at the centre of their vision? The candidates are few. There are some excellent isolated studies like Norton (1984) and Round (1993), and attention to human practice rather than theoretical ideas is indeed prominent in medievalist studies in general. Yet most works of this kind deal at close range with specific texts and specific periods, rarely attaining a large-scale explanatory vision. Even the so-called 'cultural turn' hailed in the proximity of Bassnett (1991a) and Lefevere (particularly Lefevere and Bassnett 1990) assumes rather than elaborates an explanatory vision: it skips across fairly shallow waters, pointing to some kind of general cause behind translation but not giving many substantial details about social history (I will return to this in chapter 3).

On the other hand, the engaging collective volume *Translators Through*

History, edited by Jean Delisle and Judith Woodsworth in 1995, presents an array of fascinating detail about human translators and could indeed claim to escape from the fixation on theory; it could become a seminal document for a future history of translators. Yet one must ask if this work does not also contain a quiet warning about the temptation of instant humanization. Who is actually writing this history, and according to what critical criteria? Is all this information really needed? Is it enough? To decide, we would have to know what problems the individual chapters are designed to solve. What are the guiding hypotheses? Why mention these translators and not others? How do we recognize a person as a translator (surely through translations, or in terms of a theory)? Do translators make their own decisions (if not, surely many non-translators should be mentioned)? In short, as soon as we leave the relative comfort of past theories and venture into the world of actual translators, methodology becomes a very real problem requiring some very real answers. Good storytelling is not enough, even when the main characters are people.

One cannot start studying a field just by collecting fragments that look like they might have something to do with that field. There must also be careful thought about what we are looking for, how we are likely to find it, and how the field itself is to be constituted. There must be some attention to method. More important, questions of method must necessarily be formulated on the basis of what has already been done in a given field. Even if everything that has preceded us were absolute rubbish – and it isn't –, even if we were going to import wholesale methodologies from other sciences – and we aren't –, we should be able to say why what has been done is rubbish, according to what methodological faults, and how our future non-rubbish is going to correct those faults. It is not possible, I believe, simply to turn our attention to translators-as-people (rather than theories or products) and hope that some kind of automatic enlightenment will ensue. This is why, although my aim is very much to write a history of translators, this book will not grapple with the actual nature of the human translator until some nine chapters of fairly formal methodology has been sifted through. Only then might we know what we are looking for and how we could find it. There is no instant revolution; hard work is required to cross from one epistemology to another.

Let me stress, perhaps uncharacteristically, that considerable humility is also needed in this regard. We cannot pretend that translation history is virgin territory, that nothing of importance was done prior to the 1960s or 1980s, and that a few big ideas – theories about the history of theories, about the inferiorization of intermediaries, translative transgression or translational invisibility – can now set the world aright. Much contemporary certitude should be toned down. Indeed, we would do well to assume that translation history was probably never virgin territory, at least not for long. At the latest it began a few minutes after the practice of translation itself, although it was no doubt implied in the first translator's prevision ('now I'll do something for the storytellers'). As soon as translators or witnesses explain how or why a translation has been carried out – or someone tells them how or why it *should* have been carried out – their discourse is partly historical, just as it is partly theoretical.

This is not an idle speculation. To continue the example mentioned above, histories of a twelfth-century 'School of Toledo' were by no means invented by Jourdain or his latter-day followers. In the thirteenth century Geoffrey de Vinsauf referred to Toledo as a centre where the *quadrivium* was studied, placing it alongside the universities of Paris, Bologna and Salerno (Procter 1951:8). Less definite references were circulated at the same time by Albertus Magnus and Roger Bacon. Yet most of the accounts can be projected back to about 1175, the latest likely year in which the travelling Englishman Daniel de Merlai very probably saw translators working in Toledo and decided to describe their activities in pedagogical terms, specifically mentioning the emphasis on the *quadrivium*. This means the history was formulated not in the thirteenth or nineteenth centuries but in the twelfth, at virtually the same time as the translative-pedagogical activity itself. The historical facts are immediately embedded in the historiographical account. More specifically, we can't say what actually happened at Toledo without analysing a twelfth-century traveller's reasons for associating the town with a pedagogical use of translation. More worryingly, as in Jourdain, Daniel de Merlai had a clear desire to discover something at the end of his path: "And so," he told his bishop as he justified his decision to study in Hispania rather than Paris, "since it is at Toledo that Arabic teachings, almost all in the *quadrivium*, are widely celebrated, I hurried there to listen to the world's wisest philosophers" (ed. Sudhoff 1917:6). That's it. That's quite possibly the strategic reasoning that sparked off several centuries of reference to a 'School of Toledo', down to and including Jourdain's 'college'. But it might also have been Daniel de Merlai's calculated excuse for having played truant. Whatever the case, this kind of translation history would seem to be about as old as the history of translation. The two are not lightly separated.

Not only is translation history very old, but there has also been no real shortage of it since at least the advent of systematic philology. In the particular case of scientific translations from Arabic (the work carried out in twelfth-century Toledo) historical research has been fairly constant from the mid-nineteenth century.[2] It has been real research, not in any way to be associated with a prescientific stage that was somehow transcended in the 1960s. The work has included pioneering large-scale hypotheses, careful archaeological catalogues, critical editions of translations and detailed philological syntheses, all on the same general field, combining archaeological, critical and explanatory work. There is no obviously nationalist centring (in fact, with only two Hispanic researchers, the mix could come close to that of the twelfth-century translators and patrons studied). There is no radical break between misguided and enlightened translation history. On the contrary, as we have noted with respect to Jourdain, the many mistaken hypotheses and occasional partisanship of the earlier studies were often necessary conditions for later advances.

Seen in this light, translation history is a long-term activity that is not easily upset by revolutions. New methods and theories can certainly alter interpretations and offer occasional insight. But this does not happen automatically with each new decade. Indeed, the rhythm of substantial advances could well conform to a rather slow process of development, if only because the material to be interpreted does not appear by magic. The stuff of history has to be gathered and assessed; explanation requires archaeology; solid research takes time. If translation history is to achieve long-term results, it must appreciate its own long-term history.

This is not to say there has been no fundamental change at all. In the long-term view, the impact of systems theory must surely be seen as a major shift of attention. The move has been not just in favour of a more generalist scope – the 1960s volumes achieved this fairly enough – but also in method, most basically the awareness that translation history might actually have a method, with its own concepts, procedures and results. This particular change can be dated from the insights that Itamar Even-Zohar, drawing on the Russian Formalists, introduced from 1969. The general systemic approach has also been developed by Gideon Toury, meeting with the tradition of Holmes and finding some kind

---

[2] The rhythm of research might be understood from the dates of the following book-length studies: Jourdain 1819, Libri 1838, Boncompagni 1851, Renan 1852, Jourdain 1873, Rose 1874, Steinschneider 1904-05, Berthelot 1906, Sudhoff 1914, Sudhoff 1917, Thorndike 1923, Haskins 1924, Théry 1926, Thorndike 1927, Steel 1929, González Palencia 1937, Muckle 1937, Carmody 1941, d'Alverny 1948, Clagett and Moody 1952, Minio-Paluello 1954, Clagett 1953, González Palencia 1953, Alonso 1955, Carmody 1956, O'Donnell 1958, Opelt 1959, Dunlop 1960, Schrader 1961, Lemay 1963, Kritzeck 1964, d'Alverny 1964, Clagett 1964, d'Alverny 1968, Lemay 1968, van Riet 1972, Kunitzsch 1974, d'Alverny 1982, d'Alverny 1989, Jacquart 1989, and so on.

of uneasy synthesis in the 1985 volume edited by Theo Hermans as *The Ma-nipulation of Literature*. In retrospect, the change was not really the system model itself, which belatedly extended the scientific pretensions elsewhere known as structuralism. The more profound innovation was the application of a general descriptive model to translations rather than to translation theories (translators remained nowhere to be seen, as in the Holmes map above). This has had at least three effects:

First, systems theory has enabled fragmentary philological studies to be placed in a wider picture, unifying translation history without denying the discipline's own historical depth. A good example of this synthesizing vision is Theo Hermans' explanatory narrative of Renaissance translation (1992), which presents little new material but makes good sense of a lot of old research.

Second, since most of these studies have been based on corpora of transla-tions, the insistence on wide-scale empirical research has tended to welcome rather than isolate the perspectives of translation archaeology. Instead of being professionally opposed to the high-risk hypotheses of explainers, archaeolo-gists have virtually been invited to work out the big narratives themselves.

Third, the focus on translations rather than theories has underscored the normative role of previous theories, which have consequently become a le-gitimate part of the object of study (after Toury 1980:62). Theories can now be seen as playing a role with respect to the translation practices of their day and age. True, recognition of the historical role of theory has occasionally led to a rather unhelpful stand-off between descriptive and theoretical studies (Lambert 1988:128, 130; 1991a:31-32; 1991b; assessed in Delabastita 1991). But Holmes effectively recognized the necessary give-and-take of these areas (1972:78). Although it was correct and timely to point out that translation theories are historical, few would now seriously argue that description can exist without theorization, nor vice versa. Few would now seriously adhere to an autonomous descriptive translation studies that aspires to be value-free or pretends to indulge in no theory beyond the procedures of an idealized science. Such autonomy is neither possible nor ultimately desirable.

These three factors – explanatory integration, properly empirical archaeol-ogy, and the historicization of theory –constitute a fundamental change that cannot be ignored. I do not wish to suggest that there is or ever was a coherent group of scholars carrying out a doctrinally descriptive translation studies (the unity of a 'manipulation' or 'polysystem' group is an illusory effect of distance, occasionally operative in the United States); I am keenly aware of the many differences that separate the scholars named above, differences that keep them debating in a most productive way (so when I mention Toury in the next few chapters, I mean *only* Toury). Yet there was a moment when a fundamental change came about thanks to a group effort, and it is that change, now distanced in time, that I wish to identify as the lasting contribution of systems theory. A later chapter in this book will seek to assess the virtues and shortcomings of this particular part of our recent history.

The present in which I write is thus marked by an incipient history of translators, which pays little attention to method, and by an established systems theory, which pays little attention to translators. Both sides tell stories (the fundamental difference is between human and abstract characters); both might productively dialogue not only with each other but with the histories of translation theories as well. Part of my task is to suggest ways in which they can do this.

Before closing this introductory overview, let me insist that translation history also has a partly foreseeable future. Where are we headed? One might expect action analysis and deconstruction to play out their roles, reorganizing and reinterpreting some of the collectively accumulated data. Yet perhaps the most desirable change will come from certain collective undertakings. As I have worked on this book, at least five such projects have been in preparation: Delisle and Woodsworth's *Translators through History* mentioned above, the Oxford *Guide to Literature in English Translation*, the Fitzroy Dearborn *Encyclopedia of Literary Translation*, the *Routledge Encyclopedia of Translation Studies* and the De Gruyter *Handbuch zur Übersetzungsforschung*, all of which include large helpings of history. If these projects are to constitute some kind of composite landmark in translation history, they will probably do so through the various degrees of teamwork and collaboration involved. I doubt there will be any profound agreement about concepts and methods, at least not between different research teams. Yet the very fact that researchers from different fields are at last coming together to work on translation history should stimulate changes in concepts and methods. Ideally, the wider vision gained through collaboration will promote increasingly productive interrelationships between archaeology, criticism and explanation.

Reasons for doing translation history

Any research should be justifiable on at least two grounds. First, it should not have been done before. Second, the people carrying out the research must have an interest in it. Both conditions have to be fulfilled if the work is to make any human sense. But neither condition is sufficient for research to become a meaningful and fruitful group activity. Neither condition, nor their combination, can say why the research should be written up, communicated, debated and, somewhere along the line, paid for. Some wider justification is required. The following are further possible reasons for doing translation history.

Translation history can fulfil a service function with respect to the humanistic disciplines concerned with describing individual cultures. At every point where a culture has changed through contact with another culture, the conceptual tools required to grasp the process go beyond those normally used to describe internal cultural dynamics. This is of some importance in situations where the methodology normally used to describe internal processes effectively precludes the substantiality of external forces. Some Marxist historians, for example, were so convinced that historical truth lay in internal class struggle that they saw intercultural processes as inessential. All real change had to come from the inside, not from the outside. Fortunately, there are many historical phenomena that cannot simply be brushed aside by such inside knowledge. They require at least the hypothesis that substantial change can result from intercultural processes, just as Althusserian Marxism was prepared to admit international processes as a series of 'overdeterminations'. This means that intercultural aspects, although not able to replace internal knowledge of cultures, must be accounted for and integrated through appropriate concepts and empirical research methods. Translation history is one way of formulating such concepts and approaching the necessary research.

Second, translation history can provide information and ideas that may prove useful for policymakers in the field of general language and culture as well as translation (since translation is a linguistic and cultural option). To take a prime example, historical perspectives could prove vital when formulating a future language policy for Europe. They should play a role as soon as one calculates the cost of symbolic recourse to translations in the European Union. If planners are not to abandon the ideal of huge translation flows, they will have to integrate even more computerization into most text-production processes; massive machine translation will increase the many situations where foreign information comes in recognizably translational language; the wholly human-translated text should become a relative luxury. Of course, this will be anathema to teachers who currently extol the virtues of naturalizing translations, who want it all to be human, and who thus risk relegating many fields of translation to the level of a cottage handicraft industry. Yet the advent of recognizably translational language need not be so alarming for anyone aware that European philosophy and science worked with literalist translation techniques for many centuries, developing quite successful ways of reading and using recognizably translational language. Greater knowledge of the past can give us wider frames for assessing the future.

Another reason for studying translation history is potentially at odds with the compatibilist arguments given so far. Most benignly, it posits that translation history can be of indirect service to social groups of intermediaries, be they translators, negotiators, traders or whatever. This does not mean history should teach these people how to translate. Our service function is rather more abstract. Translation history might help these groups affirm their intercultural specificity. More problematically, it might affirm a kind of specificity that is not wholly compatible with histories and theories of what might be called sedentary cultures, the cultures that stay in place, the ones that have states and money to subsidize their products.

This is worth explaining.

Some people currently study translation history because they are interested in the birth and evolution of individual cultures, particularly smaller or regional cultures that have consciously used translation programmes for the formation of linguistic or literary identities. It is perhaps no accident that various descriptive procedures suited to this study have been developed in places like Holland, Belgium, Israel or Quebec, where researchers cannot ignore the problems of such cultures. This is an entirely legitimate reason for doing translation history (of course, it is also a reason why subjective engagement might dress in the clothes of objective science). Our discipline can indeed provide valuable lessons to anyone concerned with the formation of a sedentary culture. Yet this need not be our sole calling. After all, sedentary cultural communities of all kinds, big and small, have long projected their specificity and substance by writing about their past. Not much changes if they should now decide to write about the translations of their past. Yet something could possibly change if translation history were to be written in a slightly different way, with reference to a non-sedentary past.

The basic problem is that sedentary cultures have projected so much specificity and so much substance that the very concept of culture is now difficult to envisage in non-sedentary terms. A cultural identity is supposed to be what one is, here and now, or deep down because of birth; translations are sometimes supposed to reflect this primal substance. Identity is less frequently thought about in terms of what one is becoming, where one has come from, or where one is going. A culture seems always to be *in* a certain place (remarkably less in a certain time); it belongs more than it moves; it can be mapped and tied to a certain stretch of land. The very term 'culture' says so, coming, as it does, from the verb *colere*, to till the land, to engage in cultivation, farming. Culture would thus be gained by staying in one place, breaking open soil to sow crops and to raise animals, establishing a temporal permanence requiring political organization and defence. From this permanence, eventually, come the commercial centres where the products of cultivation are exchanged, along with their language, requiring translation.

According to this history, exchanges of products and their language must always take place *between* existing cultures. The people carrying out exchange are made to appear secondary, inessential to the primary cultural business of staying put and producing from the land. Most histories of cultures find little place for uprooted intermediaries, who flicker around the chapter divisions as momentary and isolated figures. Intermediaries are accorded little history of their own. They own little land; they come later; they cause only marginal changes; they have no long-term power and often no voting rights. At best, they bring news and diversity. At worst, they spread disease, cause trouble and take away profits.

To say that intermediaries, like and along with translators, have culture – or even have a special kind of culture – would perhaps be to contradict etymology. Yet it would not be an altogether idle argument. We can at least imagine that intermediaries have temporary intercultures, even without cultivation. Many others would be in the same drunken boat. The native peoples of Australia prohibited breaking open the soil for agriculture or mining, and yet they would certainly have what most of us would call culture. Nomadic culture is no more a contradiction in terms than is a culture of intermediaries. Anthropologically, it gives the movement of intermediaries some claim to primacy over sedentary cultivation. Intermediaries might pleasingly be placed alongside hunters and gatherers, who had longer and healthier lives than farmers. The nomads were there before the farmers and will probably remain after. Physical movement was there in the beginning and might yet be there in the end. Translation history has the privilege of recounting part of that movement. It need not be reduced to the desire for sedentary belonging.

There are good reasons why general history should nowadays be interested in issues of interculturality and transcultural movement. As productivity increasingly ensues from information rather than land, sedentary cultures are becoming difficult to map. Their conceptual sovereignty and historical boundaries are becoming indefensible. Cultural change is increasingly the prerogative of those who move information. But those people, some of them translators, have only vague ideas of where they come from and in whose collective interests they should act.

The ideal history that makes me want to do translation history is not primarily about sedentary cultures. It concerns the movement of people and texts. It could be a story of wanderers, frontier dwellers, children of culturally mixed families, human hybrids. For as long as they have no coherently written past, these intercultural groups can have little clear vision of their present position and future potential. Rather than simply complement histories of established cultures, translation history might help write a non-sedentary future.

That's why I do translation history. It's also why, of course, I'm interested in maps of the project. Beyond the boundaries, no one needs maps more than the traveller.

2. Importance

To begin at a beginning, one of the first things you need when doing translation history is a question to be answered. The question should be selected with care; it should ideally be in some way problematic, of consequence, or simply important. Just one important question is usually enough for any project; two or more can complicate life rather quickly, although any researcher usually spends time wandering from question to question, trial to error, before reaching anything worth calling important. The more common mistake, though, is to have no regard for importance at all, answering numerous unimportant questions, producing miles of data and analyses, then watching one's work do no more than sit on selected shelves. This is a serious shortcoming in translation history, where many fields are admittedly so obscure that they tend to be of concern to only a handful of similarly obscure experts. Some regard for importance is surely necessary, right at the beginning, before we go barking up fruitless trees. Yet how can we be sure we are asking an important question? How can we define this importance? And how can we make sure the importance isn't just for us?

What is importance?

Let's suppose research is based on a question to which we want to know the answer. That much is easy. For instance, here we have a manuscript tradition with numerous variants and we decide to ask what the translators most probably wrote. We have already seen how Marie-Thérèse d'Alverny asked this kind of question with respect to a comma and proper name, coming up with a fairly convincing answer: the name 'Johannes' very probably referred to the translators' patron (Archbishop Johannes of Toledo) and not to the supposed translator (Johannes Hispanensis or John of Seville or of Spain). The question was asked and answered, in this case on the level of archaeology. But why was this particular question of importance? After all, medieval manuscript traditions have countless variants; many thousands of similar questions could be asked; few of them would merit all the work d'Alverny invested in analyzing this one particular phrase. Why do some questions become important?

In d'Alverny's case, the question was important not because it was difficult to answer but because it had been answered differently by other researchers. Jourdain had hastily accepted one answer ('Johannes' as the translator) so as to build up the reputation of the French archbishop Raimundus (who had commissioned a further translation from Johannes Hispanensis). D'Alverny could use an alternative answer to *question* Raimundus' reputation as the founder of the

School of Toledo, in fact to question the entire idea of a School of Toledo. Note carefully: her answer became a mode of questioning, breaking any one-to-one relationship between questions and answers. More simply, the philological details were of major explanatory consequence. Further, at the end of her analysis d'Alverny suggests why the initial question had been so hard to answer. The misconstrued proper name not only concerned the patron of the translation but also hid the identity of the more likely translator, someone called 'Avendauth', whom d'Alverny suggests was Jewish. The problem, posits d'Alverny, was that the Jewish influence on twelfth-century Toledo had been covered over by centuries of Christian redactors and historians, who usually interpreted in favour of the more native Hispanic or French influences: 'Should we not ask,' wonders d'Alverny, 'whether the doctrinal syntheses of Israel had an earlier and more direct influence?' (1964:43). This wider question properly belongs to historical criticism; it reveals the researcher's motives for questioning commas and proper names; it locates another kind of importance. D'Alverny's original question was thus important on at least two counts: first, she could answer it in a way that others had not, and second, her answer led to a much wider question that others had failed to ask.

This example contains most of the elements we need for a basic understanding of importance. On the one hand, there are countless problems of detail and identity that may or may not be worth solving. On the other, there are major questions concerning wide issues that are subject to disagreement and debate. I suggest that 1) the second level of questioning can give importance to isolated questions on the first level, just as 2) an answer on the first level can support further questions on the second, and 3) this can happen in a way that avoids most one-to-one relationships between questions and answers. When these three initial conditions are met, we are dealing with a question of importance. The hypothetical inferiorization of Jewish translators made the name 'Johannes' important, indicating why others had failed to ask questions about this particular point. Big questions can make little questions important, and this process can in turn lead to new questions of importance.[1]

---

[1] A more formal description of this process would have to define what makes one question 'bigger' (or 'wider') than another, at least in situations where the two are related and can to some extent be compared. We may think of this relative size as being both objective (the amount of world one has to look at in order to answer the question) and subjective (the number of people or social positions likely to be interested in or affected by the question). Much of my discussion here will assume that these two aspects correspond to each other, such that a question involving a lot of world will automatically interest or affect a lot of people. This might be true if there were no such things as fields and their corresponding disciplines.

What exactly is importance? The quality is obviously not inherent in any particular object. Something can only be important or unimportant *to someone*; the situational relation to the subject is essential. Mechanistically, we might suppose something is important to us if we are prepared to expend energy to get it, to keep it, or to avoid it. D'Alverny obviously thought her question was important enough to go hunting for 45 manuscripts of the same translation. Yet the fact that she went to all this trouble does not in itself give a measure of importance. Individual effort would more properly concern a subjective theory of deprivation-based value, according to which the value of an object can be measured in terms of what an individual would sacrifice to gain or retain it. Countless researchers deprive themselves of social life, money and good sleep in order to produce books on questions that are nevertheless of little importance. The key to success is not mere suffering.

What makes d'Alverny's question properly important is the fact that some-one else could also have thought it was important. In the distant medieval past – goes the argument – hidden hands might have considered the role of Jewish translators so important that it had to be covered up. A nineteenth-century French historian could then capitalize on this inferiorization in order to create a heroic French archbishop whom various generalist sources still describe as the founder of the School of Toledo. At least some effort had been expended to avoid precisely the answer that d'Alverny managed to substantiate. That's why her answer is important in a way that narrowly subjective value can never account for. It is able to disturb the answers of others.

In this sense, importance could be seen as a measure of the effort expended by some people to answer a question in a way that other people want to avoid.[2] Importance is not just for someone but also in relation to someone else; there is always some degree of intersubjective disturbance or conflict involved. Of course, in situations where translations are automatically inferiorized or rarely discussed, the fact of doing any kind of translation history at all may become important. At the other extreme, as soon as everyone agrees on a particular point – for example, that an implied comma should be moved and 'Johannes' should be read as 'Johanni' – this particular question will become unimportant. The attention of researchers can then move on to more pressing issues.

---

[2] My interest in importance goes back to I. A. Richards (1924:47-51), who equated the term with a measure of disturbance caused by one appetence or aversion for other appetences or aversions. Without subscribing to all the psychomechanistic principles that this involves, I am interested in recasting the description on the level of social relations, focusing on the element of 'disturbance'.

To summarize, I am suggesting that in addition to the three initial conditions mentioned above, a question is important when there is disagreement about its answer and this disagreement bears on some wider question of explanation. We shall return to these principles when dealing with the role of past translators and translation theorists, since importance concerns both the subject and the object of translation history.

Once you have an important question, you logically try to determine what kind of answer you are likely to find. A possible answer should take the form of a hypothesis, which is no more than a statement of what is to be substantiated or falsified. In the above example, some of the pertinent hypotheses would be: 'This translation was done for Johannes', 'The translator was a Jew called Avendauth', 'The role of Jewish translators has been understated or suppressed', and so on. Hypotheses can be on any level, from the archaeological to the metaphysical. They can be formulated as positive or negative propositions ('The translation was *not* done for archbishop Raimundus', etc.). As a general rule, though, the positive or negative form of the hypothesis corresponds to the answer you expect or want to find, the answer on which you are going to bet your research efforts. In this kind of practice, initial hypotheses tend to be substantiated or falsified only to a certain degree, often requiring formulation of a new hypothesis, leading to further testing on the object, then an even better hypothesis, and so on. Hypotheses multiply. At the same time, results obtained on one level (say, the name 'Johannes') may require modifications on another (for instance, the role of Jewish translators).

The question-and-answer process quickly blossoms into networks of interdependent hypotheses that, together, propose simultaneous explanations on several levels. Such networks might be called 'models', since they present multifaceted explanatory accounts of an object. D'Alverny, for example, has an implicit model that relates the inferiorization of Jewish translators to the misinterpretation of certain texts and the operation of a certain Hispanic ideology. An opposed model might hypothesize that Jewish translators were truly subordinate, that the main intellectual in mid-twelfth-century Toledo was the apparent Hispanic Gundisalvi, and that the question of one proper name is quantitatively irrelevant anyway. Thus, the answering of any one important question – over and above the many run-of-the-mill questions that spawn hypotheses – may require the construction and testing of a more or less elaborate model. The jumps forward in this process, involving the formulation of hypotheses and the construction of models, might fairly be called the fruits of speculative thought, which is obviously an intimate part of any historian's practice. All this is well known. It is the basic stuff of intelligently empirical research.

My main point is that the motor behind the whole investigation process must remain the important question to be answered. If you lose sight of that, your hypotheses and models risk becoming unimportant. In themselves, empirical methods are not enough.

Against blithe empiricism

Almost everyone I know has problems: family, health, love, children, wars, environment, worries about the future, worries from the past, things they want, things they don't want, a string of objects and goals they consider important. If intellectual work is to be done purposefully and for more than aesthetic contemplation, the aim must surely be to answer questions of importance. Further, if such work is to be done with some degree of involvement or even passion, the aim must be to tackle questions that are relatively close to our lives. Historians of translation have no real reason to be different in this regard.

   Some claim that the development of hypotheses requires dispassionate judgement, objectivity, calm, science, or at least an outmoded stereotype of science as emotionless inquiry. At one extreme, this view would maintain that good research comes from simply looking at the world and telling someone what you see. According to such an ideally descriptive position, no explicit initial questions are necessary and any outright subjective engagement would automatically disengage the researcher from serious scholarship. Hypotheses and models would be no more than ways of 'synthesizing research' (so Frank 1992). This approach could even imply that we read all the books before thinking about how to make sense of them, or indeed before reflecting on why we should have read them in the first place. True, the culture of erudite scholars does tend to fall on its feet, synthesizing enough conclusions to stimulate more reading. For most of us, though, time and eyes are precious; not everything can be read; the erudition of others is likely to inspire occasional admiration and little else. From our pragmatic perspective, there are reasons to doubt that hypotheses and models merely enter at the last minute to synthesize an open-ended adventure through texts. The general belief that such methodological things constitute a mopping-up phase might even be associated with a widespread 'descriptive fallacy': it falsely supposes translation history will come to us without us ever having to go to it. We would just have to wait and describe.

   At another extreme, some researchers invest rather heavily in the concepts and methods of field-formation, formulating questions that actually become answers before anything is really described. This might take the researcher out into the world, but it more often stifles productive importance. An illustrative case is the rudimentary assumption that translations are facts of target cultures only, which leads to the constitution of an object comprising "translations as facts of the culture which hosts them" (Toury 1995:24). The axiomatic status of this supposition too often means that all subsequent hypotheses and models necessarily confirm the point of departure, even to the extent of overriding the perceptions and opinions of historical translators. We shall return to this later.

A similar example of the same logic would go something like this: Translating is by definition a teleological action; let's look at translating as a teleological action; behold! we find that all translating is a teleological action, no matter what individual translators think they are doing (some think they are following the dictates of source texts). A more curly one is this: Translation history should be an empirical science; here is how you do empirical science; so here is how you do translation history. Or this one, our very own: Translation history is about dynamic intercultural groups; we look at such groups; we find they are full of translators. Or more generally: Translation is important; let's look at translation; see, translation is important, isn't it?

What's going on here?

Such reasoning is an element of any field formation. This is quite understandable: If intercultural groups (or target cultures, purposes, etc.) are important to us, we look closely at them; we tend to look less closely at other areas. This can also concern historical periods: not by chance am I more interested in the international movements of the late nineteenth century than the great Romanticisms of the first half of the nineteenth century; my models work better in one field than they do in the other. Any researcher might be expected to focus on aspects that are likely to verify their initial assumptions. Yet this should clearly not become a long-term indulgence. At some point the basic field-forming propositions should also be formulated as important questions. Until this is done, our notion of importance is operating in a strictly one-to-one way, finding immediate answers to all its questions, producing potentially massive tautologies on the level of theory, and sweeping a lot under the carpet.

One way around both the descriptivist and tautological traps is to insist on the multi-layered nature of importance and the tension that it sets up between various levels. Before reading and describing all the books or before assuming that translations belong to target cultures, that they are teleological actions, or that the world needs empirical science, translations or whatever, we should be able to say what kind of important question is to be addressed by reading a particular set of books (and not others), by looking at target cultures only (rather than intercultures or cross-cultural relations), by privileging final causes (instead of Aristotle's other causes, for example), by counting objects (thus spending less time on ethical or speculative thought), by focusing on intercultures (rather than independent sources and targets) or by studying translation (rather than second-language acquisition, for example). Thanks to their disputed nature, questions of importance should suggest what kinds of considerations are likely to be left out of our answers, and thus what aspects of the object we are likely to overlook. If we become aware of this, hopefully by elaborating our particular place in questions of importance, descriptive passivity and tautological theory can often be avoided; researchers might even discover they actually have a position, whether they want it or not.

A slightly more rigorous way of avoiding one-to-one questions and answers is to insist on the formulation of hypotheses and models that can be tested on precisely the kind of material where they seem most likely to fail. Many starting assumptions can be submitted to tests of falsification rather than eternal justification. For example, the assumption that all translators belong to target cultures is fairly easy to check, if and when the terms involved are clearly defined. The same should be true of hypotheses concerning intercultures, on the same conditions. On the other hand, a proposition such as 'all translations are teleological' is not easily submitted to any falsification test; it can be allowed to stand if and when it is of some importance in a wider context (if and when someone actively denies the proposition), and it can be calmly ignored when of no such importance (or when one simply refuses to believe it). At base, the circularity useful for the construction of fields and disciplines may be more efficient than universal Popperian falsification. Yet wherever possible, criteria of importance should require that our fights be taken at least some way into enemy territory, overrunning established fields and breaking academic ranks when necessary.

Beyond basic fallacies, three specific features of current empirical studies have much to do with our notion of importance. First, the principles of empiricism are often formulated without distinguishing between the human and non-human sciences. Second, depersonalized research tends to be promoted through appeals to 'intersubjective testability'. Third, as an apparent consequence, some approaches incorporate a strange social asceticism, as in Gideon Toury's assertion that "it is no concern of a scientific discipline to effect changes in the world of experience" (1995:17). Empirical scientists just sit there and produce descriptions, come what may, important or unimportant. Let's tackle these aspects one by one.

Why should no fundamental distinction be made between the human and the non-human sciences? Doesn't something rather special happen whenever people set out to work on the products of other people, rather than on superconductors, quarks or wood? Whether you like it or not, translation history places us in the same world as the stuff we are dealing with. We are inescapably in the human sciences, the humanities, the part of business where the subjectivity of the researcher – or the intersubjectivity of the research community – is just as social and just as historical as the translators and translations we are looking at. Yet it is easy to hide this fact by focusing on textual artefacts and then dissipating subjects into systems, as if the past were irrevocably dehumanized. It is easy to seek a method that would function like some kind of processing machine, complete with hypotheses and models able to cut up any historical object into manageable pieces and stick it back together in an immediately understandable way. If the method is right, it can be applied indifferently to virtually any object and by virtually any person, since intersubjective testing will ensure the same result. To be sure, we are told that every application of a hypothesis tests and refines the analytical principles, working ever onwards toward some universal truth. Yet where in this process is the object recognized as being specifically human? Where do straight empirical methods mince with the actual starting points, the initial questions that are surely the very condition of any intersubjectivity testable result?

In stressing importance, I am proposing a method that is activated right at the beginning of any research project, both in the selection of the important question and in the concomitant engagement of the researcher's subjectivity. We cannot simply draw a few translations out of a hat then apply the recommended method. One should have good reasons for working on *this* particular object in *this* particular way, and the reasons should in both cases minimally concern people, human values, not abstract results.[3]

This leads to Toury's problem of whether or not scholarship should try to change the 'world of experience'. If you have an important question, or the social world around you is asking questions of importance, wouldn't it seem vital to try to answer precisely those questions rather than others? And wouldn't such an activity necessarily bring about some kind of change, be it direct or indirect?[4]

---

[3] This involves a classical ethical problem that may be illustrated as follows: A medical researcher discovers a cure for a tropical disease; the cure is applied; the population increases; food becomes scarce; the population's standard of living declines. So what was more important: the disease as a medical field or the population's standard of living? I suspect something similar is happening in translation research, where the field is set up so that we solve strictly translational problems, without ever comparing the costs of translation against those of language learning or the development of multilingual communities.

[4] The contradiction behind Toury's claim becomes blatant when he asserts that "translation activities and their products not only can but do cause changes in the *target* culture" (1995:27). If this assumption applies so well to the past, why shouldn't it apply equally well to current research activities and their products? Toury's failure to subjectivize translation history results in elective blindness to his own place in history.

One of the ironies in Toury's work is that he has a commendable track-record of dealing with important questions. When virtually everyone was analysing source-text determinants on translations, he proposed that translations were determined by their role in the target culture. When virtually everyone assumed that translations can and should read like non-translated texts, he was one of those who described social tolerance of specifically translational language ('interference'). When pedagogues have most insisted that researchers should find ways to improve the standards of translations, he has most insisted that researchers should describe translations independently of any preconceived standards. One could also add Toury's semi-heretical interests like pseudotranslations and 'native' translators, not to mention his work as a translator and translation critic within Hebrew letters. But the point is clear enough. Here we have a researcher who apparently does not want to bring about any specific change and yet constantly deals with questions that are important in precisely the sense outlined above. How should we read his claim to empirical neutrality?

One answer might be found in the French sociologist Pierre Bourdieu. When asked whether sociology was properly a 'science', he replied that it had the specificity of a *science qui dérange*, roughly a 'science that upsets'. Why should sociology upset people? Because, says Bourdieu,

> it reveals things that are hidden and sometimes *suppressed*, like the fact that success at school correlates not with "intelligence" but with social background and more exactly with the cultural capital inherited from one's family. These are truths that technocrats and epistemocrats – that is, a good number of those who read and finance sociology – do not like to hear. (1980:20, italics in the text)

The description certainly belongs to the French 1980s. Yet it applies uncannily well to Toury's research interests, which should indeed upset many of those who read and finance translation studies. It might also apply to d'Alverny's archaeology, the findings of which were first published in a collective volume where almost everyone else sang the praises of identifiably Hispanic translators. To delve into a question of importance inevitably means that some people are going to be upset. Yet Bourdieu is not interested in being an academic lout. Like Toury, he insists on descriptive science. He even talks about this science producing truth, although the conditions of his kind of truth go beyond cold objectivity or neutrality:

> The possibilities of helping to produce truth depend on two main factors: the interest one has in having a truth known (or inversely, in hiding it from others and from oneself) and the capacity one has to produce it.

> As Bachelard put it, there can only be a science of that which is hidden.
> Sociologists are best armed to discover what is hidden when they have
> the best scientific weapons [...]. And they are most "critical" when their
> conscious or unconscious intention is most *subversive*, when they are
> most interested in revealing that which is censored or suppressed in
> the social world. (1980:22-23, italics in the text)

Bourdieu sees the researcher as being consciously or unconsciously interested
in asking certain questions and answering them in a certain way. From this
perspective, sociological science, with all its paraphernalia of questionnaires,
statistics and concepts, becomes a weapon that can be used to win a fight, just
as Toury uses an idealization of empirical science as an instrument for challenging other people's beliefs about translation. There is no reason to refuse the
use of these tools (nor others: deconstruction, for example, is a very powerful
weapon that can be pointed in almost any direction). Intellectual weapons are
part of any method. The point, however, is that the researcher's subjectivity
need not be equated with them. It is wrong to believe that the person doing
sociology is a sociologist and nothing else, or that a translation scholar believes in the virtues of translation and nothing else. The instruments (tools,
weapons, procedures) can only give important results when used to answer
important questions. Intersubjectively framed subjectivity must inform the
decision to work on one question or another, making the selection in terms of
importance. The researcher's subjectivity is there at the beginning, prior to the
instruments. Thus, no matter how neutral the white-coated experts might want
to appear – and Bourdieu admits that sociologists have great personal interest
in appearing to be neutral – the decision to peer into certain domains and not
into others must always come back to the personal or collective interests of
the people carrying out the research. In this sense, despite Toury's claim to
neutrality, he must have some basic desire to bring about change in the world,
even if the only change is that other people are made to think twice.

Does Bourdieu want to bring about change in the world? Yes, of course he
does, since he admits that researchers have personal and collective interests at
stake. On the other hand, Bourdieu also knows that change does not ensue from
the sociologist's efforts alone. His ideal sociology is a way of giving a voice
to social groups that would otherwise be overlooked or excluded from public
debates. This too might be applied to translation history, which could give a
voice to otherwise silenced translators. Unfortunately, such a vision cannot be
applied to Toury's science, which not only feigns indifference to what the world
might make of it but also allows scant room to translators as subjects. Unable
or unwilling to ask important questions about its own subjective bases, this

descriptivism is peculiarly unable or unwilling to ask important questions about the subjectivity behind the texts called translations.

The lesson is this: Before we adopt someone else's methods, we should think about what question we want to answer, and why it might be important. Such thought should become part of the method itself.

Personal interests

Although translation historians ideally ask questions of importance, I certainly do not want to suggest we must have overwhelming personal desires to find certain answers and hide others. Some degree of subjective involvement is a good and necessary thing, since there would be little substantial motivation without it. Yet the first check on our motivated questions should be self-critical awareness of why we want to study a particular stretch of history. This check can have both negative and positive aspects. On the negative side, prolonged self-reflection can become intellectual lethargy, blocking rather than guiding the study of history. On the positive side, though, if you're looking for an important question, it often helps to ask why you're already looking in one direction rather than another.

If I were to formulate the personal interest I had in working on the School of Toledo, I would have to think back to how I got there in the first place. As is so often the case, I stumbled into the field almost by accident. I was asked to write an encyclopedia article on the history of translation in Spain; I had no special expertise in medieval translation; I had to start from scratch. As I read, I began to suspect that much previous research had indeed been conducted in the interests of Spanish national glory, effectively covering up the role of intercultural groups like the Jewish and Mozarab translators, as well as various travelling Italians and Englishmen. What d'Alverny had to say was of considerable importance in this respect. But why should I, as an individual, care about this? Subjectively, I couldn't help but care, since I was at that time working as a foreign translator in Spain, teaching with some difficulty within the power structures of a Spanish translation school. The problems I experienced in the present inevitably coloured my view of the past. When I asked, with reference to twelfth-century Castile, 'How would a foreign translator be received in a Spanish translation school?', the question was formulated in terms of my own situation, even though I tried to answer it in terms of Girardus Cremonensis' relation with the Toledo cathedral. I supplied the question; history responded with a kind of answer (Girardus, I believe, would have been received as a threat). This is an extreme case of the kind of subjective involvement that strict descriptivists might want thrown straight out of court, while psychologists could dismiss it as a mere delusion of grandeur on the part of the researcher. Yet does personal involvement necessarily lead to bad history?

In this case, I don't think the results were all that bad. The initial question was personal. But I had to express it in the form of testable hypotheses (the central one being that 'translation in twelfth-century Castile was mainly carried out by intercultural groups'); I had to form the object, collecting data on translations and translators; I had to find enough evidence within the object to test my hypotheses, reformulating them where necessary; I eventually produced a model that I hope is of large-scale explanatory importance for numerous aspects of this particular historical object. In short, the outcome of the research was something more than the personal interest I started from. Although I asked the questions thinking in the first person, the answers were *there*, in the third person. I took my problems out into the world in search of solutions.

By the time I'd done enough of this particular research to have a tentative result – and I still have enough personal interest to keep working on the twelfth century – my investigation had taken the form of general field-forming hypotheses addressing questions far wider than my own. What is the nature and role of intercultural groups? How have these groups been dealt with by nationalist historians? How can the groups negotiate with sedentary cultures?

At the stage when answers to such questions become possible, the researcher can hope to find some kind of social support. This is essential. Some degree of assistance, no matter how symbolic, is always necessary, no matter how much tenured academics flourish the autonomy of research. Important history not only *should* concern more than one person, it *must* do so in order to be exchanged, in order to give returns on the time and effort invested. But who is going to swap anything for a few ideas about twelfth-century Castile? The market demand is not automatic. Few Spanish nationalists are likely to support work on such problems (this would be a measure of negative importance). Of course, the Spain that is rediscovering its multicultural past might yet be interested. More helpfully, a scholarly journal of internationalist allures, edited by remarkably intercultural translation historians, did recognize some interest and published a first version of my research. In the end, the initial problem led to findings that hopefully involved a measure of importance beyond my strictly personal concerns.

Research and client interests

Whatever our personal concerns, the questions we work on must be important to someone or to some social group. Even before we use methods that ensure we can't impose just any personal desire on the world, there is a kind of initial constraint built into the fact that research depends on more than the existence of a self-proclaimed researcher.

Whether we like it or not, someone is supporting our research, directly or indirectly. Support may come from a university, a government, an international organization, a local foundation, a publisher, a research community, a family that has to put up with us, and hopefully readers who are also prepared to lend us time and attention. Let me lump all these people together as 'clients', by which I mean they are the people to whom, sooner or later, we have to sell our research, if only in the metaphorical sense of getting them to feed and house us. Without external support, the lone researcher would be left muttering in a room. The need for this broad client support means, of course, that personal problems are never sufficient justification for carrying out research. There must also be some regard for the interests of others. They too have a stake in importance.[5]

The relations between strictly individual interests (what the researcher considers important) and client interests (what others think is important) are notoriously tricky. There are usually different priorities requiring some kind of compromise. This is best explained by a few examples from the laboratory.

As I have mentioned, a series of minor accidents left me with a contract to write an article on 'The Spanish Tradition' for the *Routledge Encyclopedia of Translation Studies*. This was not a particularly welcome project: in 5,000 words I had to cover some eight centuries of translation history. The real problem, though, was the title. How could I write on a 'Spanish tradition' if I suspected there was no such thing? Julio-César Santoyo had already lamented that Hispanic translation theories "constitute no tradition; they have no genetic interdependence" (1987:19), and I had little evidence to suggest there was substantially greater continuity on the level of translation practice. Worse, the hypothesis embodied in my client's title ('there is a Spanish tradition') was by no means the hypothesis I wanted to pursue (I was interested in intercultures). And yet, for the client, it was apparently important that this historical section of the encyclopedia be divided into countries with translation traditions, like a United Nations of sedentary states. If not, how could the world be organized?

I initially dissented by suggesting the title 'Translation in the Iberian

---

[5] A possible exception here might be the kind of subjective importance proclaimed by sovereign professors: such is the only way I can understand Vermeer's blunt first-person stance in statements like "An interpretation functions within *our* – better, *my* – situation, within which, if fruitful, it is legitimate for me" (1996:7); or again, "The interpretation [of historical data] is *my* interpretation" (1996:9, italics in the text). The individualism of this interpreting 'me' would be mere arrogance if it did not at the same time project a history composed of similarly sovereign individuals.

Peninsula'. I supported this with a draft article that explained why Spain, as a composite of languages and cultures, shared a substantial past with Portugal and, as far as I knew, had little substantial translation tradition of its own. The draft text was a compromise in that I accepted the client's implicit hypothesis and then set about trying to disprove it. In the process, of course, I also learned to modify my own initial assumptions, finding that five centuries of hegemonic Castilian involved translation practices that might as well count as an established if contested tradition. Yet the title remained a sticking point, even if I conceded to the term 'tradition'. Some argument ensued as to what is or is not 'Spain' (the modern state certainly cannot be identified with the past of Castile). These disputes, upsetting at the beginning, gradually exhausted themselves. We compromised again, settling on the title 'Spain, translation in' (for reasons of alphabetical order) and I gave up trying to explain why my Basque, Catalan and Galician friends would still be unhappy about the word 'Spain'. My client was eventually satisfied and I was paid, which might represent bottom-line success. One learns to give and take; one learns by giving and taking.

There's a sequel to this story. As I write, I find myself in the position of a client or client's agent responsible for organizing the Iberian Peninsula chapter of the De Gruyter *Handbuch zur Übersetzungsforschung*. Yes, this time I've avoided 'Spain'; I've won the title 'Iberian'! It wasn't easy. I complained that the article originally envisaged as 'Translation in Spain' had been allotted just a fraction of the pages conceded to German, English and French translation cultures, thus grossly under-representing the role Hispanic translators have played in European history. As a researcher, I was quite prepared to upset the expectations of my clients. But then these particular clients very cunningly won me over by inviting me to reorganize the topic as a long chapter, paying due attention to multiculturality and this time, thankfully, not presupposing the existence of any national or language-bound tradition. I then had to coerce various historians into contributing to the chapter. This is where the problems started.

In outlining the chapter, I wanted to ask questions about the roles played by intercultural groups in the complex flows between the various Iberian languages (which historically include Arabic, Hebrew and Latin). Consequently, I organized the chapter into chronological articles. As I contacted the specialist historians, however, it became clear that few of them had much interest in working this way. Portuguese experts justifiably wanted a separate article for Portugal; Catalan specialists wanted the same for Catalonia; as did Galicians for Galicia (the Basques have not yet insisted). As much as I tried to impose a model of closely interwoven cultures, the actual researchers thought it was more important to hypothesize the interrupted development of semi-independent cultures, along the lines of Spain's current political organization into semi-independent *autonomías* or self-governing regions. What was logical for me was not so logical for them, and vice versa. The tradition of traditions dies hard! In this case, the necessary compromise has fallen the side of the specialist historians, since one of the functions of the *Handbuch* is to present the research that has been done, and much of the recent research has indeed been done in terms of separate cultures. Not gratuitously, many of the research grants now available in Spain are financed by the regional governments. My weight as a client is obviously less than that of semi-independent cultures eager to rediscover the translators of their past. Once again, you have to give and take.

This brings me to one of the most important elements in the setting up of any research project: the art of getting funding. Much could and should be written about the ignoble skills of writing research proposals, since they are an inevitable part of our business. Some tricks of the trade are fairly clear. Good mileage can be obtained from technical references to methodological problems, extensive bibliographies, a few drops of arcane terminology, in short anything that can make you look like an expert that a client might want to trust. But before all the expertise, you must always be able to say, in the simplest of terms and usually in the first paragraph, why your work is important and why it should be of some importance to the people likely to pay you. Monied clients sometimes want certain questions to be addressed; they often want other questions avoided; they are also players in the formation of importance. At this most basic of levels – the selection and formulation of a question of importance – there is no impersonal neutrality.

The recognition of client interests need not involve selling your soul. I believe that a sincere search for important truths will always win out in the end, come what may. Yet while we're waiting for justice, many strategies and subtle compromises are possible, over and above the widespread tactic of promising goods that you have no intention of delivering. The real art lies in being able to make some really abstruse question sound worthy of social support. Does any funding body – or its social constituents – actually get excited or upset about details of the School of Toledo? Who beyond a few academics would really care how Wagner and Nietzsche were translated into French at the end of the last century? In its defensive mode, the formulation of a problem can be a justification of a certain obscurity. On the ideally positive side, however, the need to sell our research should force us to ensure our questions really *are* worthy of support; we should be able to formulate questions that really *can* arouse passions among those distributing funds. This is one reason why the notion of importance links small questions to big questions, since big ones are hopefully those that most people can grasp.

My example here concerns work on the French-German literary translations of the 1890s. How did I get there? In this case, the trajectory was far more academic than accidental. Following my work on Toledo and several other case studies, I had formulated the general hypothesis that translation norms are intercultural. To test this hypothesis I wanted to work on a translation situation involving two very distinct cultures; I sought an object where there was no obvious intercultural community and where translation norms were apparently very culture specific. That is, I wanted to test my hypothesis precisely where it seemed most likely to be invalidated. If I could prove it there, it would be far stronger argument in other fields as well.

As such, the problem was academic in a fairly noble sense, involving no more personal passion than my genuine interest in interculturality. But I needed support, in this case a grant from the Humboldt Foundation in Germany (for which, by the way, I have nothing but sincere praise). In case justice wasn't on time, how could I make my academic problem sound like a client problem as well? How could I make it *be* a client problem? As might be expected, my proposal in this case highlighted the importance of translation for transcultural understanding, particularly in the context of European integration (this was the time of the Maastricht Treaty) and very particularly with respect to French-German *rapprochement* or *Annäherung*. This sounded like a problem that Germans were likely to be interested in; it certainly had wider appeal than a merely academic hypothesis. In a sense, my personal problem was made to be compatible with what I projected as a possible client problem. For this or other reasons – solid academic virtues would no doubt have been enough for the Humboldt Foundation – the Germans decided to support my research. That's how I got there.

The strange thing about this particular case is that the projected client interest (German culture in the context of European integration) eventually became more important than my personal question (interculturality). After about a year of financed reading, I came to believe that France and Germany could have formed some kind of alliance in 1895-96 (the prime evidence is a well-known cultural survey published simultaneously by the *Mercure de France* and the *Neue Deutsche Rundschau* in 1895, at a time of touch-and-go negotiations between the two powers). The European Union might conceivably have been initiated about a century ago. Perhaps we could have been spared the trouble of two world wars! The crucial question was to determine what got in the way of that possible alliance. What were French and German translators doing at the time? Were they for *rapprochement* or against it? This problem turned out to be far more important than any abstract speculation on intercultural translators.

What happened was that my opportunistic invention of a possible client interest effectively became my personal interest. It led to a hypothesis that, although too outlandish to figure as such in a research proposal, was important enough to keep me motivated for a long time. The formulation and pursuit of the hypothesis was also stimulated by political events in the years during which I was carrying out the research, as enthusiasm for Maastricht turned into widespread disillusion, national votes on European union were uncertain, and a war in the Balkans seemed unstoppable (that too had happened a century ago). The hypothesis became a personal problem to the extent that I very much wanted translators to be a force for mutual understanding, with all their good work perhaps being undone by a handful of stupid politicians. That was my desire. Had there not been dead and wounded Bosnians on my television throughout the research period, I might have been inclined to see 1871-1914 as a long period of European peace, perhaps mirroring the Cold War peace I grew up with. But the bodies were there (albeit only on one side). I could not help but see the 1890s as a time of great tension and negotiation. My hypotheses concerned the relation between translation and war, not peace.

The results of that research are complex and will partly be recounted later in this book. Let me just admit that my personal desires turned out to be ingenuous. I certainly found many translators associated with intercultural locations, especially Alsace-Lorraine. But the key players, on the French side at least, were remarkably Germanophobe. They were among those who did the most damage to any project for *rapprochement*. My academic hypotheses might still be saved in a modified form, since many of the translators were of intercultural origins. But numerous ideological riders came to naught. Exposed to falsification, they were indeed falsified. History answered my questions in ways I had not expected and certainly had not hoped for. When our questions are important, even our failures can be important.

Subjective interests and humility

In the previous chapter I argued that translation history should make greater room for translators as people. In a sense, the object should be subjectivized (as Bourdieu would say). In this chapter, as a corollary, I have argued that room should also be made for researchers as people. That is, we should be objectivizing the subject (as Bourdieu also puts it). There is more to this than neat formulas.

If we recognize our subjective engagement in research, several things become possible. First, we can be self-critical about our personal interests, correcting our bias or blindness when necessary, sometimes searching for inner criteria of importance,Which might reach back as far as the reasons why we at some stage decided to study the humanities. Second, we can gain greater insight into the interests and strategies of the people within our historical object, the translators of the past, simply by trying to put ourselves in their place (there is no better way of discovering why we're *not* in their place). Third, and perhaps most essentially, we tend to ask questions about the subjectivity of other researchers, not to debunk their findings as mere opinions but in order to appreciate that they may have very good reasons for taking up positions we cannot share. For instance, when I work with Catalan clients or colleagues, I constantly have to bear in mind that the affirmation of their national culture, with its long past and longstanding repression, is far more important to them than it is to me. Their results are quite valid, their empirical methods are sound, but the initial questions they ask tend not to correspond to mine. One must understand and respect that difference. It's a question of working with people.

Some might say this kind of subjective importance promotes arrogance on the part of the researcher. I am unworried by such reproaches. This is because I suspect the contrary has just as much chance of being true. If we are prepared to put a good deal of ourselves into our research, we should be able to approach the research of others with a degree of humility. We should try to look at the world through their eyes before we agree to disagree. If this can be done, there need be no radically opposed positions, no simple right and wrong in questions of importance. We are all people trying to see the world from our respective positions, and all positions are open to change through dialogue. No matter how much deconstructionists have projected radical otherness, I believe there is a primary though asymmetric sameness from which different kinds of importance can be understood and engaged in. This principle could apply to our relations with other ages, other cultures, and other researchers.

Our task is now to find out why the work of translators might have been important in the past.

3. Lists

Our problems become questions, occasionally of importance. Some questions can be answered quite easily, by thinking about them or by looking at the places they have come from. Other questions, though, concern a quantitative order where we have to grasp more world than the one that gave rise to them. Such questions must be answered on the basis of more than we already know. Once we have a question of this order, we necessarily constitute some kind of object likely to help us answer it in one way or another. In translation history, the object usually comprises translational documents (either translations as documents or documents on translations). This is because documents are all we have in our libraries and it is ostensibly by producing their translational variety that anyone becomes a translator. True, translators do much else as well; they are also humans. But in this field we can only reach those other activities and that humanity through translational documents. There is no instant humanization. The real problem is instead how to select the translations we are going to include in our object, which should be a not-yet-known world. How should we locate and sieve them? And what kind of pitfalls await us when we start from the indications most at hand, namely the lists of translations we find in our books and libraries?

There are two basic approaches to these problems. Both have their relative advantages; neither should exclude the other. The first involves the use of lists to extract corpora, which can then be subjected to a series of operations including the application of working definitions, the plotting of distributions across space and time, and explanatory analyses of the resulting forms. This method might be called reductive, since it starts from a large list and attempts to reduce it to a smaller field of some more specific importance; its common (though not only) mode of operation is more conventionally called deductive. This is the method I will adopt here and in the following two chapters. A second method, which we might call incremental, theoretically avoids the need for lists by working outward from a small area, gradually building up a larger object piece by piece, using a mode of operation that is mostly (though not only) inductive. Anyone for whom lists and quantitative methods are anathema might like to jump straight to this second approach, elaborated from the beginning of Chapter 6. For the rest of us, lists now constitute a way of getting our hands dirty.

The kinds of lists I'm interested in basically comprise bibliographical data on translations (what was translated when), although the basic principles could apply to any resulting lists of translators, places of publication, translation theories and translator-training institutions. I will soon make distinctions between catalogues and corpora as different kinds of lists. Yet the essential focus of this chapter is on the general nature of lists as basic tools for translation archeology.

Reasons for lists

Little history can be construed from the analysis of isolated translations. Worse, quite superficial history can result from hypotheses that are pumped up after summary testing on just one or two cases. Here is one such hypothesis: The rise of the printing press coincided with the inferiorization of translators as non-original writers. This is an argument put forward by Susan Bassnett, who appears to believe in it quite wholeheartedly ("sono assolutamente convecuda..." 1991b:23). The argument sounds important, since it suggests the interesting causal hypothesis that the printing press led to inferiorization, technology led to ideology, as in good materialist mechanics. Is this a valid historical hypothesis? It certainly works if one's only references for medieval translation are Bassnett's two examples: uncited troubadours and Chaucer. If these examples are representative, translators who worked prior to the printing press were by no means held to be inferior authors; inferiorization thus came later; the printing press was therefore the cause, QED. A wider survey of medieval translation would nevertheless have no real trouble locating cases where translators were duplicitously inferiorized within religious and philosophical practices several centuries prior the printing press (cf. Norton 1984:59-89; Copeland 1991:52-53). Indeed, medieval ideologies of the translator's inferiority tended to function as a mode of professional self-protection: particularly when advancing dissident knowledge, writers could protect themselves by claiming to be 'merely translators', as might have been the case with the Toledan scholars who used church resources to transfer contestational secular science. Reasons like this had nothing to do with printing presses; a certain inferiorization was functioning well before the technology that might otherwise appear to be at its base. To appreciate this, we have to look at more than a few isolated cases. When no checking is done, such argument-by-example risks becomes an exercise in self-verification.

A more respectable form of much the same process might be unearthed from the methods underlying works like the *Oxford Guide to Literature in English Translation* and the Fitzroy Dearborn *Encyclopedia of Literary Translation*, which are being compiled as I write. The first step in both these projects has been to draw up lists of the major foreign authors and genres, then to survey the various English translations of each. This procedure is no doubt well suited to 'guides'. But guides to what? Obviously, in the absence of any actual cataloguing of past translations, the guides can only really show us around the editors' apparently intuitive knowledge of who the most important foreign authors are. If left there, the method would surely find little objective world beyond the one it already knows, elaborating present assumptions in the guise of historical and even 'encyclopaedic' knowledge. In practice, though, some surprises will certainly turn up on the intersubjective side of business; contributing experts will disagree with their briefs; dialogue should lead to countless revisions of initial assumptions; teamwork will hopefully make up for the lack of a properly empirical foundation. Yet the frame for those surprises and revisions will remain the civilized paradigms of unquantified intuitions. Such pragmatism, although quite English, is not necessarily the best way to proceed.

Our first reason for drawing up lists must thus concern problems of framing. Just as any text gains meaning and function from its genre and context, so translational documents should ideally be placed within a context formed by other translational documents, particularly those that would otherwise be excluded from our intuitions. This should give the researcher a wider vision, hopefully a vision allowing the quick testing and discarding of weaker hypotheses. True, knowledge of contexts does not necessarily require the compiling of long lists (no elaborate data base is needed to question Bassnett's hypothesis about the printing press). Yet lists help force the recognition of contexts, and do so in a way that can make us revise our more disposable impressions. A brief story might illustrate the point.

At one stage I was fascinated by the number of pseudonyms used by late nineteenth-century translators working between French and German. I thought the translators' use of professional names would help me identify some kind of interculturality. A data base of sorts was readily available in the translator and author indexes of the Bihl/Epting and Fromm bibliographies (described below). Examination of these lists led to a series of whimsical hypotheses, each of which was based on a handful of examples: Some translators used pseudonyms because they considered their translations inferior to their more authorial products; others used them to appear exotic; those working into French often hid their Germanic origins; those going into German sometimes pretended to have French origins; women translated as men; men translated as women; and so on. However, when I drew up relatively complete lists for translators' and authors' pseudonyms, producing custom-made corpora designed to answer my questions, I found no clear statistical differences between the two columns (translators and authors) on any of these counts. Nor were there significant differences between the four periods used to cover the nineteenth and early twentieth centuries.[1] The

---

[1] The lack of chronological variation may be related to other unsuccessful attempts to locate significant changes in nineteenth-century authorship. Altick (1962) worked on a list of 1,100 British writers, analysing their class background only to conclude that "the author-class remained relatively constant in its make-up" (403). One might otherwise expect authorship to

hypotheses might have been interesting, but they could not be substantiated in terms of any quantitative tendency or anomaly. So I went back to the drawing board. The prime function of lists is to falsify first impressions. As in sagacious gambling, you should know when to cut your losses.

Getting data

The basic problem with lists is that you have to find suitable things to put in them. This can be a problem in cultures where bibliographical traditions are weak. In one such field, at least three researchers in Brazil – Paes (1990), Milton (1993) and Wyler (1993) – have lamented the meagre references available for a history of translation in their country. In fact, each writer has regretted that previous scholars have not done the necessary groundwork. Sooner or later, these individual lamentations will have to give way to research teams prepared to compile the lacking data.

A more serious problem with lists is that they inevitably depend on previous lists of one kind or another, usually catalogues compiled by publishers or libraries, although there is an increasing number of specialized bibliographies of translations.[2] Unfortunately there seems to have been little thorough discussion

---

have widened, in accordance with the very significant social changes in readership: Laurenson (1969), working on a much smaller corpus of 170 writers, does indeed claim that were was a drop in the percentage of upper-class writers (314). Note, though, that both these lists turn blind eyes to interculturality, in Altick's case by explicitly excluding 'writers whose family background and the major part of whose education were non-British' (1962:390). I can only suspect that a good many translators were thus left out. As far as I know, no significant list of translators' social identities has yet been compiled. The construction of such a list could benefit from the work done in the field of authorship, particularly from approaches like that of Ponton (1973), whose questions concern not where writers come from but where they finish up (i.e. official recognition, prizes, etc.).

[2] Although my discussion here will focus on modernist fields, where the problem is more often the excess rather than paucity of data, the role of lists as ideological preselections also affects research on medieval translations. Our knowledge of translation in twelfth-century Castile, for example, is heavily dependent on the list of Girardus Cremonensis's translations drawn up by his students or *socii* after his death in 1187 (McVaugh 1974). Thanks to this list, Girardus has probably been attributed more translations than anyone else in the twelfth century, gaining the status of "perhaps the greatest translator of all time" (Van Hoof 1986:10). Nevertheless, there must be serious doubts about how many of these translations he could have done himself (Jacquart 1989:110); some translations have certainly been attributed to him wrongly (d'Alverny 1964:34). The list puts an unfair spotlight on this one particular translator, considerably dimming the work of those around him. Before we can use the list, we should carefully consider the reasons why his *socii* compiled it, and indeed who those *socii* were.

of how these kinds of lists are related, especially with respect to the specialized bibliographies. The lists are there, some are more complete than others, and that's about it. To compensate for this lack, I propose to describe a few shortcomings in this quantitative aspect of translation history.

The difference between catalogues and corpora

The four works I am about to describe all call themselves 'bibliographies'. This is unobjectionable. Bibliographies comprise references to written or printed documents, in this case translations. But some bibliographies are more properly called 'catalogues' and others are better known as 'corpora'.

Let translation catalogues be lists of translations within a specified field for which the ideal is to have data on *all* the translations. The main function of a catalogue is to approach maximum completeness so as to enable any particular piece of information to be found. Corpora, on the other hand, are better seen as lists of translations drawn up according to strictly controlled criteria – of which relative completeness may or may not be one – in order to test a hypothesis or a set of hypotheses. The degree of completeness necessary for a corpus should depend only on the nature of the hypotheses to be tested (this point will be taken up at length below).

One might say a corpus is a special-purpose catalogue and a catalogue is a general-purpose corpus. Yet the distinction is not quite so trite. The movement from catalogues to corpora in fact involves forming an object of study; it recognizes that although archeological data are found, history has to be modelled. Catalogues alone do not produce good historical knowledge.

Shortcomings in bibliographies: four examples

Bibliographies are sometimes thought to be ideologically neutral, since their aspiration to completeness is ostensibly an extinction of subjectivity. Yet all bibliographies incorporate criteria that concern rather more (or less) than completeness. This means lists that look like pure catalogues are often unwitting corpora; they promulgate agendas that are more or less concealed. Since these aspects are mostly unappreciated – there is little critical discussion of bibliographies as such – and since more bibliographical work deserves to be done – particularly in the field of English-language translations – the following pages take a fairly detailed look at the criteria behind no less than four translation bibliographies. Generalists are invited to fast-forward. For the rest, my comments are formulated from the perspective of an only moderately satisfied user.

- Anselm Schlösser, Die englische Literatur in Deutschland von 1895 bis 1934. Jena: Verlag der Frommannschen Buchhandlung Walter Biedermann, 1937. 6,493 entries. 535 pp.

Schlösser sets out to study the reception of 'English' literature (everything non-American) in 'Germany' (wherever German is spoken, a definition of some importance in 1937). Since the data from periodicals and reviews only reflect reception by literary critics, Schlösser chooses to draw on publishers' catalogues, which he believes will reflect the general reading public. He thus draws up a list comprising all the catalogued translations and, in a separate list, all the works published in English in Germany (that is, nontranslated English-language works). The lists are analyzed in terms of the age of the source texts (modern/older literature), genre, the most published authors (assumed to be the most read), the publishing houses and the major translators. The analyses are presented in tables, graphs and an explanatory narrative. The study could be a model of its genre. If only we knew what important question it had set out to answer.

Schlösser's only truly operative hypothesis would seem to be that publishers' catalogues are significant because they somehow reflect the 'general reading public'. Yet this belief is never tested or questioned, even when it is openly contradicted by a struggle between two publishing houses that consciously flooded the German market for English-language publications in 1933. If a market can be flooded, then publishers' catalogues cannot directly reflect a reading public. To get from the catalogues to the public with any degree of certitude (although we don't know why we should do this), greater account would have to be taken of publishers' strategies as a major category of mediation.

In the absence of any visible question to answer, Schlösser's lists are defined in terms of catalogues, aiming for total coverage within a field. The problem is that the field is defined through the exclusion of material catalogued elsewhere. The first half of the nineteenth century had been studied by Sigmann; the American novel in Germany had been studied by Vollmer for 1871-1913; Shakespeare reception had been covered by Schücking-Ebisch. So Schlösser avoids most of the nineteenth century, leaves out American literature and makes no mention of Shakespeare. This is perhaps a good way of delimiting a useful catalogue (one has to do something that has not been done before). Yet it is a very strange way of constituting a corpus for the study of reception, since there is no guarantee that the most significant information is not precisely that which has been left out. Can we be sure American literature followed a separate reception process in Germany? What is the good of distinguishing between canonized and recent literature if one leaves out the most canonized author? Despite all the analyses, we are left with a catalogue that, quite apart from being full of holes when compared with later surveys of the period, is of little use as a corpus.

• Liselotte Bihl and Karl Epting, Bibliographie französischer Übersetzungen aus dem Deutschen 1487-1944. Bibliographie de traductions françaises d'auteurs de langue allemande. 2 vols. Tübingen: Max Niemeyer, 1987. xviii + 1311 pp. 12,289 entries.

As is indicated in Landwehrmeyer=s preface to this work, the Bihl/Epting bibliography of translations from German into French is very much part of the relations it tries to reflect. The initial plan was drawn up by Karl Epting when he was director of the German Institute in Paris during the Nazi Occupation. The French bibliographic sources had been conquered; they could be resystematized by German hands. The original idea would appear to have been Epting's alone; a first card-index was carried out under his control. As such, the project was not entirely separated from a certain direct interest in translations, since the German Institute in Paris published French versions of Hölderlin following the 1943 centenary of the poet's death. Epting not only conceived the catalogue, he helped produce titles for it as well. He obviously attached some importance to the place of German culture in the French language.

Epting's initial work was later revised at the University of Tübingen, mainly by Liselotte Bihl from 1979. The data were checked with the Catalogue des Imprimés at the Bibliothèque Nationale in Paris and sometimes with the actual publications, adding numerous entries and correcting many others.

The classification is by periods and genres, in accordance with Epting's original plan. The periods begin with the advent of the printing press and correspond to French political regimes, the dividing dates being 1789, 1815, 1830, 1848, 1870, 1918 and of course 1945. Although I have elsewhere praised this style of periodization because the divisions affect both the cultures concerned, subsequent work with the catalogue has dampened my enthusiasm. Paradoxically, the periodization tends to hide the effects of political ruptures, since considerable re-elaboration is needed to locate the translations immediately before and after each historical watershed. The periods also make the translation history of individual works difficult to follow. Similar problems ensue from the six genre divisions. In principle, no genre is excluded, resulting in miles of children's literature, popular novels and ephemeral tracts that are unfortunately absent from other catalogues and whose titles sometimes make good reading. Yet the genre divisions themselves are occasionally obstructive. For instance, 'archeology' is with literature (genre 1) but 'history' and 'prehistory' are with geography (genre 2), 'anthropology' is with mathematics (genre 4) and 'sociology' is with law (genre 5). Any corpus to be extracted from these categories has to weed out a lot of unwanted material.

This kind of problem is nevertheless surmountable, since data-processing has blessed the bibliography with indexes of authors, translators and publishers. Without these indexes, the genre range and periodization would probably make the work unusable. With them, just about everything is possible. The information one requires can be selected and recompiled, albeit manually.

The obvious lesson to be learned is that period and genre divisions are not really useful in catalogues. All that really matters is that indexes allow the information to be reprocessed by the user, who can then extract corpora. In fact, the Bihl/Epting catalogue should probably not have become a book. It would be far more useful as a simple data base available for editing on demand. Rather than follow fixed period or genre divisions, one should be able to select fields on the basis of actual dates and key-words in titles.

In this case, the bibliography's main attraction is its relative completeness as a catalogue extracted from catalogues. Yet there can be no illusion of total coverage, even after so many years of work. The entries were not systematically checked against the card indexes at the Bibliothèque Nationale (xvii), thus allowing for considerable *terra incognita*. When constituting a corpus of French translations of Wagner (described at the end of the next chapter) I had no real trouble finding 23 editions omitted in Bihl/Epting. Corpora must be prepared to venture beyond even the most impressive catalogues.

- Hans Fromm, Bibliographie deutscher Übersetzungen aus dem Französischen 1700-1948. 6 vols. Baden-Baden: Verlag für Kunst und Wissenschaft, 1950-1953. 27,790 entries.

Fromm's bibliography was compiled in 1946-49, at a time when German libraries were understandably in considerable disarray. The prime data come not from libraries but from publishers' catalogues, as was the case with Schlösser's work. Surely it would have been better to wait for the libraries to be organized? But the historical moment called for the bibliography as a reorganization and reorientation in itself. Sponsored by the French High Commissioner for Germany, the work was part of a wider attempt to redress past conflict through cultural *rapprochement*. Interestingly enough, at least seven anthologies of French poetry were published in German in 1946-48. Like the anthologies, Fromm's bibliography is concerned with indicating and extending the place of French literature within German culture.

Fromm excludes items for which the original French titles could not be ascertained (thus excluding not only pseudotranslations but also ephemeral publications not found in the unnamed French catalogues). He also omits all musical and illustrated works in which the text is of incidental or secondary importance (thus introducing a grey area with respect to opera, to which we shall return in the next chapter).

Note also that titles are included as translations from the French *language*, regardless of the author's nationality (French, Belgian, Swiss, Canadian). This creates a problem with respect to the many Germans who wrote in French, from Frederick II down. Which side of the border are *they* supposed to be on? Fromm solves the problem by giving these cases in a separate list, which is not inconsiderable (some 553 separate works written in French by German authors). Obviously, the general criterion of nationality was not important, but the criterion of *German* nationality was extremely important. The bibliography is by no means value-free.

•   Joseph Jurt, Martin Ebel, Ursula Erzgräber, Französischsprachige Gegenwartsliteratur 1918-1986/87. Eine bibliographische Bestandsaufnahme der Originaltexte und der deutschen Übersetzungen. Tübingen: Max Niemeyer Verlag, 1989. 908 pp.

The research for this bibliography of German translations from 'contemporary' French literature was carried out in 1984-87 at the University of Freiburg as part of a wider project on the German reception of French literature. Given the dates, the compilers obviously sought no temporal distance between themselves and their object. This should perhaps not be surprising, since similar proximity characterized the work of Schlösser, Epting and Fromm. All these lists were indeed 'in' translation history. What is surprising, however, is the way the compilers in this case suppose their work should directly affect the object.

The bibliography was based on the "impression that the transfer of contemporary French literature in West Germany is *stark defizitär*" (ix), which I understand to mean something like 'so quantitatively deficient as to create a deficit'. The economic register of 'deficient/deficit' is most peculiar. Reference to a 'trade deficit' would imply Germany receives more French goods than France receives German goods. A deficit means you have to *export* more. But here it clearly means that Germany should *import* more, since the importation of culture is obviously a good thing (for whom?, to what end?).

The bibliography proceeds to support this view by rigging its measurements in terms of an enormous criterion of abstract literary quality: a 'reception deficit' is apparently only meaningful in relation to "qualitatively valuable literature" (x). The bibliography thus attempts to list all that is best in contemporary French literature, indicating the works that have been translated into German and those that have yet to be translated. Of course, the result is reams of untranslated titles. Would they all have to be translated in order to cover the apparent deficit?

The actual procedure used to select the best French works leaves much to be desired. The compilers attempt to quantify the results of French canonization, then criticize this canonization as 'francocentric' (xvii) and finally add fifty of their own favourites once they realize that the 508 most canonized authors are too old to be truly contemporary. The result is a methodological potpourri of idealization and critique, illustrating one of the dangers of the mixed discourses we mentioned in chapter one.

So much for the bibliographies I have used or would like to have been able to use.[3]

The compiling of catalogues is an entirely legitimate and useful activity. If treated as archeology, it should be welcomed by those less-self-sacrificing souls like myself who seek the more immediate results made possible by specific corpora. Despite their unfulfilled ambitions to completeness, catalogues are necessary for the construction of corpora. However, if future catalogues are to become properly functional in this way, some could perhaps benefit from the following shortlist of a user's desiderata:

First, a catalogue should serve as a data base and no more than a data base. Since corpora can be extracted from such a base, period and genre divisions are not required and, if used, should be surmountable. This means one should be able to extract corpora based on alternative divisions. When access is facilitated in terms of key words, dates, authors and translators, the building of corpora could even be a relatively painless affair.

Second, if a catalogue is to be a catalogue and nothing but a catalogue, coverage should be as complete as possible, without criteria of quality or quantity, and within the widest possible boundaries. This is vital in the study of lyrical

---

[3] Lest the above comments give the impression that bibliographies are getting worse with time, note should be made of some apparently excellent work on German translations from Swedish and Italian literature (Quandt 1987-88, Hausmann 1992). Nor would I like to give the impression that all the substantial bibliographies are by Germans. There are several classic catalogues produced by non-Germans (although Morgan 1922 and Duméril 1934 are still concerned with translations of German literature), not to mention the *Index Translationum*, the Leuven project on French translations from all sources, and many minor checklists and restricted corpora.

expression, where translations published in periodicals and anthologies are often more influential than those published in individual books. When one catalogue includes such information and another does not (Fromm does, Bihl/ Epting does not), corpora requiring the two catalogues are simply blocked by unreasoned selection criteria.

Third, the existence of possible lacunae should be indicated clearly, along with the exact procedures used to compile the catalogue. When this is done, users of the catalogue will at least be aware of the areas in which any extracted corpora are likely to be weighted on one side more than the other.

Such is the potential of catalogues. They are useful to the extent that they are relatively complete. But is there ever absolute completeness? More to the point, at least for people like my Brazilian friends, how can we do historical research in situations where we know our data are not even remotely complete? And what can we say to the many other researchers who, in slightly darker reaches, are not yet aware of any possible incompleteness at all?

Completeness in history and geology

The compilers of the above bibliographies made few claims to be doing critical or explanatory translation history. Nevertheless, various groups working in descriptive studies, notably in Leuven and Göttingen, have deployed considerable resources to draw up lists that *are* presented as the bases for rather more than straight archeology. These lists are still probably best thought of as catalogues since, as far as I can tell, most of their selection criteria are based on an initial striving for target-side completeness; there are very few mentions of any rigorously selective representativity. The researchers have set out to locate all the translations appearing in a given language in a given genre in a given period. The aim of the exemplary Leuven project on French translations of the early nineteenth century is correspondingly described as being 'to study' the field (Lambert, D'hulst and van Bragt 1985:149). Similarly, a Göttingen project on translation anthologies, outlined by Frank and Essmann (1990), assumes that the pertinent categories will arise from the constitution of extensive archeological lists. In both these cases, the constitution of the list appears to precede the asking of any important question, thus apparently circumventing the need for a problem-specific corpora. This in turn allows the ideal of completeness to be extended beyond the strict terrain of catalogues, becoming a criterion for the production of explanatory translation history itself. The resulting leap from quantity to quality, very much a question of faith, merits a few remarks.

The desire for completeness is closely bound up with the ideal of empirical research being devoid of subjectivity. And yet the lesson to be extracted from our brief survey of bibliographies must be that there is always some subjective agenda at stake. Even if the lists were absolutely complete, their delimitations, if nothing else, would still respond to questions that were considered important, even if not declared as such.

A more specific desire for completeness is associated with Lieven D'hulst's claim that "the aim of any analysis, be it microsystemic or macrosystemic, is to discover systemic laws" (1987:17). Since systemic laws are believed to exist independently of the researcher, the aim of analysis must be similarly independent, allowing for no subjective intervention in the constitution of lists: "if the researcher's aims are to determine their criteria of selection," says D'hulst, "any analysis of a system will remain 'incomplete'" (1987:17). Heaven forbid!

Wait a minute. Wasn't the researcher's aim just described as being 'to discover systemic laws'? And isn't this aim being used to determine one enormous selection criterion, namely 'completeness' itself? Obviously, if a researcher has any other aim – not everyone is inspired by systemic laws – then other selection criteria could be valid, including those that are derived from the researcher's own interests. To accept incompleteness is to live with the researcher's subjectivity. It also means watching out for the subjectivity at work in even the most rigorously compiled lists, especially the scholarly subjectivity that pretends to suppress all other subjectivity.

None of this should suggest that a certain striving for completeness is without value. For strict catalogues, it is clearly one of the prime values. But what about corpora drawn up to address specific questions? If maximum incompleteness is the kind of argument-by-example cited at the beginning of this chapter (where lists, if you will, are reduced to one or two items), there are clearly degrees of relative completeness that usefully force us to go beyond our immediately subjective expectations. In my foray into translators' pseudonyms, the available lists were complete enough to make me abandon a few minor hypotheses, and yet they were also incomplete enough to ensure that the hypotheses could be tested and thrown away with the minimum of effort they deserved. I had no reason to hunt out a longer list of names. If, however, my hypotheses had turned up something of importance, I would have had cause to compile a more substantial list able to confirm, refute or refine the hypotheses. And then perhaps an even bigger one, and so on until I would eventually have exhausted importance, viable hypotheses, available object items, or personal interest in the question.

The problem is not whether or not a corpus should be complete. It is instead whether or not our questions are important enough for us to invest in a certain degree of completeness. Obviously, the more important the question, the more effort should be put into compiling a corpus able to test answers to that question.

My thinking with respect to this problem, indeed with respect to quantitative methods in general, comes from my sometime involvement with geological fieldwork. Here I indulge in extended analogy.

For some years I wandered around the hills and savannahs of Australia and southern Africa converting multinational capital into a not unsuccessful search for gold. At each stage in a prospecting operation, the cost of compiling information has to be related to the probable value of the result. One needs just enough information to confirm or deny the pertinent hypotheses. For instance, if I want to ascertain the general presence of gold in a large mountainous region, one of the most efficient quantitative methods is traditional panning in streams. The information is unsystematic and imprecise, but it is cheap and provides good indications about where further information should be sought. Researchers like Amable Jourdain and Susan Bassnett are basically panning in the streams of translation history. Theirs is a useful art that should be not be rejected out of hand. In fact, no thesis topic should be decided before the more accessible streams have been panned.

A second level of testing might be a geochemical survey. This involves taking soil samples from systematic gridpoints over a wide area and assaying for mineralization (generally not for gold, since the assay costs are prohibitive). Although the survey gives information that is more precise than panning, it by no means involves completeness. It might be like selecting the title-form of every tenth translation and using selected paratextual variants (mention of translator, term used for the translation, etc.) as surface indicators of more profound phenomena. Or again, in my nineteenth-century work I keep rough track of whether poetry is rendered as verse (rhymed or unrhymed) or prose, since the information is easy to obtain (I don't have to read the poems from beginning to end) and it could indicate the working of more important cultural processes (mainly the relation between translation and the general nineteenth-century prosification of lyrical expression). Some lists are useful not because they are complete but because they are relatively easy to compile. Cost-effectiveness counts.

Sources as sifted sands

But beware of extended analogies! If doing history were really the same as geology, I'd still be out there looking for gold. It isn't, and I'm not. There are reasons for this.

One of the differences between the human sciences and geology is that, in the humanities, information isn't just lying on the ground waiting for you to come along. The drawing up of lists requires considerable work by individuals or teams. Such work is also diachronically collective or shared; it is carried out in more than one human frame, even when we think we're all alone in the library. This is because any list of translations must be to some extent depend on previous lists, and thus on someone else's criteria. As a result, there can never be any guarantee of absolute completeness, since there are always reasons to mistrust or disagree with the products of someone else's labour. More important, necessary dependence on others means we should be wary about doing whatever seems easiest. Since lists select certain items and allow them to be transferred across space and time in a way that non-selected items cannot, they constitute a highly conditioned mode of not just presence (the items listed may still be present in our libraries) but highly enhanced presence (we can locate the listed items, whereas the others have to be hunted). Despite cost-effectiveness, the most easily constituted lists are often the most ideologically pre-cooked.

This could be the case with the Leuven project mentioned above, the one that D'hulst was working on, the one that has produced a bibliography of French translations for the period 1810 to 1840 (Bragt 1996). This is a commendable and exemplary project, particularly since the data-collection procedures have been made very explicit (Bragt 1989) and the bibliography is available on CD-ROM. But what kind of completeness does it attain? All the information for the catalogue was drawn from a previous catalogue, the *Bibliographie de France*. This source was in turn based on the French *dépôt légal* system, which obliges printers to deposit duty copies of their publications. The source of this particular completeness is thus a form of centralized state control over printing. Not gratuitously, this same state power enables the researchers to formulate their object and their aim in terms of systems. Nevertheless, even in this most apparently complete of cases, the *Bibliothèque de France* was found to have ?a small percentage of lacunae, imprecisions and contradictions@, a minor incompleteness that was inevitably compounded by reliance on the researchers' personal ability to identify translated titles (Bragt 1989:174). The result is a catalogue that aims for "complete restoration" (173) but which must settle for representativity, since the result is described as being "at least representative of translations published as books" (174).[4] There is no absolute completeness.

Clearly, when you depend on just one previous source, you also depend on the criteria used in that source. The fact that the *dépôt légal* system began in 1810-11 fixes one limit to the Leuven bibliography. That much was out of the researchers' hands. But also, in the same way, the fact that the *dépôt légal*

---

[4] "la restauration complète" ... "au moins représentative des traductions publiée en volume".

was a measure of state control inevitably fixes geopolitical limits: since the catalogue excludes French-language translations produced by publishers not based in France, it cannot accurately represent the French language in the Netherlands, Switzerland, or other properly intercultural situations (remember that Fromm's catalogue lists some 553 works that Germans wrote in French or translated into French, many of them published in the Germanic states). This limitation is not minor; it is certainly not a detail whose importance would be lost on researchers working in Belgium. The 'system' of these translations has inevitably been inherited from the political configuration of the French state, reproducing national criteria by excluding intercultural spaces. This could be a high ideological price to pay for relative completeness.

At the other extreme, a carefree shunning of completeness can incur an even higher price, particularly in situations where no compensation can be made for bias inherited from previous sources. This concerns research like Paul St-Pierre's work on '2750 randomly-selected' translations into French and English (1993), where all the empirically based conclusions must remain suspect for as long as no one tells us exactly what the term 'randomly selected' means. In the humanities, where every source has been elaborated by living people for living purposes, there is strictly no such thing as a 'random selection' of texts. If an explicit statistical process was involved, what information was it based on? What catalogues was the researcher working from? What selection criteria were involved in those catalogues? The problem is not so much that the term 'randomly selected' might coincide with a path of least resistance (a quickly constituted corpus can always throw up interesting hypotheses for further research). The problem is that we have to know how much further testing, with what kind of modified corpora, will be necessary before such surveys can lead to any kind of gold. In the humanities, the real mistake is to act as if the information were just lying on the ground, all glittering with the same immediate value.

One might argue, of course, that the traces of previous bias gradually disappear as corpora become bigger, to the point where, lost in the huge dimensions that are nowadays quite manageable, bias becomes virtually irrelevant. Although this argument has yet to be effective in translation history (St-Pierre's 'random' corpus is much smaller than the bibliographies we have been discussing), it certainly finds expression in corpus linguistics, particularly for the analysis of English. The only problem is that large corpora require funding of an order that in itself implies national or state interests. Just as the *Bibliothèque de France* invites one to consider the political limits of France as a pertinent frame of analysis, so the British National Corpus (of English-language texts) fixes national limits that are hard to circumvent. Intercultural groups, which mostly lack such financial means, risk being sidelined. Serious work is required if they are to be extracted from the sedentary cultures in which their records are embedded.

Completeness is always relative and conditioned by interests that extend well beyond those of the individual researcher. Our task must be to work with incomplete sources in such a way that the catalogues can be converted into useful corpora. At every stage, of course, the cost of the transformation must be in proportion to the importance of what we want to find. Continued analogy might push the point home.

Gold exploration has a series of fairly expensive research methods that go well beyond panning and geochemical grids. One can excavate and sample trenches, drill through a target area, and finally, the actual mining is perhaps the only way to obtain any kind of complete information about exactly how much gold is in a certain location. In each case, the cost of the research method must be less than the value of the information obtained. In the final analysis, the mining of the gold must cost less than the gold itself. If not, there would be no reason to aspire to any kind of completeness at all.

Just as only small areas are actually mined for gold, so only relatively small areas of translation history need be analyzed phrase by phrase, comma by comma. For the rest, the art lies in knowing when to call it a day.

The historian as reader of indexes

I'd like to close this chapter with a brief illustration of what it can be like to read through lists of translations. Even in the most apparently objective and depersonalized modes of research, there is still a thinking person engaged in the process. Not surprisingly, the inevitable tedium of lists means that much of one's more subjective thought is given to labour-saving devices. You look at previous catalogues and, in the case of periodicals, at minor lists like indexes, tables of contents, and the like. You become a reader of indexes. If you have had any measure of humanist training, you soon feel guilty about leaving vast stretches of text unread. You've started to *count* texts instead of reading them. Words that might otherwise have gained some kind of life are left in the graveyard of things.

As I go through *fin de siècle* periodicals, counting pages of prose, pages of verse, and translated pages of each, there's not much time to read many words. Yet it sometimes happens. Here in *Die Insel* of 1901 (2.4:261), I read Hölderlin's 'Hälfte des Lebens'; I remember having first read the poem fifteen years previously; I wonder if the midpoint of my life was in between; I note that the poem is not listed in the corresponding table of contents – had it been sneaked in for me, to punish the reader of indexes? – then I flick on through the pages, silently lamenting the unread but counted texts. Do we really want to mathematize the humanities for the sake of 'intersubjectively testable results'? What should I do with my very personal guilt, in the face of all the lists?

In defence of lists, even those that are all boxed and binned into corpora and statistics, let's not forget there is also lived experience behind their quantitative story of struggle and processes within a given human group, in a given place and time. As we watch the curves move like water flowing in a stream, now this way now that, swelling between poles like verse and prose, we should seek out what the movements might respond to, what they might say as practical reason exercised by a diffuse collective subject. If read in humanist terms, the numbers, like Hölderlin's poem, might yet show something of the human in history. They too should represent something from the past that can be read in terms of our present. Although terribly unpoetic, their story might yet be told as lived experience. This could also be one of the tasks of translation history.

4. Working definitions

By 'working definitions' I mean the explicit criteria used to select items for a corpus. This often means deciding what is or is not to be regarded as a translation or as a member of a specific genre. It means developing and applying some basic concepts concerning the object to be studied. By extension, the general problem of working definitions also touches on technical operations like fixing the chronological, geographical or cultural boundaries of a list. These last-mentioned problems will be mentioned here briefly and dealt with more fully in the following chapters. My prime concern in this chapter is with ways of defining translations.

Common sense might suggest that problems involving definitions should be solved prior to the actual compiling of lists; you decide to study a certain field before you go out and create a corpus to represent that field. In practice, though, most of the serious problems with definitions crop up in the course of actual empirical work. This is because the very function of the object is to take us beyond the world we already know. We cannot foresee all the borderline cases that will have to be decided one way or the other, and the very nature of the material often alters the terms of any starting definition. After all, if we knew exactly where and how the most important questions were to be answered, there would be no reason for compiling lists in the first place. Stable definitions thus tend to be formulated toward the end of work on corpora. This is why I have dealt with the general problems of lists (in the previous chapter) before considering how to solve the more specific problems of working definitions.

Why some information has to be thrown out

The main practical problem with lists is not really that they are incomplete (if you know *why* they are incomplete this is not a major problem) but that they quickly give more information than one can deal with cost-effectively. As you start digging away in a particular area, you tend to find far more translations than you expected, especially once you go beyond traditional secondary sources and start rummaging around in complementary bibliographies, publishers' catalogues, private papers and the like. A certain joyous abundance is usually to be blamed for rather uncomfortable numbers of borderline cases. Exactly what degree of 'imitation', 'adaptation', 'rewriting', 'version' or whatever is to be included as a translation? Should there be any radical distinction between intralingual and interlingual translation? How can genre limits be fixed *a priori* when one of the things history does is change genre limits? Where should period limits be established? According to what criteria? Should selection be based on the limits of the target culture (which always has to be defined), the target language (rarely the same thing as a culture) or combinations of a target language with selected source cultures and/or languages? As we saw in the previous chapter, these questions are often answered haphazardly. In most cases, the problems can only be solved once strong hypotheses have been formulated. You have to know – and reformulate if necessary – exactly what is to be tested. You have to know what kind of gold you're looking for.

Let me simplify the problem in terms of the distinctions proposed in the previous chapter. When swamped by items, you basically have two ways out: either you keep going and make the list as complete as possible (a catalogue, for future researchers) or you reduce the list to representative dimensions adequate to the specific problem to be solved (a corpus, for your own purposes). You either produce a catalogue or a corpus. If you want a catalogue, you put things in. If you want a corpus, you throw things out. If only actual research were that simple.

Working definitions concern the basic criteria by which catalogues and corpora are constituted. Since their most effective work is when they take you from a catalogue to a corpus, they are most useful as ways of throwing things out. It would be wrong, however, to suppose there is any immediate jump from a catalogue to a corpus, or that just one working definition will guide all the leaps we require. In practice, catalogues are extracted from other catalogues, just as small corpora are extracted from large corpora, and big ones are built up from small ones. Since there are many possible jumps, there is scope for many working definitions, not all of which need be of the same kind.

In what follows, I will argue that there are two main kinds of working definitions: 'inclusive' and 'exclusive'. The inclusive variety is used to group as many items as possible from a list (say, to retain the translations that figure in a list of books); its aim is usually to construct an initial corpus wider than the field one really wants to study. Exclusive definitions, on the other hand, select items of importance from within an initial corpus.

The way these two operations work is perhaps most easily be explained with respect to periodization. When I set out to study French-German translations, my initial field was the fairly conventional period 1871-1914, delimited by wars. However, my first corpus of translations, extracted from previous catalogues (Bihl/Epting and Fromm) was for the period 1830-1945, consciously overshooting the mark by many decades. This corpus was constructed using essentially inclusive definitions, since I wanted as much material as possible in order to have a rough overview of the terrain. On the basis of this first corpus, I could identify several phenomena of importance occurring quite specifically around 1892-1904, which then became my period of interest. To reach this second, more restricted corpus, I had to throw a lot of material out, using a series of exclusive definitions. I found limits that concerned translations, not wars. I located an area worth mining.

Thanks to this process, you can start with one object in mind, go beyond it just to make sure, then redefine your object in terms of whatever you discover. Inclusive definitions are followed by exclusive definitions. Big corpora can be reduced to manageable dimensions, and the cutting down is arguably carried out in terms of what the corpora themselves reveal. This is fairly clear when we are talking about periodization. But when the idea is applied to working definitions of translations (or cultures for that matter), the process quickly becomes obscured by the dust of futile debate.

In defence of definitions

Since we are dealing with translation history, let me now focus on the limit most likely to concern all our research projects. At some point a distinction will have to be made between translations and nontranslations. Borderline cases will have to be disentangled, some going into the translation corpus, others onto the heap of nontranslations, and still others – why not? – constituting a special list of borderline cases. Any criteria we invent to solve these problems must involve a working definition of what-a-text-must-have-if-it-is-to-be-a-translation ('translationality' is a simpler term), not as an eternally fixed truth but as a strictly operative set of distinctions considered suitable for a particular question, applicable to a particular corpus, and particularly changeable if they turn out to be unsuitable. The frustrating problem, though, is that several camps oppose the very idea of having a definition of translation. Here is a quick survey of the opposition:

- Descriptivists of various persuasions tend to criticize exclusive definitions as being inevitably prescriptive in that they involve some evaluative notion of what a translation *should* be, in fact an implicit distinction between good and bad translations. To avoid the smell of prescriptivism, some descriptivists try to absolve the researcher of all responsibility in this respect, pretending to locate their definitions wholly in the object under study.
- For relativists of all kinds, definitions tend to be imperialist in that they impose our ideas about translation on the ideas of other cultures. According to this argument, we cannot fully know the limits of translations in other cultures because we can never fully liberate ourselves from our own culture-bound modes of thought.

- On a related tack, deconstructionists and their sympathisers tend to regard all definitions as being unacceptably essentialist, and exclusive definitions as being downright reactionary.

In the face of this three-pronged attack, dare we still separate translations from nontranslations? Of course we should; we must. Whatever particular objection we want to grapple with, we still have to apply some kind of definition just to break our lists down to manageable sizes. Either that, or we abandon quantitative research altogether. For as long as we find some virtues in lists, one of the functions of working definitions must be to save us from unimportant or impossible work, which is another way of saying that definitions allow us to seek worthwhile work. They should be working definitions in every sense of the word. The best way to reply to the purists is thus perhaps to point out that, in formulating and applying exclusivist limits, at least we can see our hands getting dirty; we should know enough about work to want to make it count. Yes, we are using some kind of initial evaluation (we opted for an initial field), yes, we are asking our own important questions (not those of unknown cultures) and yes, our definitions are motivated interventions that cannot help but work for or against processes of historical change (our definitions are moving in the world). All of this ensues from our desire to deal with important questions. Further, in the process of applying inclusive then exclusive definitions, along with any number of necessary loops, we can be taken beyond at least some of our unreasoned evaluations and unfelt cultural blinkers. In fact, if working definitions are formulated and applied with more rigour than common sense, they should force us to measure our preconceptions rather than impose them directly on the world. As long as we have no illusions about what we are doing, as long as working definitions are applied strictly and reworked explicitly, no transcendental crime need result – although we can always be damned for the imperialism of seeking knowledge, and the socialism of counting human facts.

Inclusive definitions

Considerable confusion on this point has been spawned by what seem to be descriptivist attempts not to define translation. The most notorious case is Gideon Toury's recommendation that, when compiling lists, "a 'translation' will be taken to be any target-language utterance which is presented or regarded as such [i.e. as a 'translation'], on whatever grounds" (1985:20). This seems to pass the buck from the researcher in the present to the target culture in the past. It looks like relativist largesse, an elegant cop-out, making the object work while the subject just 'describes'. But is it?

Toury's working definition has been criticized by Ernst-August Gutt, among others, because it can only concern usages of the English word 'translation' (1991:7). Strictly speaking, this is correct, since Toury put the word 'translation' in inverted commas, citing it as a word from the English language. But as Toury has since made clear (1995:33), his object was intended to comprise certain functions for which he, Toury, uses the word 'translation' and for which other cultures can use as many different words as they like. In the 1995 version of the above phrase Toury consequently replaces the inverted commas with the term 'assumed translations' (inverted commas mine!), unfortunately without stating exactly who is doing the assuming.[1] Toury thinks he has solved the problem. But there are many other problems involved.

The main catch is that, as soon as Toury describes the functions of an 'assumed translation', he effectively gives a definition that can be imposed directly on all possible cultures.[2] Like Quine's jungle linguist (1960), descriptivist researchers would arrive in a foreign community and ask to see not 'translations' (English word, inverted commas) but whatever satisfies their understanding of what a translation is (actual functions). That is, in terms of Quine's thought experiment, they try to locate a functional rabbit they can identify as such before asking about how the foreign community identifies it as a rabbit. In Toury's case, this means looking at

> ...any target-culture text for which there are reasons to tentatively posit the existence of another text, in another culture and language, from which it was presumably derived by transfer operations and to which it is now tied by certain relationships. (1995:35)

There you have it, a working definition, and a particularly inclusive one at that, far more suited to a catalogue than a corpus. This definition no doubt suites Toury's specific research purposes; it has its virtues. My humble point, however, is that some such definition must be given, by the researcher and in the present. Despite the apparent largesse, there can be no question of the research process simply allowing each culture to make its own selection of what is to be considered a translation. There is no real relativism here.

The sticky problems bubble up when we have to use our definitions to exclude

---

[1] "...assumed translations; that is [...] all utterances which are presented or regarded as such [as translations] within the target culture, on no matter what grounds" (1995:32).

[2] This was very clear in 1985: "...the translation procedure should be regarded as universally acknowledged in situations where translating is indeed performed" (23).

specific texts; even inclusive definitions must be called on to do a bit of excluding. Let's try Toury's definition with the following examples:

- Pseudotranslations (original texts falsely presented and received as translations): Yes, if a certain target culture at one time believed they were translations (if it had 'reasons to tentatively posit the existence of another text'), pseudotranslations can be included in a list of translations. In this case, the list of 'assumed translations' includes texts that target-culture recipients assume to be translations.
- Unmarked translations or 'pseudo-originals' (translated texts falsely presented and received as originals): Yes again, if the researcher can locate the likely originals, there are 'reasons to tentatively posit' the translational status of a pseudo-original. Example: I was reading my daughter a Catalan bedtime story, sight-translating into English, when I came to the lines "Correu! Correu tant com pugueu! / No em podreu agafar, / perquè sóc l'Home de Massapà!" (it rhymes in Catalan). My English translation, after some stumbling: "Run, run, as fast as you can, / You can't catch me / I'm the Gingerbread Man!" (which also rhymes). Although nothing in the Catalan book marks the text as a translation, I can't help supposing the Catalan text is a translation of the story read to me in English when I was a child. So I have reasons to think it is a translation. But be careful: I have no foolproof reason to assume the story was not Catalan before it was English, nor that it didn't come from some further language. There must always be doubt concerning the classification of pseudo-originals. In this case, of course, 'assumed translations' are texts that *the researcher* assumes to be translations, widely extending the target-culture criteria pertinent to the case of pseudotranslations.
- Weakly marked translations: Between the above extremes, there is a wide range of cases where significant doubt arises and Toury's definition becomes an inadequate guide. For instance, here I have a catalogue of some 371 *fin de siècle* versions of the Salomé theme (Dottin 1983). Some of the versions are strongly marked as translations, others are not, but in almost all cases it is possible to trace the narrative elements back to crosscultural antecedents or 'traditions' (the dancer in the late nineteenth century was either Salomé or her mother Herodias/Herodiade, the main reference versions being Wilde's and Flaubert's). All kinds of transformations are at work here, from major genre and media shifts to radical rewriting and significant parody. At what precise point do these transformations stop being 'transfer relations' and start becoming original creations? In other words, in terms of the above definition, where is the cut-off point between translations and nontranslations?

Toury's broad criteria can be used to assume that virtually anything is a translation until proven otherwise; Toury doesn't really tell us how to prove a text is *not* a translation. One could conceivably regard all versions of Salomé as translations of the pertinent texts in the Bible (Mark 6, 17-19; Matthew 14, 3-12), especially if we concede that addition and omission are legitimate translative strategies (Toury does concede this). But if we throw everything into the soup, surely we start doing comparative thematics rather than translation history? More to the point, our corpora soon become so large that we can't really do very much of importance. This is one reason why I suggest we should be a little firmer than Toury. In constituting our corpora, we must be able to use properly exclusive definitions of translation, of which I shall now propose one.

Defining translations from paratexts

Toury's working definition, cited above, is of the run-of-the-mill inclusive kind ('A translation is/does x, y and z'). We now have to locate some kind definition able to state explicitly what a translation is *not* ('A translation is not/does not do x, y and z'). This is much harder and rather less popular. Yet there are more than practical reasons why it should be done.

The first reason has already been mentioned: No matter how many re-searchers elaborate their private definitions and go in search of functions instead of words, someone has almost always done the same thing before them. This is the lesson of lists: virtually all our lists depend on previous lists, so all our working definitions have to confront and perhaps compensate for previous selection criteria. In fact, considered carefully, there are no real rabbits running around in translation history. They're all dead, mummified as documents, until we make them run for us. This means there are *no functions* to which we have access except through language and, more specifically, through the filtering language of lists. Thus, when Toury checks to see if his three criteria are fulfilled in any particular case, he has to rely on the words used in the presentation and reception of a translation as a translation (or as something else) and in the sources – the lists – that initially brought this case to his attention.[3] We can invent as many definitions as we like, but we cannot impose our criteria directly on the material world. We can try, but someone else always got there first.

One way to recognize the substantiality of the object is to retain as much

---

[3] This is the point where Gutt's critique becomes truly pertinent, and where Toury fails to understand the critique. From a deconstructionist perspective, Toury commits the deadly sin of considering words transparent to the world, in this case to 'functions'.

as possible of its surface level, its words, before reducing it to a series of functions that may or may not fit our definitions. In the case of translations, these surface fragments are most usefully the 'paratexts', a term used by Genette (1978) to cover all the textual material that introduces a text proper (cover, author's name, title, blurb, table of contents, and so on, although Genette strangely fails to look at the translator's name or other translational signs, which are clearly parts of paratexts). Elements of paratexts – not the 'text proper' – are carried over into publisher's catalogues, library catalogues and the lists of all kinds by which they eventually come to us. Obviously, what is carried over is not the 'function' of the text as a translation or nontranslation but the words by which it might so be marked. As far as possible, the words should be reproduced in our own lists. If the paratext says 'imitation', 'frei nach Zola', 'wortgetreu in deutsche Prosa' or whatever, that is exactly what should appear in our corpora, quite independently of the functions we may later attribute to or construe from these terms.

Close attention to paratexts might be able to locate a key difference between translation and nontranslation. Whereas the comparative study of contents tends to discover continuous gradations of possible transformations – as in the case of the Salomé theme – paratexts function within a discourse where there is a fundamental discontinuity between subject positions. Basically, if a paratext distinguishes between a translator and an author, the corresponding text is presented as a translation. On a slightly more subtle level, if a paratext allows different discursive slots for an author and a translator, then the text may be said to be a translation (working definition!). If not, then not (working exclusive definition!).

Note carefully what is happening here: The defining discontinuity of a translation is not just on the nominalist level of external language ('this is a translation because the cover says it is a translation'); it is a function of a discourse that we receive ('this is a translation because the person who says "I" is not presented as the producer of the discourse'[4]). The words are there, in whatever language, but we interpret them as markers of a specific function that we define as a constitutive feature of translations. This is very close to Toury's definition give above, except that here the focus is on a discontinuity that results from explicit interpretation;

---

[4] Plus, of course, a series of more variable conditions: there are references to a previous text in a different or distanced language (a translation is presented as being of something); there are no markers of reported speech (the first person is not the producer of the translational discourse); there are no markers of radical quantitative change (a summary or a table of contents do not count as translations); self-translation is read in terms of two coinciding subjectivities. More conditions may be required for future leaks, but not many more: the definition need only serve its purpose as an instrument of research.

we are dealing with a definition that we make work; it is of no strict concern to us what exact concepts any other language or culture might use to talk about translations (although such questions certainly have their interest). All we need to categorize is our reception of the defining discontinuity (or of some wider function, if we want to be inclusive). Some examples might illustrate the way this discontinuity can indeed sort sheep from goats.

Consider the case of Tarchetti's Italian translation of a story by Mary Shelley (described in Venuti 1995:161-167): Mary Shelley's name is absent from the paratext, Tarchetti's name is present, and the text is followed by the note 'dall'inglese' ('from the English') in one edition and 'imitazione dall'inglese' ('imitation from the English') in the other. This could indicate plagiarism, which is Venuti's main concern. But is it properly a translation? Venuti is not sure. For him, the paratexts "offer only the vaguest indication of the relationship between his Italian version and Shelley's tale" (1995:162). For our working definition, though, this is most definitely a translation, since the note 'dall'inglese' points to a space not filled by Tarchetti, thus allocating him the role of translator. In this case, our definition turns out to be slightly more inclusive than Venuti would probably like, but that is of no real concern. You set the definition up, you apply it like a machine, and you see what results it gives.

Problematic cases abound in medieval texts, which constitute a minefield for any exclusive definition of translation. Should we make a radical distinction between translators and the numerous other rewriters (editors, scribes) who also contributed to chains of transformed texts? What should we do when an ostensible translator is also an original author and a merciless editor, all in the one text? The great risk, of course, is that we might disregard the result altogether, categorizing, as Jeanette Beer puts it, "a millennium of translative vitality as one thousand years of non-translation" (1989:2). Yet an exclusive paratextual definition of translation might nevertheless wade the tide and have something to say about medieval practices, especially to the extent that our working definitions at this stage strictly concern the products, the texts, and not the producing person or activity (we shall consider the specificity of the translator in due course).

On the level of the outgoing text, all kinds of interesting ruptures can be observed between medieval translational discourse and various first-person paratexts. Is it of theoretical consequence that these paratexts (most obviously the references to 'me the translator' or to 'my author') should become authorial asides scattered throughout the text, making the translator into a kind of narrator or reader's guide? Examples would be Jean de Meun's translation of the Abelard-Heloise correspondence (Brook 1991) or Wace's rendering of Geoffrey of Monmouth's *Historia Regum Britanniae* in his *Roman de Brut* (Durling 1989,

Allen 1991). A more extreme case is a fifteenth-century English translation from Old French, where the reader has to wait more than 2000 lines before the translator interrupts the story and mentions that, by the way, the text is a translation (Hosington 1991:234). Nice to know! Surely the interruption is a paratext, as are all the asides, narrator's comments, marginal notes and even, in some medieval manuscripts, changes of colour or period-marked handwriting that indicate ruptures between a covert translating (non)voice and the overt translator-commentator as a framing voice? Surely these are just more complex cases of the paratextual phenomena we observe in our own age? Admittedly the differences between voices will tend to be of more importance to us as researchers than they might have been to medieval readers and patrons (the earlier readers probably sought the story or the information; we're more interested in how the story or information got to them). Yet there is no reason why an exclusive definition of translation should condemn the Middle Ages to the purgatory of nontranslation. In fact, an exclusive defini-tion could well reveal why medieval specificities should be of importance to general translation studies.

One major question remains. Can our discontinuity consistently identify non-translations? Yes, if we operate blindly, any original or 'pseudo-original' is going to be classified as a nontranslation, even when there is convincing archeological data to show that it was produced by translative processes. A curious borderline case here is the final two volumes of the *Blätter für die Kunst* (1914, 1919), where the purest form of group expression is obtained by paratexts devoid of names, neither authors' nor translators'. By the same stroke these zero-degree paratexts suppress all possible indication of translational status. According to paratextual criteria, there are no translations in these volumes.[5]

This conclusion is far from satisfactory, of course. Sooner or later the re-searcher's own knowledge must also play a role; other kinds of definition can be made to work. If we have firm archeological reasons to believe that A is a translation of B, even in the absence of paratexts to this effect, then we are going to create our own paratext, classifying A as a translation if and when that suits the purposes of our research. Remember that our fundamental discontinuity had

---

[5] This criterion proved reasonably efficient on my nineteenth-century corpora of lyrical texts because copyright laws, which had developed since the middle of the nineteenth century, had made literary authorship conventions relatively strong. The restriction to lyrical texts further strengthened authorship conventions, since the genre was at that time still largely based on the expression of subjectivity. This meant there were virtually no weakly authored texts in the field under study (nothing like an unsigned tourist guide or cooking recipe). When there is strong authorship, the status of translations is marked with corresponding strength.

to be interpreted by *us* in the first place. Yet this does not mean we can forego the entire question of paratexts. Cases where we have had to supply the paratext are not translational in the same way as those where the discontinuity was more clearly inscribed. A pseudo-original is a translation for the analyst who calls it a pseudo-original (sorry about this!), but it is also a pseudo-original. If we forget about paratexts, we forget about this difference.

Corpora of borderline cases

Working definitions, like love, should be as blind as possible, incorporating an element of conscious heresy or irrationality into their carefully verbalized form. The more exclusive a definition, the more it will force us to make categorizations that go against the grain of common sense. Paratextual discontinuity, for example, can give us apparent nontranslations that were produced by entirely translative processes, and apparent translations that were not. What method supports such madness?

It is possible, of course, to be as blind as your definitions. I could say that my object comprises only translations presented and received as translations, that I don't care about the rest, and that I'll use the paratextual-discontinuity criterion come hell and high water, so there. It's nevertheless more fruitful to think about what your object has done to your definition (and vice versa). You can do this by bringing together the broken pieces, the unsolved or doubtful borderline cases, and constituting a restricted corpus of considerable heuristic power.

The interest of borderline cases has certainly been recognized by Toury in his analysis of pseudotranslations, which he shows to be extremely useful tools for locating what a community expects of translations (Toury 1995:41-52). One might equally bring together pseudo-originals and ask why their translational status was suppressed. All the 'imitations', 'adaptations' and the rest should also give us information about the status of translation within the object. Further, the paratextual status of translators' and authors' names in such cases, along with poorly marked references to source texts, might be expected to show ways translators indicated their belonging to a culture or interculture. Whatever the case, borderline corpora most usefully force researchers to reconsider their aims, sometimes to the point of reformulating the approach to the initial field itself.

Let me illustrate this with an example from research on translator training, which I believe should be a legitimate part of translator-centred translation history (since the institutions, although only formalized in recent years, have a very rich and complex history, and they may well define translators just as much as any strictly paratextual genre does). When compiling a list of 'translator-training institutions', Monique Caminade and I had to decide whether to include all or just some of the institutions that responded to our questionnaire. Although we had hypothesized an unappreciated diversity of such institutions (and a suppression of this diversity by a handful of large European and North American institutions), if we had adopted a wide inclusive definition (say, 'all institutions that have courses on translation') we would have had to list virtually every university language department in the world, constructing a plurality that would have surprised no one and would quickly have exhausted us in the process. On the other hand, to adopt a narrow exclusive definition (say, the 23 institutions that are currently members of the CIUTI[6]) would have meant not only reproducing a list that already existed but also adopting the criteria of the very people we thought we should be questioning. An intermediary solution would perhaps have been to draw up a Toury-like list of rabbit functions (for example, 'university status', four-year programme', 'limited language teaching'). Yet this would involve fairly arbitrary evaluation criteria and, more seriously, attach immediate truth value to the information that was sent to us (some 'translator-training' programmes look great on paper but have very little to do with translation in practice). Between these possible solutions, our strategy was to include only those institutions that gave a degree, diploma or certificate mentioning the words 'translation', 'translator', interpretation', 'interpreter' or cognate terms. This was our exclusive working definition, which worked reasonably well in that the resulting list was of a manageable yet surprising size (about 270 institutions), we avoided having to make functional assessments (we merely cited the words that were sent to us) and there proved to be no problems determining the equivalents for the particular words 'translation', 'translator', etc. (it was a happily closed interlingual field). For those very practical reasons, we applied the working definition blindly. Of course, we wound up with a mixed bag of odds and ends. What should we do with an institution that was excluded by our definition but was a member of the CIUTI? How could we explain cases like Japan, where translators and interpreters appear to be trained but where we could find no institution meeting our criteria? What should we do with the British Institute of Linguists, which is included by our definition (it gives diplomas) but doesn't actually do any training (it only organizes the exams)? Studying these borderline cases, we were forced to go back and reaffirm our reasons for undertaking the survey. Since we wanted to reveal diversity, yes, all these cases should be included with some kind of distinctive status. So we devised a series of secondary working definitions

---

[6] Conférence Internationale des Instituts Universitaires de Traducteurs et Interprètes, officially founded in 1964 to promote the training of translators and interpreters and to ensure the quality of its member institutions

or wild-card rules (e.g. 'In countries where definition 1 gives 0 items yet translators are trained, relax the degree-diploma-certificate condition'). These rationalized borderline cases were then included in our list, albeit marked with asterisks.

To close this chapter, I would like to recount how working hypotheses were formulated in two quite different projects, both of which will be picked up later. The examples are far from pretty, since working definitions naturally eschew conceptual elegance and correspondingly durable success. Working definitions are valuable only to the extent that they work on a particular corpus, with respect to particular preconceptions, and in view of a particular cost-effective result. Little of the following material will see the light of day within serious explanatory history.

How Wagner sneaked in

My research on translations between French and German at the end of the nineteenth century was initially focused on lyrical texts, since I was at one stage attempting to see if translation was causally related to genre prosification (cf. Pym 1992b). Roughly described as 'translations of/as lyrical texts', the field had to be defined in a way that was quantitatively and qualitatively practicable. Further, the catalogues I was working from (Bihl/Epting and Fromm) were far from perfect. The task of formulating definitions was neither easy nor conclusive.

Given the deficiencies of the catalogues, the corpus had to be constituted from a lowest common denominator, leaving out re-editions and translations appearing in anthologies and periodicals. Within this restriction, a 'translation' was accepted as any text listed in either bibliography, since the application of a functional or exclusive definition at this stage would have required too much effort for too little reward. 'Lyrical texts' were also defined in a consciously inadequate way, resolving borderline cases by accepting as lyrical any translation paratextually described as a 'poème', 'poésie', 'chanson', 'ballade', 'Lied', 'Gedicht', 'Lyrik' etc. but excluding explicit distinctions between verse and prose, since one of the aims of the research was to test hypotheses concerning the prose translation of lyrical texts. There were no obvious cases where a 'lyrical' translation was made of a 'nonlyrical' source, although I wasn't exactly digging for such possibilities.

Despite their ragged nature, these working definitions actually gave quite nice quantitative results, leaving me with a reasonably extensive yet manageable and balanced corpus of translations in the two directions (252+298 titles). More important, it made me reconsider my initial field. As noted in the last chapter,

Fromm's catalogue was ambivalent about including musical works, and I was similarly fearful of taking on genres that I did not spontaneously consider to be potential literary expressions of first-person subjectivity. My working definition was thus formulated in such a way that most music and opera was left out (i.e. I deleted items listed as musical scores in the Bihl/Epting catalogue). This made life simpler and me happier, at least until I came across a major borderline case: Wagner's libretti in French translation, called *poèmes d'opéra*. Did I really want to study Wagner? No, not really (it is a major undertaking). However, thanks to the term *poème* in the translational paratexts, I had to let him gatecrash, since my working definition said that anything calling itself a poem was enough of a poem to be in my corpus. My empirical methods obliged me to look carefully at Wagner. And I am eternally grateful to my working definitions. Although consciously inadequate, they saved me from producing some even more inadequate explanations (to be continued in the next chapter).

How Salomé revealed her importance

My final example is quite different. It hopefully illustrates one of the ways working definitions of translations can be useful in the wider study of cross-cultural influences.

As mentioned above, I once tried to find out why the Salomé theme was so fashionable at the end of the nineteenth century. My initial hypotheses had to do with the social role of women and the relative impotence of men artists, although I also hoped the theme would indicate how various national modernisms were interrelated. A catalogue was available (Dottin 1983), to which I could add 17 versions to finish up with a corpus of 389 items. This number was good for distribution curves (see next chapter) but still far more than I had time to read or analyze, especially in view of the modest and general nature of my hypotheses. I could construct a relatively inclusive definition of an underlying functional 'topic', understood as a structure accounting for almost all the variants on the level of plot. This actually allowed the catalogue to be extended in at least one significant case.[7] But I needed a corpus, not a catalogue. Something had to be excluded.

In this case, after considerable experimentation, my working definition was

---

[7] The topic was defined in the following way: four characters – a prophet, a king, the king's second wife and her daughter – are narratively interrelated in such a way that the prophet is beheaded at the instigation of the wife and/or the daughter. A version of the theme was considered to be any text received such that any part of this structure would be expected to activate all other parts. The significant text thus included was Baudelaire's prose narrative *La Fanfarlo*.

used not to chop off segments of the corpus (poems, plays, stories, etc.) but to locate versions that were in some way strong, central or even important. The definition stated that 'strong versions are those most embedded in the 389-item corpus', where embeddedness was defined as the quality of a text that functions as the source or reference underlying a paratextual discontinuity in a further text (in this case not necessarily translational). This, I hoped, would give me the texts I needed; it should have located those that were in some way the most important for cross-cultural relations. In practice, the definition forced me to look closely at the ways the various versions of Salomé were interrelated. In some cases the connections were very clear, the zero-degree case of a connection being, as chance would have it, straight translations. When Mallarmé's *Hérodiade* was translated by Hovey in Boston in 1895, by Brennan in Sydney in 1904 and by George in Berlin in 1905, the text was undoubtedly of some importance at that particular moment and in the very narrow milieux concerned. Yet other forms of rewriting could also indicate importance. Ezra Pound's very free version of Laforgue's *Salomé* (1920) also projected importance on paratextual grounds, whether or not it would pass anyone's test as a legitimate translation. The same held for the Strauss opera, which was based on Wilde's play. After some hesitation, I decided the working definition could also apply to performances that were in some way represented in my inherited catalogue (through programmes, libretti or whatever), such that the Strauss opera was considered thrice embedded because performed in Paris, Milan and New York all in the same year, 1907. My definition was no doubt too liberal for most purposes, especially since it failed to distinguish between translation and performance. Yet the result was useful in this particular case: I extracted a shortlist of just 15 strong versions, the analysis of which was able to relate the theme's major variants to a concrete distribution network. Further, these strong versions could be weighted in terms of the number of secondary texts they had spawned, thus furnishing an extendible central corpus that could have comprised just three texts (weighting of 5 or above), seven (4 or above), ten (2 or above), or the whole fifteen. The corpus could be adjusted to the amount of effort I wanted to invest in it.

I mention this project because it had a special concern with importance. In the previous chapter I described importance as a measure of disturbance, which may be both positive and negative (positive for some, negative for others). Applied to the problems of working definitions, this enables us to consider not only the items that become embedded in a list through positive repetition (positive importance indices) but also items that have in some way been actively prohibited from gaining such embedding (negative importance indices). We must consider the whole range of *negated* translation or performance, from state censorship through to refused publication. We might pay special attention to the more or less radical transformations used to overcome or circumvent negation. All such cases should in theory indicate the negative side of importance, since they all imply a situation where the desired translation/performance was so important that someone didn't want it to take place. In the case of the Salomé corpus, strictly negative importance concerns just a few versions: Massenet's opera was refused in Paris in 1881, Wilde's play was banned in London in 1892, as was the Strauss opera in Vienna in 1905. Remarkably enough, these counts of negative embedding actually reinforce the distribution of positive embedding: the most negated items were often also the most translated and/or performed. Importance was manifested on both sides.[8]

This particular kind of importance, measured in part by translations and distributed over the historical object, could scarcely be attributed to the researcher imposing a set of entirely subjective definitions. Something important had come from the object itself, and working definitions, rough and ready, had allowed that importance to surface.

---

[8] Note that the indices of negative importance are in this case projected on a corpus of positive mentions (i.e. texts that reached a public elsewhere or at another time), so we are not dealing with texts that were negated entirely. The construction of a wholly negative corpus (i.e. of texts that were refused and never saw the light of published day) is conceivable but would require vast research energies, since there are few negative lists to begin from. Projects for such negative histories have nevertheless been devised (see Coste 1988) and Venuti makes good use of the negative indices found in readers' reports leading to publication refusals (1995:253-260).

5. Frequencies

When lists have been compiled, one of the few things you can immediately turn them into is a frequency curve. You plot the distribution of translations over time. The resulting graphs may not always be eloquent but they do offer a satisfying sense of control over otherwise unruly data. The curves can confirm or deny the countless minor hypotheses, suspicions or hunches that surface as one goes along compiling the lists. They also offer relief from the tedium of bibliographic data. Yet there is more than quiet fun at stake.

In what follows, I would like to show a few easy ways to manipulate frequency distributions, plus a few ways you can avoid being manipulated by them. The discussion will be kept quite simple, with no mention of anything remotely resembling mathematics. Anyone planning to make frequency distributions the basis of historical explanation is well advised to grab some expertise from a standard textbook or a qualified colleague. In the present situation, however, my main interest is in the cunning pictures and prose in which statistics are presented. Lists become numbers, but they also become iconic and natural language.

Statistics and importance

Much of our modern image of the social sciences is based on statistics, mainly percentages and their tendencies. We believe a given society can be divided into groups that can be conjugated in numerical ways: '30% of the unemployed are under 25', 'working-class children have 30% less success at school than do middle-class children' and so on, in a general malaise that erupts into news reports, informal discussions and almost any invocation of objectivity.

The ideological use and abuse of statistics is notorious. Much depends on small evaluative phrases like 'only 30%' or 'as much as 30%', which suggest the percentage is significant with respect to a usually unexplained expectation. If '*only* 30% of the unemployed are under 25', the implication is either that a) some kind of tendency meant the figure was *expected* to be higher (perhaps as opposed to 50% for the previous year), or possibly that b) the researcher feels the figure *should* be higher (perhaps because unemployment liberates the soul, creates grounds for revolution, or whatever). Both implications concern tendencies: in the first case the tendency is based on previous data, in the second, it ensues from wilful projection. In the entire range of cases, from the most apparently objective through to the most apparently subjective, the selected tendency relates the otherwise insignificant '30%' to a question of underlying importance.

A statistic is only significant with respect to a question of importance. If no such relation is in evidence, the statistic is a mere number.

The movement from numbers to importance always involves a degree of selective processing. This means the reader of frequencies must look very carefully at what is being said. Lawrence Venuti, for example, is not above producing strangely manipulative sentences like the following:

> British and American book production increased fourfold since the 1950s, but the number of translations remained roughly between 2 and 4 percent of the total. (1995:12)

Notice the 'but'. Venuti obviously wants the number of translations to be higher; he went looking for these figures and cites them because he thinks the ratios of translations to nontranslations are too low (although what this has to do with an incease in book production is far from clear). To help his argument, he presents graphs where the numbers of published books are very tall black columns and the published translations are very short white counters (one of his graphs is reproduced here as Figure 3). Graphic representation is also manipulation. Yes indeed, 2 and 4 percent are very small quantities. The argument looks convincing. Unless one stops to think about the nature of the values being processed. According to Venuti's graphs, book production increased almost fourfold (3.94) and the number of translations increased almost threefold (2.92) over the period concerned. That is, book production increased *and* translation production increased. 'And', not 'but'.

Venuti nevertheless justifies his 'but' by comparing the low English translation percentages (2 to 4%) with much higher percentages in France (9.9%) and Italy (25.4%). What do these figures actually say? Do they mean English-language cultures are deprived of translations? Or are there other kinds of value at stake? Consider the quite compatible fact that, for years quite central to Venuti's period of analysis (1960-1986), the *Index Translationum* lists more than 2.5 times as many translations in Britain and the United States (1,640,930) than in France (624,830) or Italy (577,950). We can be fairly sure there were far *more* translations into English than into French or Italian. This is something Venuti hides from us, and yet it is surely just as significant as the percentages of total book production. Despite having much lower ratios of translations to nontranslations, English readers have many more translations available to them than do French or Italian readers. So who is worse off? What kind of culture does Venuti want us to live in? What question is he really responding to?

This is not the place to pursue all of Venuti's arguments. Suffice to say that

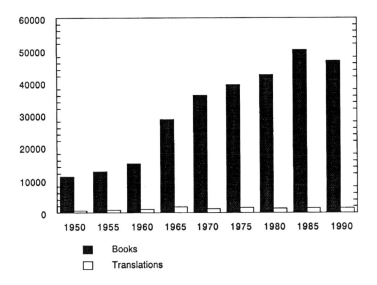

Figure 3
American publishing: 'Total book output vs. translations'
(from Venuti 1995:13)

he, like the Freiburg researchers cited in our discussion of lists, is worried about an apparent 'trade imbalance' in translations to and from English, although he never tells us exactly what a world of perfectly balanced translational trade would look like. This is worth some thought.

If all languages were spoken by exactly the same number of people and were used for the movement of the same amounts of cultural capital, Venuti might happily command something like a 25% translation rate all round. The world's translators would be overjoyed then overworked. Yet since languages are very unequal in the extent of their use and even more unequal in their access to international publication, there is absolutely no reason why their translation rates should be at all comparable. Rather than expect the same percentages, it is safer and more interesting to hypothesize that, assuming similar crosscultural communication parameters, the more restricted the use of a language, the higher the ratio of translations to nontranslations in that language.[1] There is no kind

---

[1] Think about it. Imagine a world where 90 texts are in language A and 10 in language B. If half the texts in both languages are translated into the other language, A will have 5.5% translations to nontranslations, B will have 450%. Even if language A were used by idiots and only one of their texts was worth translating, and all the texts in language B were so brilliant that they were all translated, the rate for A would still only be 11%, on a par with 10% for B.

of planetary paradise to be found by imposing standard translation ratios in the interests of a 'trade balance'.

Be careful of statistics. Ask what the numbers really represent. Are they reasonable in terms of prosaic thought? For example, Venuti's graphs indicate that more books are published in Britain than in the United States, even though the United States has about four times as many people. Does this mean British people read four times as many books? Or are the British books being exported somewhere? Why doesn't Venuti tell us about this? What interest does he have in treating Britain and the United States as just one culture?

No statistical distribution of translations, be it across time or space, is entirely neutral.[2]

Diachronic distribution

Little effort is needed to produce a diachronic distribution curve. All you really have to do is select period intervals appropriate to the required details and the hypotheses to be tested. This can be as tendentious as you like. Consider Figures 4 and 5, which both represent the foundation dates of the translator-training institutions mentioned in the last chapter (Caminade and Pym 1995). Figure 4 groups the dates into 30 periods or 'bins'; Figure 5 groups the same dates into 32 bins, which means that each analytical period is slightly shorter. If I wanted to argue that translator training is in full expansion and has a bright future, I would obviously use Figure 4. On the other hand, if I were convinced that the expansion of this field peaked in 1992-93 and that translator training faces a more uncertain future, I would show Figure 5. Same data, different hypotheses. Note that there is no extensive cheating here, since the optimistic vision of Figure 4 surreptitiously lumps the more recent data with everything post-1990, whereas the pessimistic message of Figure 5 comes from naïvely assuming that all the data from 1993 and 1994 were immediately located by researchers working in 1994. As much as absolute honesty might be the best policy, the graphic presentation of frequencies cannot help but express a certain inclination one way or the other.

---

[2] Similar manipulations concern the rapid rise in the number of translations over recent decades. For countless translator-training brochures and introductory texts on the subject, translation is all that counts: we are in the age of translation; we should be training more translators, studying more translations and getting more research funds. Seen within a wider statistical frame, however, this is the age of text production, of which translation is just a part. Pedagogues and theorists should be drawing out the consequences.

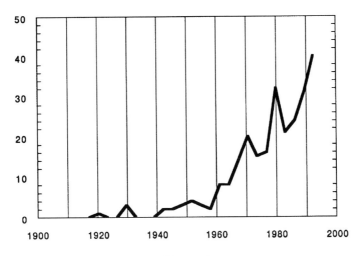

Figure 4
Translator-Training Institutions
Sample of 270 from all countries
Frequency of foundation, in 30 bins

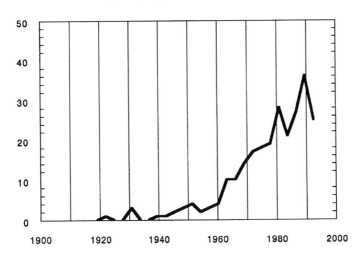

Figure 5
Translator-Training Institutions
Sample of 270 from all countries
Frequency of foundation, in 32 bins

This does not mean that the frequency curves automatically bend in accordance with the researcher's desires. You start off with certain questions; you formulate hypotheses in terms of the kind of answers you are looking for; but the actual plotting of frequencies is a constant test of both the initial hypotheses and the interests that underlie them. Our first ideas about the world can be wrong; some statistical concentrations are so objectively great that no amount of alternative binning can make the curve bend any other way. Note, for instance, that a deceleration in the 1980s is reflected in both the above graphs. As we go out into the world, we must expect the object to modify our initial expectations.

In the case of my Salomé corpus, period divisions of virtually any size would give a very obvious curve peaking in the 1890s (Figure 6 is based on twenty-year intervals). This concentration confirmed one of my more obvious initial hypotheses, namely that Salomé was a *fin de siècle* theme, which is hardly a transcendental revelation. When I tried the distributions for different cultures, however, things became a little less banal and a lot more messy. I soon had a string of minor distribution curves, few of which included enough data to indicate anything significant. The only solution was to work by trial-and-error, trying different hypotheses and sets of data until the world decided to agree that some kind of significance might be at stake. In this case, the meaningful division turned out to be between French and non-French versions. Once this distinction was plotted diachronically, a certain story became immediately obvious, in fact so obvious that only a fool like myself would have failed to recognize it in the first place. The distribution showed that Salomé was dominated by French versions in the 1880s and early 1890s before being taken over by Germanic versions after 1900, when she was flung out toward a very wide periphery. Work on frequency curves thus pushed my findings beyond the initial hypotheses. Further, the more developed hypotheses were well supported by several testimonies from the period, notably Vaucaire's 1907 comment that the versions by Oscar Wilde and Richard Strauss had definitively overtaken "notre Salomé bien française" (1907:147).

Other cases can become rather more complex. Figure 7 shows the basic frequency curves involved in my work on late-nineteenth-century translations of lyrical texts.

Despite the problems with the catalogues used as sources (see chapter 3), the distribution of this particular corpus turned out to be deceptively neat. The German-to-French flow clearly peaks in the 1890s and is overshadowed by a French-to-German movement peaking around 1910. This 'twin peaks' model is remarkable in that when one direction increases, the other decreases, suggesting that something went from German into French and then, after some transformation, from French into German. Of course, the curves don't tell us much about *what* could have moved in this way. At some point one has to return to the corpora.

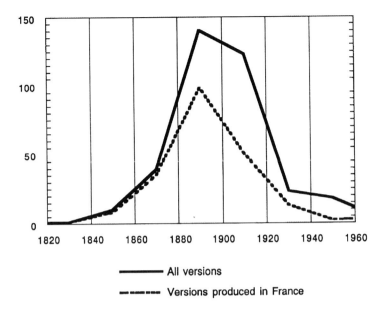

Figure 6
Diachronic distribution of 371 versions
of the Salomé theme

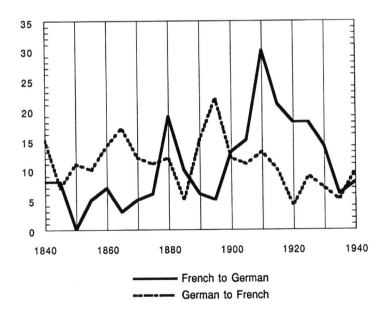

Figure 7
Translations of lyrical texts, from Bihl/Epting and Fromm
(showing 'twin peaks')

Close inspection of the lists constituting these peaks shows that much of the movement into French comprised translations of Wagner's *poèmes d'opéra*, precisely the ones I originally wanted to leave out. There were of course many other texts caught up in the general flow, but the frequency of the libretti translations (107 titles) nevertheless gives a neat parabola of sorts (see Figure 8):

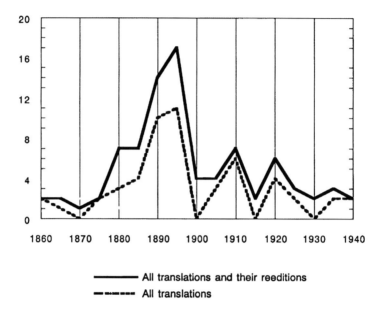

All translations and their reeditions
All translations

Figure 8
French translations of Wagner's operatic poems

Although the peak here comes slightly later than the general one shown in Figure 7, it does fit in with an interesting explanation of the entire movement. One might hypothesize that Wagner was translated into French, that the translations influenced post-Symbolist aesthetics, and that the result was translated back into German. None of this had been foreseen in my initial hypotheses, which were based on an unsophisticated notion of poetry as the stuff of poets rather than musicians. But the late nineteenth century thought otherwise. The French Wagner was indeed idealized as a poet. The hypothesis that his influence extended right through post-Symbolism and back into German can moreover be supported by readings of Max Nordau (1892-3 I:267-332), who opposed both movements, and Edouard Dujardin (1931:94, 166, 190), who claimed that Wagner's influence not only helped prosify French verse but eventually culminated in Joyce and beyond. Not that Nordau and Dujardin were wholly neutral observers of these influences. They were key players on opposite sides of the importance equation, Nordau opposing the movements, Dujardin announcing and promoting them. The quantitative phenomenon was unexpected but perhaps not entirely illusory.

Frequency curves are able both to falsify hypotheses and to suggest further hypotheses. Yet this does not mean everything can be done by drawing lines, which are in any case only as good as the data they represent. In the particular case of the late nineteenth century, subsequent research has shown that the cultural functions of lyrical translations had more to do with periodicals (*petites revues*) than with book publication. My next step was to extract corpora from a systematic reading of the main literary periodicals of the period, starting with Dujardin's *Revue Wagnérienne* (1885-1888). The distributions based on the general catalogues of translated books had little to say at this stage of investigation. But without them, I could not have formulated the new hypotheses; I would not have paid attention to Wagner. Although quantitative methods cannot in themselves write good history, they can certainly help us head in the right direction.

Retranslations, re-editions and nontranslations

You might have noticed that Figure 8 includes a curve factoring in re-editions of Wagner translations (i.e. cases where the same translation was reprinted or brought out in a second, third or n'th edition by the same or a different publisher). This curve closely follows the distribution of 'all translations'. The decision to use these re-edition data is based on the same reasoning behind the use of embedding as an index of importance in the case of Salomé (see the previous chapter). Here, the resulting curve is comforting in that it closely corroborates the Wagner translations as a *fin de siècle* phenomenon. Not only were there more translations at that time, but there were more re-editions of previous translations. This might be considered a good index of public demand. Yet it should point more precisely to some kind of object-derived importance.

The integration of data on re-editions is justifiable on two counts. First, in this case the information was there, in our lists, so it cost virtually nothing to find. Second, the readily available data for this period include no statistics on print-runs or actual sales, so we have no convenient way of calculating how many translations went to how many people. The frequency of re-editions can thus replace the missing information by giving a rough approximation of when there was a public demand, as well as what kind of translations there was a demand for. This is a cheap way of producing interesting results.

As you might have come to expect, frequencies that are as neat and comforting as Figure 8 tend to suggest something has been fudged. Consider carefully what the curves represent. Surely one would expect re-editions to concentrate at some point *after* the high-point of translations? Of course, the magic corroboration has ensued from the decision to *add* rather than separate translations and re-editions, thus hiding various kinds of chronological shifts. It has also concealed information on *first* translations, which simply disappeared into a far greater corpus, as well as the specific distribution of *retranslations*, which do not necessarily share the same reinforcing logic of re-editions. So as not to hide anything, Figure 9 gives the distributions of the re-editions alone, the first translations, and the retranslations (i.e. translations of libretti that had already been translated into French). The picture is not quite so neat.

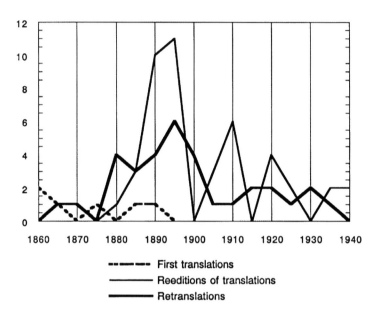

Figure 9
French translations of Wagner's libretti
First translations, retranslations and re-editions of translations

Here we discover numerous displacements. The first translations were carried out well prior to the peak of apparent demand, which is still somewhere in the mid-1890s (the mutually exclusive retranslation and re-edition curves really do confirm each other at this point). In fact, the first translations came relatively hot on the heels of the first German editions. But then a war got in the way in 1870-71; France lost; Wagner celebrated the defeat in a farce (*Une Capitulation*); the French were not amused, and no translation of Wagner was published in Paris between 1869 and 1879. Profiting from this gap, in the 1870s and 1880s a significant number of translations and retranslations were published in Brussels and an even greater number were carried out by Belgians (notably Wilder and Kufferath). There was thus not only a significant diachronic lacuna as a result of the French defeat but also a geopolitical displacement toward Belgian intermediaries. Unfortunately, the graphic focus on diachronic relations fails to show this second phenomenon. In fact, it actively conceals it by lumping everything together as 'French'.

Further factors are also hidden or overlooked by this mode of analysis. For example, the moment when the 'embedding' curves (retranslation and re-edition) really take off coincides very exactly with the publication of the prestigious *Revue Wagnérienne* (1885-1888). How should this coincidence be reflected? More to the point, why should it be reflected in quantitative terms? True, the *Revue Wagnérienne* made a few waves by explaining Wagner to certain literary coteries in Paris. Unfortunately the periodical carried only a few translations of libretti (20 pages in the whole series), which were in any case absent from our original corpus (they were not in book form). The *Revue Wagnérienne* moreover lacked an adequate distribution network (it was sold at the entrance to the Lamoureux concerts in Paris) and remained of quantitatively negligible proportions. Even if it had been included, it would scarcely have made a dent in the above graph. The role of quantitative analysis is in this case to challenge the assumed importance of such phenomena.

Could we nevertheless see the *Revue Wagnérienne* as the cause of the 'embedding' curves suddenly jumping up? It does indeed occupy the right place at the right time. Once again, though, care must be taken not to force conclusions on the basis of mere statistics. Several other factors were shaping the numbers. Most important, the Wagner translation rights were retained by Schott & Söhne of Mainz, which signed an agreement with the Belgian translator Wilder in 1885, the same year as the *Revue Wagnérienne* began publication. Wilder set about translating and retranslating; Schott brought out bilingual and multilingual editions in Paris, London, Sydney, Mainz, Brussels and Leipzig (through Breitkopf); the curves bounce up all over the place. The embedding would seem to have been caused by international publishing agreements. A better explanation, of course, would be to see both factors as causally linked, such that the elitist and Parisian *Revue Wagnérienne* opposed Wilder's 'vulgarized' Wagner (which it certainly did) and thereby created a debate of importance that continued right through to the 1890s (when the opposition framed Ernst's literalist translations). These debates took on war-like dimensions in the Paris of the 1890s, which would in turn explain why there were so many retranslations, and even why the re-edition curve becomes so erratic.

Clearly, although distribution curves can help us locate and sometimes identify quantitative phenomena, they cannot tell the whole story. Attention has to be paid to data that are qualitatively important although quantitatively insignificant (the *Revue Wagnérienne*), as well as to the actual causes of phenomena like re-editions and retranslations. The numbers alone indicate some disturbance, but they can never explain the causes.

Retranslation and its reasons

Cursory analysis of the Wagner corpus would suggest that retranslations were the fruits of some kind of debate about how a particular text should be rendered. When there are disagreements over translation strategies, there are likely to be several translations of the same text, especially when the text is complex enough to admit widely divergent versions. Is this a generalizable hypothesis?

Let me refine the terms a little. Periodical retranslations of texts like the Bible would appear to be quite a different phenomenon, at least when they have relatively wide expanses of time or geography between them and would seem to be responding to long-term processes of linguistic or cultural change in the target community. A similar logic would apply to retranslations separated by synchronic boundaries (geopolitical or dialectological), where there is likely to be little active rivalry between different versions and knowledge of one version does not conflict with knowledge of another. These might be called 'passive retranslations', at least to the extent that they have relatively little disturbing influence on each other. However, retranslations sharing virtually the same cultural location or generation must respond to something else, especially when they give pronounced parabolas like those in the above graph. Let us look briefly at three cases of this latter phenomenon, which we might label 'active retranslation':

- In twelfth-century Hispania, a kind of active retranslation could occur in the production of several versions of the one text, all by the one translator. The manuscript tradition analyzed by Clagett (1953) suggests that Adelardus de Bada (Adelard of Bath to his friends) produced three versions of Euclid's *Elements*: the first version directly from an Arabic text, the second one adding didactic commentaries and omitting much of the proofs, the third putting the proofs back in. It would seem the three versions were intended to carry out different pedagogical functions for different readers. Hence active target-based retranslation.

- In thirteenth-century Castile, a clear case of active retranslation occurred in 1277, when Alfonso X commanded 'Bernaldo el arabigo' and Abraham ('alfaquí') to carry out a second translation of Al-Zarkali's Acafea (Al-Safi'ha), correcting a version he had ordered and received some twenty years earlier from Ferrando de Toledo (see Ballesteros Beretta 1984:817). Same patron, same text, virtually the same target language, but now the king seems to have returned to the translation business with renewed enthusiasm for correcting his translators' Castilian. Hence a commanded retranslation.

- In fifteenth-century Spain, a French book on warfare – Bouvet's Arbre des batailles – was translated into Castilian twice, once for the Marqués de Santillana, and again, at about the same time, for the Marqués's arch political rival Alvaro de Luna (Schiff 1905:379; Alvar and Gómez Moreno 1987). Although the translators were different, the translation strategies appear not to have been significantly different. What counted was no doubt the book's content, to which neither rival patron wanted the other to have exclusive access. Hence retranslation.

These three cases certainly prove no general causality behind active retranslations. Instead, they suggest a variety of possible causes. In each case, though, the fact of retranslation differs significantly from a simple count of re-edition. Whereas re-edition would tend to reinforce the validity of the previous translation, retranslation strongly challenges that validity, introducing a marked negativity into the relationship at the same time as it affirms the desire to bring a particular text closer. Because of this negativity mixed with crosscultural movement, active retranslations are a particularly subtle index of historical importance.

Once again, care must be taken to understand what we are analysing here. A comparison between two or more passive retranslations (i.e. first + subsequent translations) would tend to provide information about historical changes in the target culture (for example, free verse became common in English, so Homer was retranslated accordingly). Quite apart from being often redundant (the information thus revealed could have been obtained without doing translation history), such a procedure can only affirm the general hypothesis that target-culture norms determine translation strategies. The comparative analysis of active retranslations, however, tends to locate causes far closer to the translator, especially in the entourage of patrons, publishers, readers and intercultural politics (although clearly not excluding monocultural influences from any side). The study of active retranslations would thus seem better positioned to yield insights into the nature and workings of translation itself, into its own special range of disturbances, without blindly surrendering causality to target-culture norms.

A general diachronic hypothesis

Let me close this chapter with a broad working hypothesis that is perhaps more whimsy than anything else, since it comes from looking at the shapes of frequency curves rather than at any properly explanatory material.

All the above distributions form parabolas of one kind or another; they rarely remain at any constant background hum. Further, looked at closely, they are peculiarly erratic, jumping up and down rather than forming smooth curves, and this seems to happen at almost all levels of analysis (my smaller-scale curves for individual periodicals also jump mercurially). Is there any reason why translation should be associated with quantitative instability rather than relative invariance?

One might reasonably expect translation to respond directly to the ruptures of wars, revolutions, economic cycles and the general crosscultural distur-bances of the modern era. However, when we analyze a more distant object like the datable translations from Arabic carried out in Hispania in the twelfth and thirteenth centuries (147 items), we find remarkably similar patterns, with remarkably few corresponding wars or revolutions:[3]

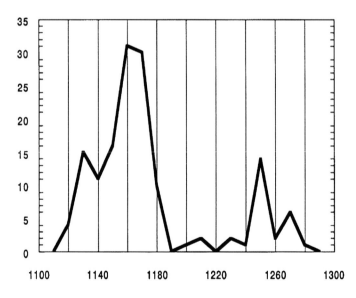

Figure 10
Datable translations from Arabic in the Iberian peninsula, 1100-1300

---

[3] I include Figure 10 in order to question the concept of a unified 'School of Toledo': the first major peak was into Latin and was sponsored by the church, the second major peak, after 1250, was mostly into Castilian and had Alfonso X as its patron.

Are these curves merely the result of unreliable data and distortions by centuries of partisan historians? Historical filtering undoubtedly darkens the glass we are looking through. Yet such massive concentrations must surely suggest something was there in the twelfth century and again in the thirteenth. Sheer quantity can indeed shine through some degree of historical distortion, especially if we know how to adjust our vision. In this case the message crystalizes into uncannily familiar parabolas.

Could these roller-coaster frequencies be due to the nature of translation itself, at least as we find it in the more central cultures? There are good reasons for taking the hypothesis seriously. As a relatively expensive strategy for crosscultural communication, translation may well be viable for short-term projects only, eventually giving way to alternative strategies involving language learning (when there is more material to be communicated) or noncommunication (when not). More disturbingly, a similarly parabolic distribution can be found in the recent history of translator training (Figure 5 more than Figure 4), which could reflect some kind of fluctuating short-term demand for translators and thus perhaps a parabolic demand for translations, translation studies and even translation history. Are these curves suggesting that social interest in our endeavour will soon decline? Perhaps we should be preparing for wider or alternative fields of study. This, at least, is a working hypothesis that we might find important enough to test.

6. Networks

I would now like to deliver the promised alternative to the use of corpora, exclusive definitions and frequency distributions. The reasons for seeking an alternative should be obvious enough: the reductive method, in moving from large overviews to small areas of importance, has considerable trouble deciding borderline cases, locating causes, describing heterogeneous fields, representing significant displacements and assessing negative relationships. This could be a lot of trouble. An alternative method, which basically involves tracing networks by working bottom-up, from the small to the large, might be able to tackle these aspects a little more successfully. Even better, it can be used in combination with top-down reductionism.

The following pages give examples of how an incremental method can help build up networks of past relations. I will then deal with ways of representing the resulting networks, mainly through a mode of mapping that has healthily little respect for international borders.

Reconstructing networks from within

A simple kind of networking is common enough in studies of medieval translation. Small corpora of retranslations or adaptations are arranged according to the probable links connecting each particular version with the others. These links usually represent assumed initial causation. The researcher might propose that text A was translated from text B, which was a reworking of text C, and all this formed a branch P which ran parallel to branch R through several centuries and cultures. When this kind of networking can satisfactorily interrelate all the texts in a particular corpus, the term 'reductive' is certainly an unkind description of the procedure. If all the items find a place, the method is obviously neither reductive nor incremental; it would have more to do with causal structuralism. However, such initial-cause networking can also be properly incremental in places where, as often happens, one or several 'missing links' could explain the phenomena in a more satisfactory way.[1] Was text A really a direct translation of

---

[1] Straight philological examples are provided by C. W. Marx (1991) on transmission from Anglo-Norman to Middle English, and Kalinke (1991) on medieval Norse-Icelandic translations in eighteenth-century manuscripts. A more ideological example might be the debate between French and Spanish researchers as to the existence of a Hispanic version of the Alfonsine astrological tables. One side is convinced that such a manuscript must have existed; the other seems equally convinced that the original tables were French (see Poulle 1987). One of the methodological functions of networks should be to insist that such debates be grounded on material possibilities.

B, or could the apparent errors and omissions be explained by an intermediary version, by a previous version, by manuscript variants of B or by later changes in copies of A? Whenever such hypotheses are formulated, for whatever reason, the researcher sets out to locate particular links. The method reaches out beyond the established corpus; it thus becomes incremental.

In general, incremental methods can be used whenever initial corpora turn out to be inadequate. In medieval studies this usually means trying to compensate for missing data. In modernist studies, on the other hand, corpora are more commonly inadequate because there is too much information or, more exactly, because there is an abundance of information on too many different levels.

Take my sally into the French reception of Wagner. As I have noted, the explanatory hypotheses soon reached a stage where they could no longer adequately be tested on lists of books. Here and in parallel studies of modernist aesthetics, most of the action must be located in the periodicals, the *petites revues* that littered the period and occasionally constituted the true collective masterpieces of modernist aestheticism. A corpus of book publications could only take me so far. I had to take a good look at the periodicals. But which ones? Just on the French side? What about the Belgians, the Germans, the rest? Where should I begin?

The problem has a frighteningly quantitative dimension. According to the sociologist Alphonse Boubert, who was there at the time, some 1,748 periodicals were published in Paris in 1889, of which 56 specialized in literature (cited in *La Plume* 1/1, 15 avril 1889). For the German side, Schlawe (1965) lists some 64 'significant' literary periodicals for the period 1885-1910. Since I had no time to analyze 56+64 periodicals, the field had to be reduced. This could have been done on the basis of secondary sources (literary histories of the period). In this case, however, rather than hack away with working hypotheses, I tried to use the genres and links present in the historical object. This required attention to crosscultural relations or minor circuits set up and exploited by the periodicals themselves. The method is best demonstrated by example.

In a letter to the Parisian periodical *La Plume* (15 mai 1893), someone called Carl August noted that Germany, like Britain, had no real equivalent to the French *petite revue*. Indeed, we learn, the new German publication *Blätter für die Kunst* was the only periodical corresponding to the French model. It was also the periodical that Carl August, under his full name of Carl August Klein, just happened to have been publishing since 1892. His letter indicates the extent to which this particular German periodical was based on a particular French model. And French publication of the letter indicates a certain French desire to reflect the reflection. This was perhaps a relation of some importance, an interesting place to start.

La Plume and the *Blätter* thus select each other. They form a link of a kind that is far more causal than any mere coincidence along a frequency curve. Further, a series of such links can form a self-selecting circuit, constituted without great need for any excessive *a priori* criteria. Other contacts were in evidence. The Belgian periodical *La Wallonie*, when reaching its final issue in 1892, warmly recommended the *Blätter für die Kunst*. Not surprisingly, *La Wallonie* is itself frequently mentioned in the columns of *La Plume*, as indeed are several other French-language publications rallying to the post-Symbolist cause, one of which was *L'Ermitage*. Slightly previously – late 1891 and early 1892 – *L'Ermitage* had published verse by Stefan George (the index says 'Stéphane Georges') in German with French translations by Albert Saint-Paul *en regard*. George was of course the founder and main figure of the *Blätter für die Kunst*, published by our friend Carl August (Klein). George would in turn translate verse by his French translator Albert Saint-Paul, published in the May 1893 issue of the German periodical. There was a clear relation of exchange between the two poets. Yet the relation also existed between the periodicals, as was confirmed in 1892 when 'Karl August' (the same publisher of the *Blätter*) was published in *L'Ermitage*, this time arguing directly against the Munich naturalist-nationalist periodical *Die Gesellschaft*. And so the network grows.

So far we have located positive links between *La Plume* (Paris), *L'Ermitage* (Paris), *La Wallonie* (Brussels) and the *Blätter für die Kunst* (Berlin), with a negative connection with the more nationalist and naturalist periodical *Die Gesellschaft* (Munich). The more research one does, the more items enter the fray and the more nodes the network acquires. The research can be as controlled or uncontrolled as you like. It would be possible to formalize and weight the possible links, since there are hundreds of strategies between approval and disapproval. Yet it is often sufficient to build up the network with a fairly subjective feel for the various ideological currents at work. In this case, some commonsense subjectivity is necessary because of the sheer complexity of the relations. The periodicals formed an incestuous little world, with poets, journalists and translators often working for several publications at the same time then changing with the wind. Crosscultural relations were similarly complex, combining commercial criteria (periodicals often acted as distribution agents for each other) with aesthetic fashions (one periodical could undertake to promote 'exclusively' Dutch or Nordic or Russian writers), with informative functions (there were many international 'reviews of the reviews') and with the overtly politicized intercultural relations of a period of alliances and misalliances. The periodicals were not just great collective texts; they were small social groups relating with other small social groups, forming a chain that can be traced from Chile to Europe to Australia, although few people at the time could have been aware of the network's entire spread. The activities of these small groups could include the selling of shares in themselves (i.e. its readers were proprietors), the organizing of banquets, the opening of public subscriptions to feed dying poets, further subscriptions for statues to dead poets, the organizing of painting exhibitions and commercial art galleries, and the publishing of books (for which the periodical would function as a sampler or sales catalogue). Anyone entering this fascinating world is advised not to chase too many links beyond the level they need.

In principle, researchers with unlimited resources and open-ended schedules could use an incremental method to start at virtually any point of a network and eventually reach something approaching its historical form, without imposing any major *a priori* criteria. However, habitually impecunious researchers like myself can use the same procedure to start at an intuited centre and progressively identify the periodicals most often entering into exchanges with other periodicals. It is enough that the initial intuition be justified or rectified whenever necessary. For instance, my actual wanderings on the French side of this case began from the *Revue Wagnérienne*, which led to the *Revue indépendante* (Dujardin was director of both) and so on, eventually reaching far more central publications like the *Mercure de France*, which was constantly looking over its shoulder at the conservative *Revue des Deux-Mondes*. As it turned out, my starting point was quite ephemeral, but this was revealed in the course of the research.

As periodicals entered this network, they were dealt with in much the same way as the corpora described in the previous chapters. Some periodicals turned out to have no significant level of translations and were consequently retired (although significant absences of translations must be kept in mind). Eventually, I cut my losses and settled on just six of the more central French-language periodicals and seven German-language ones, along with a small test-circuit of three 'international' periodicals that were multilingual. I located and listed all the apparent translations in this corpus, thus meeting up with the reductive method.

The incremental approach is often a question of necessity rather than desire. When compiling our list of translator-training institutions, for example, the only previous corpus we had was a list of national translators' associations. We wrote to them, receiving something like four replies from the whole world. Thus returned to square one, we had to proceed institution by institution, asking each school or university department if they could give us the addresses of others. Lists of institutions participating in international exchange programmes soon became more fruitful than the national translators' associations; some of the larger and more prestigious schools provided addresses for institutions they had helped establish in other continents; information from Australia led to addresses in Japan, Chile and Kazakhstan; someone in Portugal informed us that a Canadian was doing the same research as us (no help was had there); and so on until, having located about 270 translator-training institutions, we eventually sighed and called it a day, or a network. The reality of translator training is that all kinds of supranational relations link institutions; there are many ways in which information is transferred across borders. Although it seemed logical to start our research from national translators' associations, such institutions turned out not to be hooked up with the appropriate networks. This particular world was not divided into nations.

A third example might bring us closer to traditional research problems. I was once asked to write on Spanish anthologies of translations. I knew of no such beasts, at least not in my period of relative specialization (late nineteenth century). How could I find some? There were basically two ways. First, I could go to a library catalogue, look up the word *antología* and select the *fin de siècle* ones that were of translations. Easy enough. But this would give me a corpus instead of a network. Alternatively, I could go through my notes on the period and try to determine if any translation anthologies rated a mention in secondary sources (histories, theories and the like), since secondary mentions could be traces of importance. Sure enough, I found a passing reference to a 1913 anthology of poems translated from French by many of the main Spanish poets of the day, arranged and annotated by Enrique Díez-Canedo and Fernando Fortún. This led to something like the following chain of discoveries: Fortún disappeared, but among Díez-Canedo's many writings was an ambivalent prologue to a further anthology called *Las cien mejores poesías (líricas) de la lengua inglesa* (1918), edited and translated by someone called Fernando Maristany; Díez-Canedo also wrote a positive review of Maristany's own poetry (1919) and Maristany, at that time an editor in Barcelona, accepted Díez-Canedo's translations of Paul Fort for publication in 1921. More important, the same Fernando Maristany had produced some seven translation anthologies from various languages over the period 1914-1920 (now I was on to something!). Further, his repeated anthology-title 'Las cien mejores...' (The hundred best...) had come from the nontranslational anthologies his work was based on, namely Adam Gowans' *The Hundred Best (Lyrical) Poems in the English Language* (1903) and Auguste Dorchain's *Les cent meilleurs poèmes (lyriques) de la langue française* (1905). These English and French titles were parts of a rather profitable international 'Hundred Best' series of nontranslational anthologies in English, French, German and Spanish, organized by the British firm Gowans & Gray. Although the Spanish member of this series – *Las cien mejores poesías (líricas) de la lengua castellana* (1908) – had been compiled by Marcelino Menéndez Pelayo, who had remarkably little to do with the milieux of Maristany or Díez-Canedo, it was more than coincidence that led Díez-Canedo to edit a contestational anthology called *Las cien mejores poesías españolas*. And so on. Maristany and Díez-Canedo could thus be placed in an international network that led back to Spain, where they differed significantly from each other. At the same time, however, both were opposed to Menéndez Pelayo's more nationalist tradition by the very fact that their work was internationalist and translational. In short, the links multiplied in such a way that hypotheses could be formulated to explain the 1913 anthology's local context, its place in an international network, and a few pertinent debates of importance.

Few of these factors could have been located with the same ease had I started reducing a library catalogue of *antologías*. Few of them could have been strung together had I relied on secondary sources or common preconceptions rather than methodological curiosity (Maristany remains an entirely marginal figure, and translation anthologies are not the stuff of conventional literary history). Indeed, this network's international connections – the chain of nontranslational anthologies – would probably have been excluded had I been blinkered by a purely target-side translation history. One must be prepared to follow the networks across borders.

Mapping networks

I have so far presented networks as an experimental alternative to straight corpus work. Yet there is more to the matter than a convenient shortcut. If networks really exist, they should be part of what translation history is able to discover. And if the above examples are any indication, the networks most pertinent to translation seem likely not to be limited to any one culture. They might be expected to relate points in different cultures (crosscultural links) and to develop in social settings shared by two or more cultures (intercultural groups). They should also have certain limits, probably areas where the connections become weaker or sparser. This would give the networks themselves a definite form in the space and time of history. In theory, of course, the more you trace the links of a network, the better you can approximate its actual historical form. In practice, any reasonable approximation to a network could be useful for solving problems of periodization and geopolitical delimitation.

If these general hypotheses are justified, networks can be mapped in a rather concrete way, just as we can map roads, railways, parts of the internet, all sorts of international networks. But there is a difference. In the case of material infrastructure, we are mapping the actual channels, the paths and connections that allow things to move. Thanks to networks, things move in some directions and not in others; or rather, they move more easily in some ways rather than others. A plan of the material links can tell you this. In translation history, though, the information that we have only really concerns displacements, always captured from details appearing after the fact. We reconstruct the movements, not the material objects that allow or obstruct the movements. Only on this basis can we assume the existence of channels, contacts and the like. More exactly, we can only really map the *transfers* that should give a more or less adequate representation of some underlying but unseen network. This is why our networks must be pictured in terms of what I would like to call transfer maps.

There is a further reason for transfer maps. Networks obviously concern more than just translations and translators. Things like literary periodicals, translator-training institutions and commercially connected anthologies allow transfers on many levels that may or may not concern translation. If we are to elucidate the specific role of translation within a network, we must first open up our range of inquiry to include nontranslational modes of transfer. This means going significantly beyond a conception of translation history as a story about translations and nothing but translations; our wider history may well be that of all kinds of transfers.[2] For the moment, though, our task is to think critically about how the raw fact of transfer can be represented. If we are mapping movements instead of stable boundaries, what kind of space are we going to work in?

José Lambert (1991b) has pointed out the considerable complexity involved in mapping the areas occupied by languages, literatures or cultures. These things are involved in constant processes of displacement, overlapping, unification and fragmentation. How should a map of contemporary European languages show the polyglot Eurocrats significantly located in Brussels? How many different colours and mixtures of colours would we need to map the cultures conveyed by satellite television? Lambert suggests literature maps cannot simply assume the homogeneity of national literatures; we should be talking about "literature *in* France, or *in* Germany", instead of 'French literature' or 'German literature'

---

[2] Such a step has twice been proposed by Even-Zohar (1981, 1990) and even by Pym (1992a, 1992c). Yet confusion abounds. As might be expected from the above comments, I use the term 'transfer' to refer to things that are material rather than mental. My networks cross time and space; the things moved are as physical as paper, bodies, sound waves, radio waves, digital signals. When all is said and done, I think in terms of geology and sociology rather than linguistics or psychology. I want to see what the ground is really like, even in this age of cybernetic space and apparently zero-degree distance. Unfortunately, the term 'transfer' also has quite legitimate uses in the sciences of the mind, which are rather less material than my interests.

(1991b:141). I believe this is a major step in the right direction. But it doesn't quite reach the spatial configuration appropriate to transfers. In fact, it seems to take homogeneity away from literature only to project it on political units, which are then allowed to define the pertinent spaces of literature, just like the French *dépôt légal* standardizes a political space even before any lists of texts are constituted. If we can get rid of 'French literature' opposing 'German literature', why not also get rid of 'France' opposing 'Germany'? Why retain the axiomatic national border? Lambert's proposed maps would do nothing to challenge the underlying cartographic assumption of a world divided into nations. And yet, as Lambert knows, cultures rarely correspond to this assumption. Nor do networks.

In order to map transfers, our only real requirement is that our axes allow the representation of movement through both space and time. Three dimensions would be ideal (cartography plus time), but we can make do with two. Any relatively homogeneous spaces (cultures, for example) should appear as a relative absence of movement. And any borders should similarly be made to appear as particular sites where discontinuous movements become especially intense, where transfers have been achieved thanks to points of change or changeover (yes, points of translation). Transfer maps might thus become a way of complementing all those maps that fill national spaces with colours. They could be logically anterior to the colour problem. Or more exactly, they could force relative homogeneity and systematicity to manifest themselves as modes of resistance to transfer.

This is best explained through examples.

Two cheap transfer maps

My first illustration involves a certain return to the ageing uncertainty of comparative literature (it concerns lyrical texts) and even to the imprecise and technically defunct notion of 'influence' (it concerns relations between poets and aesthetic movements). In short, it was a mistake of my youth. Yet it might prove instructive.

I first studied the international literary relations of the late nineteenth century in order to test the hypothesis that the aesthetic movements of the age were not directly determined by their immediately surrounding societies. I had to locate and evaluate modes of determination that went horizontally, from one society to another, basically the influences that connected the various aesthetic ideologies. These links were actually quite similar to the ones operating between the periodicals described above, although the more spectacular evidence was on the level of person-to-person influences of both the positive and negative kinds. Several crosscultural relationships were studied in detail, especially those framed by postcolonial relationships. But I also sought to demonstrate the weight and extent of the historical object, which had to counterbalance the weight and extent of traditional sociology. To do this, I tried to map the network of influences connecting post-Romantic aesthetic ideologies for the production of lyrical texts. The procedure was as follows:

- General histories were read covering the field concerned, noting all mentions of strong modifications in aesthetic ideologies ('influences') that were ostensibly derived from another culture. These secondary sources were inevitably partial or partisan overviews, in most cases complemented by historical accounts written from the perspective of the various cultures concerned. Many of my items actually came from the essays collected by Balakian (1982), where I simply marked uses of the word 'influence' and its cognates. This was easy and cost-effective. Indeed, the procedure was so cheap that I would never mention it to serious scholars.
- The individual influences were listed chronologically. This soon led to an excess of data, requiring reductive strategies to make the corpus manageable. I consciously privileged long-distance transfer, considering it the most likely to be pertinent to my hypotheses (at the great risk of automatic gratification). I also grouped the various endpoints around leading figures and, where possible, major periodicals.
- The chronologically ordered and filtered data were then accorded appropriate symbols and mapped onto axes of time and space.
- Considerable time was spent pondering the result, looking for a significant form, fiddling with the spatial axis to try to make any coherence visible, locating appropriate items if I had omitted or overlooked them, and constantly going back to step one to ask if the blank spaces really were blank.

The procedure is admittedly rough and ready. Considered carefully, it is a combination of the reductive and incremental methods outlined above: reductive in its initial phases, its constant movements between the mapping and the search phases became eminently incremental in nature. In this case, the combination of methods was justified by the heterogeneous nature of the source material (which made viable corpora difficult to establish) and the need for a large-scale overview (which made a wholly step-by-step approach impossible, since there were too many minor links). I should also stress that the actual graphic representation took the form of numerous quick fragmentary sketches used as visualization tools during the research process, often for one country or group of countries. Network maps are not just the results of research; they should also constitute a way of thinking about data.

It is thus with some trepidation that I present a product (Figure 11) whose minor polish risks concealing its many faults. So as to allay confusion, let me openly admit that this particular map was badly defined in its initial premises, depended too much on secondary sources, and remains in severe need of formalized definitions. I promise to fix it up as soon as I have a few years to spare. In the meantime, though, it has proved a moderately useful weapon against cultural sociologists who claim that international literary networks are historically insubstantial. Without having expended too much effort (drawing the final map was the hardest part!), I can at least point toward a network, suggest that it has a certain form, and insist that it be explained.

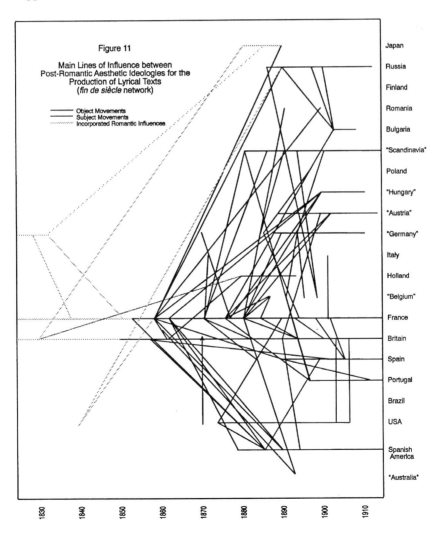

Figure 11

Main Lines of Influence between
Post-Romantic Aesthetic Ideologies for the
Production of Lyrical Texts
(*fin de siècle* network)

Object Movements
Subject Movements
Incorporated Romantic Influences

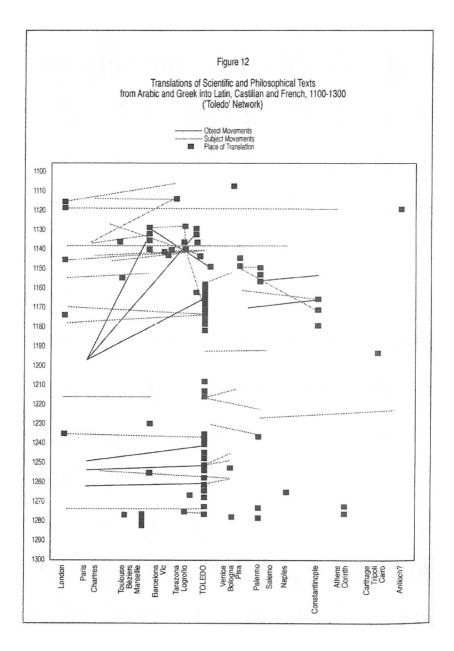

Figure 12

Translations of Scientific and Philosophical Texts
from Arabic and Greek into Latin, Castilian and French, 1100-1300
('Toledo' Network)

Before delving into the details of the actual mapping process, let me present a second map, drawn some ten years later, which represents one of the networks by which translations moved in the twelfth and thirteenth centuries (Figure 12). Although visibly sparser and more immediately pertinent to translation history, this 'Toledo' map was basically compiled using the same mixed procedures as the *fin de siècle* one. It benefited from lists that were slightly more coherent[3]; even despite the severe lack of trustworthy dates and places that plagues all medievalist research. My *fin de siècle* map had too much information; my Toledo map had too little. One looks like a network, the other doesn't look like very much at all. Something might be learned by comparing the two.

Let me now consider the various formal features of these maps: the lines, the symbols, the two axes, the limits, all the unavoidably technical details. Non-technical minds are cordially invited to fast-forward at this point, perhaps to the juicier bit at the end of the chapter, where we will ask why towns and cities have come to function as the borders pertinent to translation. For remaining readers, here is how the maps were made.

Lines and symbols

Note that both these maps have a time axis. This means we are not talking about drawing lines across traditional synchronic maps, with each map corresponding to a period. Synchronic maps could make life considerably easier, but they would risk presupposing some of the knowledge that the transfer map should help us find. Here, in the world of transfer, one of the purposes of the map is to *discover* the pertinent period limits. The same can be said for spatial limits, but that's a more complicated affair.

Both the *fin de siècle* and the Toledo maps have lines that represent movements between points. There are two kinds of movements: object transfers, which basically move texts, and subject transfers, which basically move translators and text seekers (mostly pertinent to the Toledo map). These elements merit a few comments:

• *Object transfers* (——) should be a fairly simple affair of lines linking the places of a text's production, publications, translations, retranslations, and, where possible, transcultural or post-translational receptions. If only we had all this information, and if only it all really had to do with networks. The actual mapping is not easy. For example, should points of 'first production' be part of a network? That is, should the Toledo map find places for Aristotle, Euclid, Ptolemy, Al-Khwarezmi, Al-Kindi, Abu Ma'shar and the rest? It would be a much taller

---

[3] The research was in this case fairly systematic, starting from Steinschneider's catalogues (particularly 1904-05), incorporating the additions and corrections given by Thorndike (1923) and Haskins (1924, 1929), and working through to more recent work by French and Spanish scholars, in each case noting additions and corrections. In a sense, I built up my network by following the way scholarship has built up its network.

map. But there could be no question of drawing lines directly from the places of first production to the places of translation. We know more or less how some of Aristotle's texts, for example, voyaged from Greek to Syriac to the Arabic of Baghdad or thereabouts, then across north Africa to the Latin of Hispania, while a parallel voyage went in Greek to Constantinople and Italy, perhaps an early arrival in Metz around 940, but in any case translation into Latin in Sicily, then Paris, London, and the north. These two great routes, one through Hispania and the other through Italy, extend well beyond the network we have tried to represent. Yet none of the translators had access to the place of Aristotle. In each case they were taking their text from a previous translator or custodian, building up a smaller network of more direct contacts. These were surely the links most pertinent to the way the translations were carried out (the point will be taken up later in our discussion of interculturality).

With respect to the *fin de siècle* map, a similar example would be the transfer of Poe's influence, which for much of Europe and Latin America started not from the United States but from the Paris of Baudelaire. The lines should not go straight from Poe to all his translators across the globe; one line can go from Poe to Baudelaire, then radiate out through later intermediaries, more or less.

If pursued to its limits, this mode of thought should demonstrate that all the diagonal lines are slightly illusory. Although I might know a text was translated at point X and received or retranslated at point Y, ten years later and a thousand kilometres away, I have no guarantee that the text spent those ten years progressing in a constant way to cover those thousand kilometres. In fact, it's highly unlikely that any object would be moved in such a way. The actual transfers would more probably be erratic alternations of vertical lines (movement through time) and near-horizontal lines (movement across space). Only when we have too much information (*fin de siècle*) or too little (Toledo) can cartographic licence be taken in the drawing of diagonal lines. After all, the resulting gradients are not entirely meaningless: the more vertical the forms, the slower the transfers through the network; the more horizontal, the faster things were moving. Transfers were obviously speeding up toward the end of the nineteenth century. And now, in the age of the internet, our transfers have become almost flat (although anything big from Australia or Japan still takes ages to dowload in Spain!).

• *Subject transfers* (.......) represent the movement of people who either seek texts, carry texts or convey knowledge about texts. Prior to telecommunications as we know them, subject transfers would be just about all the near-horizontal jumps behind the falsely diagonal lines described above. As such, subject transfers are especially useful when we lack good information about texts. To cite one of the examples already mentioned, sometime before 1175 Daniel de Merlai returned to England from Toledo, claiming to have brought many books with him ('cum pretiosa multitudine librorum'). Since the books are not named, we cannot really map them. But the *Philosophia* in which Daniel's claim is made (ed. Sudhoff 1917) indicates readings of Arabic science, so we might reasonably suppose some kind of knowledge transfer in this particular field. A line is required, even in the absence of data concerning actual points of production or translation. The only solution, as a kind of make-do, is to map the horizontal movement of Daniel himself. So we draw in a significant subject transfer. A similar example would be the movement of the Cuban journalist Aniceto Valdivia from Europe to Havana in 1885, where we have only vague second-hand accounts of the texts he carried in his suitcase (Baudelaire, Verlaine, probably Huysmans' *A rebours*) although we do know the suitcase was enough to set off francophile aestheticism in Cuba. Something similar might be true of the Chilean poet Vicente Huidobro, who was said to have brought Surrealism to Madrid in a Parisian suitcase (all good case studies, says Armin Paul Frank).

Perhaps the most interesting kind of subject transfers are those constituting the first step of any translation enterprise, when someone sets out to find a text to translate. What weight should we give to these text-seekers who are not yet translators? We know, for instance, that the twelfth-century scholars Hermannus Dalmata and Robertus Ketenensis left France and England respectively and moved to northern Hispania in search of Arabic science. Only when they found some Arabic science did they become translators. Similarly, Girardus Cremonensis was said to have moved from Italy to Toledo in search of the *Almagest*, the Arabic version of Ptolemy. Although these people probably did not bring significant texts with them, they certainly brought the desire and competence to help render texts into Latin. They were thus able to initiate text transfers in roughly the opposite directions to their initial voyages. If the importance of each outward voyage can be measured in terms of the subsequent translations, we might even hypothesize a certain symmetry between the subject transfers and the ensuing object transfers. Indeed, the existence of some kind of subject transfer might even be hypothesized as the condition for text transfers going in the opposite direction. In practice, of course, it is difficult to locate and represent all the pertinent subject transfers, and there are plenty of cases where people go one way and their translations go off in a different direction. There are no mechanistic rules here. Indeed, it would be dangerous to assume that people just wander around looking for texts to translate. Twelfth-century translators also moved as soldiers, diplomatic aids, commercial interpreters, students and much else. In the late nineteenth century, the Australian poet Christopher Brennan traveled to Berlin as a classics student on a scholarship, without consciously looking for the Mallarmé he would find there (yes, in Berlin) and later translate. From another end of the *fin de siècle* network, the Nicaraguan poet Rubén Darío could travel thanks to a mix of diplomatic missions, publishing possibilities and journalistic engagements, some of which involved translating. Such movements certainly set up situations allowing translations to go in the return directions, but the subject transfers cannot be reduced to this purpose alone.

Sometimes a text can be located in a place of reception but we have no adequate information about how it reached that place. For instance, around 1060 Constantinus Africanus, having arrived in Monte Cassino, produced medical translations from Arabic. In about 1130 we find his translations being used in England, retranslated in Antioch (or by a translator from there), and probably entering repertories at many points in between. Yet it is virtually impossible to say how the translations got to those places from their production in Italy. One supposes they entered a circuit based on untraceable monastic copying: a kind of circulation was to keep Constantinus' works in use until the Renaissance, despite numerous criticisms of their status as translations. This anonymous circulation cannot really be represented by our mapping procedure. The best we can do is indicate the few known points. The danger, of course, is that the resulting blank space might be confused with some ubiquitous 'general supply', when there was no such thing. A better version of the Toledo map would probably have to indicate a series of weak assumed connections so as to avoid such illusions.

• *Changeover points* (■) indicate processes that potentially mark borders between cultures. For most purposes, these points need not correspond to translations in any strict sense of the term, since historical translation principles will be analyzed at later stages of the research. The function of a transfer map should be to indicate only the general lie of the land. There are mostly good reasons to include parodies, works of plagiarism and adaptations as the results of changeover processes. A map might also show special cases like the rewriting of astronomical tables in terms of new coordinates. We find Khwarezmi-inspired tables drawn for the coordinates of Cordoba in 1126, Toledo at around the same time, Marseilles in about 1140, London in 1149, Hereford in 1178, then the apparently Alfonsine tables for Toledo in 1252, revised in 1272. If we include versions that have yet to be located or dated, the extent of this particular network becomes even clearer: astronomical tables for London compiled in 1232 mention other tables for Paris, Marseilles, Pisa, Palermo, Constantinople, Genoa and Toledo. The drawing up of a new astronomical table would perhaps not universally be classified as translation (it definitely does *not* satisfy our 'discursive discontinuity' criterion, since every reading of the stars positions an authorial subject!). But the dates and places concerned nevertheless indicate significant changeover points that can be linked up as a very definite network. The resulting image at least provides a pertinent frame for the movements of translations and translators.

An ideal transfer map would have each changeover point located on a continuous object-transfer line connecting the point of source-text production with a point of target-text reception, in each case associated in some way with the movement of a person. Yet in many areas, particularly in the medieval field, all we have is the fact of the translation itself. The directionality of a specific demand often has to be deduced. For instance, when Hermannus Dalmata and Robertus Ketenensis translated the *Qur'an* into Latin in 1141-43, it was at the specific request of the abbot of Cluny, so the transfer was very probably headed toward France. Interestingly enough, Bishop Michael of Tarrazona and Archbishop Raimundus of Toledo were also Frenchmen sponsoring translation projects in Hispania at the time, giving indications of a general movement in that direction. Hypotheses about broad translation demands are not necessarily difficult to produce.

• *Terra incognita* (   ) is an honest name for the blank spaces that are perhaps inevitable features of transfer maps. If a space is decorated with no lines or points, this does not necessarily indicate an absence of transfer activity. The blank space more exactly indicates an absence of contemporary knowledge about the matter. Of course, one might reasonably suppose there is some causal link between the actual intensity of transfer in a given space and our knowledge about it, and thus a similar causal link between blank spaces and an absence of transfer. However, transfer maps should be used in order to test this causality. Many traps have to be avoided.

To take a particularly frustrating lure, we think we know a lot about Toledo because it was the site of intensive translation activity at certain periods. But we have also gained a good deal of this ostensible knowledge because the historical concept of the 'School of Toledo' was operative for much of the nineteenth century and through to quite recent dates. Virtually every translation that cannot be located elsewhere has at some stage been associated with Toledo simply because Toledo seemed to be the most likely place for a translator to be translating.[4]

---

[4] No one really knows where the prolific translator Johannes Hispanensis did most of his work (Seville, 'Luna', on the moon?) so he is often placed in Toledo, on the strength of one preface and for the sake of neatness (everyone following Jourdain). Similarly, although we know the first Latin translation of the Qur'an was organized between Salamanca and the

The more such attributions are made, the bigger the 'School of Toledo' becomes and the more it seems a good bet for even further attributions. Such historical concepts grow of their own accord and are extremely difficult to kill off.

In the history of late-nineteenth-century literature, 'French Symbolism' is a similarly cancerous notion that attracts supposed knowledge about transfers. It has become easy and legitimate for historians to write about the influence of 'Baudelaire and the Symbolists' without ever weighting the fact that practically none of the people they include in this category would have referred to themselves as Symbolists. Nor is there sufficient appreciation of the degree to which the reception of aestheticist tenets was inseparable from the dissemination of Naturalism. By mapping what we know, we can raise a good many questions about certitudes that are as intimidating as they are unfounded. Blank spaces should not be filled with sea monsters.

The term *terra incognita* appears to have had its first cartographic use in a 1375 Catalan atlas drawn up by Yehuda Cresques, a Jew working for the Crown of Aragon (Attali 1991:154). It was a major step forward. We should share at least some of his conviction that the blank spaces may well be the areas where there is most to be discovered.

The spatial axis

Given that one axis of a transfer map should represent time, the other should logically represent space. Yet historical time has an arrow of its own; historical space does not. This fundamental difference gives rise to several difficulties and some occasionally arcane amusements. We must solve two basic problems. First, how should the spatial axis be divided up so as to give a grid? And second, since we as yet have no convenient way of communicating a three-dimensional map, how can two-dimensional space be represented on a one-dimensional line?

My *fin de siècle* map unthinkingly divides the spatial axis into countries. This merely imitated what was being done in the secondary sources I was work- ing from. But I have since become very aware that national units presuppose degrees of sovereignty that are not always adequate to the object being mapped. What should be done with Catalan literature? Should I put in all twenty-one

---

region of Logroño, the fact that one of the minor translators came from Toledo has been judged sufficient reason to baptize the resulting documents as 'the Toledan collection' (Kritzeck 1964). And again, the fascinating collection of properly Toledan documents edited by Hernández (1985) carries a preface in which 'Herman de Carintia' (the man we have been calling Hermannus Dalmata) is situated in Toledo, even though non of the published documents bears this out. These assumptions do little to help history

Latin-American republics? Should former Czecho-Slovakia figure as one, two or three countries? How many Belgiums? Should Australia appear as six colonies until 1901 and thereafter as an individual country? Not only were national units constantly being formed and reformed during the period under study but there can be little guarantee that a transfer affecting one point was automatically pertinent to a whole national or linguistic space. 'Modernism' meant one thing in Barcelona (primarily the *Modernisme* of painters and architects) and something quite different in Madrid (more given to identifying and distancing itself from Spanish-American *Modernismo*). For similar reasons, transfer to Berlin was not the same as transfer to Munich or Vienna. Writers went to Paris, but they failed to see much of France. Havana was not Cuba, yet it should not be lumped together with Buenos Aires. Sydney was not Melbourne. And so on. With respect to the *fin de siècle* network, the pertinent spatial grid should have comprised cities, mostly the largest cities of the day.

Having learned my lesson, I did organize the Toledo map in terms of urban centres, if only because countries like Spain and Italy did not exist in the twelfth century. However, the general lack of hard data required that certain urban centres somehow be grouped, since it was often impossible to say exactly where translators were working but it is nevertheless quite feasible to place them in a certain geographical region (as in the case of Johannes Hispanensis). The practical solution was to distribute the towns in such a way that they were physically close to each other on the spatial axis. Toulouse, Béziers, Narbonne, Montpellier and Marseilles, which were centres of related importance, are thus positioned as if they were two related sections. Yet they were not a country.

Once you have selected the points to be placed on the spatial axis, the next problem is to decide what order they should be given. Ideally, the order of presentation should make the general form of a transfer network immediately visible. By the same token, the arrangement of the coordinates can radically alter the appearance of the network, making several forms possible. One way around this problem is to suppose that the network itself makes certain orders more pertinent or successful than others. This can only be done by trial and error, moving between the historical object and the mode of representation.

When I did my *fin de siècle* map, I discovered that the most convincing form resulted from distributing the points more or less in the order of their geographical distance from Paris, which was undoubtedly the centre of the network. Some further reorganization was needed to categorize this distance as going either east or west. The east-west principle allowed Spanish, Portuguese and British transfers to mediate towards Latin America and Australia respectively, with Germanic mediation then heading eastwards. If the principle had not been adopted, the first set of lines would have been crossing the second, creating a mess belonging more to the representation than to the object. This actually became a tentative principle of composition: if the lines crossed each other on the map but had probably not done so in history, the map should be remodeled.

The fact that a certain mode of representation is more or less suited to a certain historical network is not a question of cheating. It instead demonstrates the pertinence of geographical distance as a mode of resistance to transfer. In the case of the *fin de siècle* a suitable spatial order also demonstrates the pertinence of an east-west orientation. A north-south principle, for example, which would mean placing traditional maps on their sides, might not have greatly altered the general form of postcolonial transfers but it would certainly have made spaghetti out of movements in eastern Europe. Yet neatness should not be considered the last word. The fact that a certain orientation can reveal a degree of coherence should not stifle the function of a map as an instrument of critical thought. We can always turn the piece of paper around, asking if the east-west ideology of *fin de siècle* progress was not concealing an incipient north-south ideology of development. Why were Africa and most of Asia absent from this network? Why did aestheticism tend to spread at about the same time and in the same directions as railways?

As chance would have it, an east-west orientation also gave reasonable results in my Toledo map, at least with respect to the meagre information I was able to incorporate. Yet alternatives were available. Although I certainly positioned Toledo as a centre around which a network should have formed, the town was geographically a frontier post from which texts headed north to Paris, Chartres, London and Cambridge, probably north-east to Bologna or Palermo, then further north to the thirteenth-century Germanic towns of Albertus Magnus. Yet Palermo and Constantinople were also frontiers of twelfth-century Christendom, producing transfers that were headed north and west, working from Greek rather than Arabic. By placing Toledo at the centre I have the lines coming from these other fronts occasionally crossing those radiating from the Iberian peninsula, even though there is little evidence that the transfers actually crossed in this way. An alternative map could have placed the more northerly destinations in some kind of centre (London, Paris, Chartres), with the Arabic-Hispanic circuit perhaps on the left and the Greek-Italian connections on the right. This would certainly give greater coherence to the textual side of business, particularly with respect to the twelfth-century. But if we consider the movements of translators rather than translations, there were indeed very significant movements directly between Toledo and Palermo-Bologna-Florence in the twelfth and thirteenth centuries. I left Toledo in the centre in order to represent these movements;

although another map, produced to answer more textually oriented questions, might legitimately have done otherwise.

Cities as borders

Where are the borders in these maps? In the case of the medieval network, probably the only feature made at all clear is precisely Toledo's association with a partly continuous vertical line indicating fairly constant changeovers between the Islamic and Christian worlds. This, I suggest, is the closest thing to a border that translation history can offer. There is no universal reason to make our field a slave to political borders. The borders between cultures are not marked prior to translation but are manifested in the very act of translating. In fact, it is often translation that first constitutes a border: a source on one side, a target on the other.

Considered anthropologically, this association of translation with intercultural borders has a certain logic. The frontier regions, the borderlands, tend to be diglossic or polyglossic and thus produce intermediaries. In second-dynasty Egypt, the interpreters used for southward expeditions came from the Nubian borderlands to the south (Kurz 1985). Yet we would not expect to find camps of translators huddled along political frontiers or standing at customs posts waiting to pounce on a book to translate. It would be truer to say that some translators have their origins in cultural borderlands, no matter where they finish up working. We might also say that such regions are reproduced, on another level, in every mixture of cultures, be it through mixed marriage, mixed education or mixed habitation. Cultural reproduction of borderlands has remarkably little to do with land. It is predominantly a phenomenon of the city, of the air that freed the peasant, of the rapid circulation of texts and people, of nonsedentary culture. And so we find translators working in the cities, or in the telecommunicational extensions of cities. Their borders, if you will, have been sublimated, their soil washed away, becoming the complex interfaces of the urban form.

It is no accident that Toledo sits on the history of a discontinuous borderline. Nor was it by accident that translators met and worked there. Translators have been creating their borders in cities ever since. Or so suggest the spatial coordinates.

7. Norms and systems

Networks are skeletons, no more than bones awaiting muscles to make them function. No matter how well we position the times and places of translators and translations, little history can ensue until we know how the translations were actually produced and received. This means reading and analyzing the translations. It also means rather more than producing archaeological lists of textual variants. We have to try to establish how transformations were produced, and within what limits. If you like, the muscles in question would be the social constraints (structures, rules, norms, conventions, whatever) that shape activity into action by contracting or relaxing, in combination or in opposition, altering their tension and thus allowing change. Somehow, we have to progress from a world of data to the dimension of abstract objects (you can't really touch a constraint). Our hypotheses can no longer just count and arrange things; considerable imaginative thought is required to model the forces that might allow things to move.

Several models will be considered here and in the next chapter: 'norms', 'systems' and a special kind of system called a 'regime'. But first we need some idea of the kind of activity that such abstract objects are supposed to constrain.

Actually reading translations

Sooner or later, any moderately diligent translation historian will read a few translations. In fact, this is best done both sooner *and* later: just as soon as you can, for the fun of it and to see how the land lies beyond the deceptions of theory, and as late as necessary, since a lot of work has to be done before you know exactly what you're looking for. The classical mistake, of course, is to read and compare miles of texts, writing a mess of notes on apparently significant differences, and never finding a way to say something coherent about the result. This trap can be overcome by analyzing translations with respect to just one or two well defined levels or aspects, always in order to test clearly formulated hypotheses.

Translations can be analyzed in several ways. The traditional approach is to compare them with their source texts wherever possible (assuming we know the translator was working from the particular text or manuscript available to us). This approach is the most difficult and often the least rewarding, since it quickly projects tangents, sending thoughts to several hundred dead-ends. Alternatively, translations can be read as texts in their own right, without reference to any anterior texts, which means they are implicitly or explicitly compared with non-translational texts in the same genre or social setting. This is easier to do, except that you can almost never be sure of stable criteria for selecting a non-translational reference text (give or take the cases where translators also wrote non-translational texts in the same genre). A third method, the one I would recommend wherever all else is equal, is to compare different translations with each other, ideally both in the same language, ideally related as active rather than passive retranslations (on which, see chapter 5). The differences thrown up by this third approach should have a reasonably direct bearing on translational phenomena, without giving way to lengthy analyses of obligatory linguistic constraints, cultural peculiarities, or anything else that can be analyzed quite easily beyond translation history. A highly productive variant of this third approach is to compare past translations with your own version of the source text, albeit at the risk of producing more details than can coherently be modelled. A further possibility is to analyze successive draft versions of a single translation (its genesis within the work of the one translator). These last-mentioned approaches can nevertheless only become properly historical when informed by a context wide enough to reveal change processes extending beyond the individual frame.

The actual method of reading and comparing texts need not have anything overly historicist about it. Inspiration can be found in the general procedures of descriptive analysis, particularly the pairing of replaced and replacing segments (Toury 1995:87-101) and the concomitant notion of equivalence as something that translators historically produce, not as a set of eternal rules they should eternally follow.[1] Some useful leads might be found in corpus-based analyses (Baker 1993, 1995), explicitation hypotheses (Blum-Kulka 1986, Séguinot 1988), Toury's 'laws of translational behaviour'(1995:259-279), or anything else likely to provide a rough checklist of things to watch out for. But one should not start with the intention of looking for everything. It is better to proceed with a specific goal in mind, keeping your eyes open in case you come across any shortcuts or signs of more attractive destinations. In most of my *fin de siècle* work I recorded the use of verse or prose (not so simple in the era of the *vers libre* and the *poème en prose*) plus quick notes on the paratextual signs (position and importance of the translator as opposed to the author). In my Toledo work the features of most interest were signs of pedagogical elaboration (explanatory apposition, marginal notes, various forms of transcription and integration of foreign terms), Christianization of pagan texts, and indications of the relationship between collaborating translators. In the case of fifteenth-century Castile, where historians

---

[1] The notion of equivalence I am defending refers to a relation operative not between a source text and a target text but between the target text and the reader prepared to believe and trust its status as an 'equivalent' of an unseen source (see Pym 1992a, 1993a, 1995b).

argue about whether Italian humanism was really understood, special attention must inevitably be paid to the translations of philosophical terms, particularly the use of neologisms. There should rarely be any question of analyzing and recording everything that is going on in a translation.

That said, one must constantly be aware that texts open many tracks leading beyond and to the side of our cursory analytical vision. One of the common shortcomings of historical studies – and indeed of contemporary translation theory – is the assumption that texts are wholly determined by their communicative contexts and immediate purposes, such that their textuality would be fundamentally transparent. It sometimes appears that adequate knowledge of sender, receiver, world and aim can allow you more or less to throw away the text itself. Some defence should be made of the opposing view that texts actively configure much of their contexts, casting out questions that may or may not hook onto a referent, an argument, a contestation, an ideology, a class or a social situation, sometimes well beyond or behind any intended purpose or immediate determinant. There are texts and texts. Some, perhaps the greater ones, release more meaning than anything invested in them by individual senders, receivers and material locations; some can reward readers seeking more world than they know. This may happen in several ways.

You might start analyzing a text in terms of translation only to find that, in cases like the Bible and perhaps Ezra Pound's *Cantos*, there is so much theorizing of translation in the text that parts of the object are suddenly on your side, informing the place of the subject. In a sense, the text got there before you did, despite all the contextual differences. And why shouldn't the text teach the historian? In other cases, texts have significance not through what they say but in what they fail to say or actively avoid. Why is it that Daniel de Merlai's *Philosophia*, the main document supporting the notion of 'School of Toledo', never once names an actual 'school' in Toledo? Why is it that in a key Latin preface from the same period, a Mozarab translator, using the first person, says someone else did the translating into Latin, while the translation itself shows no signs of oral collaboration (Riet 1972:98*, 99*n)? Such paradoxes have to be picked up through careful analysis on the level of text, especially where there is no non-textual context that might be used to resolve such issues (that is, all the context is also text). Then there are merely surprising details that might be accidental but you can never be sure. I once wondered why Robert Lowell's introduction to *Imitations* (1958) was so blatantly contradictory and unhelpful; I playfully discovered that the paratextually advertised number of poems was more than the number of fragments actually named as such; I logically counted the >Introduction= itself as a poem, or at least as a fragment with the same translational status as the rest of the book's parts.[2] There are also the very obvious things you don't see because of the trees. When hacking through Henri Albert's French translations of Nietzsche, I was focusing on aspects like versions of the term *Übermensch* and, in the particular case of Albert, the strategies by which various translation difficulties were skirted. It took me some time to see where the real game was being played, namely in the careful preselection of the texts to be translated, presenting a Nietzsche who, at least in the initial texts, was exceptionally misogynist and germanophobe. Without losing sight of our aims, we should be prepared to allow translations to illuminate areas we have incorrectly ignored. We should be prepared to learn from the texts.

The possibility that you can get more out of a text than you put into it nevertheless creates methodological problems in the specific field of translation history, and not only because of the sheer quantities of details that can be noted while reading. If I can analyze such diverse things as a wilfully misleading preface, translationally generated *vers libres*, Lowell's strange poem-introduction or Albert's particularly germanophobe Nietzsche, should all these disparate findings be expected to share the same historical status? Need I argue that any concrete reader in the past would have been aware of such things? Or should I claim that, since I found them, they exist in the present and deserve only whatever importance I choose to attribute to them? Better, can I combine these arguments, perhaps by claiming to have found features that were operative in the past but remained invisible or subliminal to previous readers?

A clean way to decide these issues is to insist that the correct object of any history is change. The features I find in a text – or the interpretations historians project on a text – can only be properly historical to the extent that they constitute or explain phenomena of change. In many cases this relation is not evident. For instance, I might be interested in counting the relative frequency of the reporting connector 'that' in corpora of English translations and non-translations, since Baker (1995) suggests (that) the explicit connector might be more frequent in the translations than in the non-translations. This is certainly interesting, but is it historical? It is something I can discover and perhaps explain in terms of an explicitation hypothesis; it is a feature that most other readers probably ignore; it may point to cognitive universals of translation that are beyond the translator's control; it may even justify seeing translational language as forming its own intercultural space, exploiting variations in numerous target languages. But it

---

[2] The story is a little more complicated. Lowell's 'Table of Contents' lists 63 translated poems but omits a translation of Rilke's 'Die Tauben'. The back-flap announces "sixty-six poems". One solution is to regard the 'Introduction' and the 'Table of Contents' as poems (63+1+2=66), since they are of remarkably little value as informative texts (see Pym 1995c).

is not a fact of properly *historical* importance until I can relate it to a process of actual change. This is not to say that connector deletion cannot be related to historical change (see Romaine 1982); nor is it to suggest that all linguistics should become historical linguistics. Yet this example should point the way to the different levels of historical consciousness involved: counting the frequency of 'that' is not quite the same thing as keeping track of the number of *vers libre* translations in the late nineteenth century, quite simply because the prosification of verse was a change process of which virtually every poetry reader was aware. The phenomenon we discover in the latter case has a very direct relation to a process of historical change: the greater the historical awareness (i.e. within our object of study), the more certain we can be of dealing with a change process. In these terms, smart interpretations of texts like Lowell's poem-introduction would be of no practical consequence for translation history and should probably be left at the level of mere sophistication, whereas Albert's misogynous and germanophobe Nietzsche should probably be admitted, if only because it was an image that would later become the object of public debate, especially around 1914. We shall return to these problems in a minute, since they require a slightly more theoretical answer. For the moment, though, I suggest a relatively simple security check: readings are only historical to the extent that they concern a change process.

Norms?

My insistence on change has a certain relation to historical approaches that describe their object in terms of translational behaviour patterns. The describers look at what translators do; they observe certain regularly repeated features; they account for these patterns in terms of social norms, assumed to be behavioural constraints that entail some kind of sanction for non-compliance (see Toury 1992, 1995; Hermans 1991; Nord 1991b).[3] As Toury says, norms are 'the main factors ensuring the establishment and retention of social order' (1995:55). As such, they are surely responsible for the field of translation making any sense

---

[3] Among the many versions, note Toury's description of norms as "basically the translation of general values or ideas shared by a community – as to what is right and wrong, adequate and inadequate – into specific performance-instructions appropriate for and applicable to specific situations" (1992:62). What worries me here is the assumption that the values or ideas are axiomatically 'shared by a community' rather than imposed in the interests of any dominant group. Note also that writers like Nord refer to 'translation conventions' rather than 'norms', sometimes distinguishing between the two (conventions would be norms not supported by sanctions). For the sake of convention, I use 'norm' here as the global term.

at all, even to the point where any old norm is better than none (such would be the desperation that, for Chesterman 1994, justifies various leaps from 'is' to 'ought'). Translation scholars are thus invited to see their object primarily in terms of regular patterns, repetitions, stability, meaningfulness and social order. Implicitly, they are not invited to see their object in terms of more primal change processes. Unaccepted transformation becomes norm-breaking, an activity that inevitably happens after the norms have been well and truly established and described. Change becomes an affair of pathology.

This is not quite a debate about chickens and eggs. True, change is only meaningful in relation to non-change, and there need be no radical discontinuity between the two terms. The real difference lies in the kinds of social contexts that are used to support the descriptions. The theorists and describers of translational norms spectacularly sideline questions concerning power relationships or conflictual social groups, an attitude that must be at least strange when discussing something as important as 'the establishment and retention of social order'. Who establishes and retains norms? The theorists of translational norms do not say, since their business is merely to describe the norms themselves, in the same way as one might describe the perfect form of an egg so as not to enter the more erratic practice of hen-pecking.

A focus on change (norm-breaking, if you must) immediately raises questions about power and social tension, whereas a focus on non-change (norm-observance, if you like) invites assumptions of social unity and homogeneity. The resulting historical visions are quite different. Change looks like deviance when considered from the perspective of norms, and non-change can be decried as false consciousness from the perspective of norm-breakers. More tellingly, since a focus on norms assumes high degrees of social agreement and cohesion, the frame of analysis used in such studies is most often the single culture. This in turn commonly leads to untested assumptions that translational norms are culture-specific and even to the strange certitude that if a norm does ever happen to turn up in more than one culture it must be as a result of 'interference' (Toury 1995:62). The underlying approach comes dangerously close to the reasoning of the French sociologist Gabriel Tarde, who believed that "when art is an agent of dissent rather than social harmony, it must be from abroad" (1895:396), as if each culture had only its own norms and all the troublemakers were by definition foreigners.

Translational norms can be discovered by looking at two kinds of material: primary texts (in this case translations), to see what translators have actually done, and secondary (theoretical or critical) statements about what translators should be doing, what they want to do, or what they want to be seen to be doing.

Some researchers prefer working on translations, since theories frequently misrepresent what translators do. Others prefer to study past theories, since there are less theories than translations and their analysis might thus seem more comprehensive and cost-effective. Yet this is not just a matter of efficiency. Although a norm-focused study can feed on either translations or secondary material, what it finds strangely difficult to deal with is a mixture of the two. The reason for this is simple enough: as soon as the primary and secondary materials contradict each other – which is usually sooner than later – you have some kind of debate on your hands, a conflict of norms, or at least a falsifiable ideology. Whatever the details, a mixed input tends to switch the focus from steady-state norms to conflicting norms, or to norm-breaking in cases where there is a clearly dominant norm to be broken. Obviously, if you're interested in the latter change processes, some of the best data will come from mixing primary and secondary material.

An example to illustrate the point: When Christiane Nord (1991b:103) claims that translation norms ('conventions' for her) are culture-specific, she cites the second-hand example of Alonso Fernández de Madrid's 1526 version of Erasmus's *Enchoridion*, which was much longer than its original. No one today would accept translational amplification on this scale, so our norms are not those of Fernández de Madrid. Therefore, implies Nord, Fernández de Madrid was working in terms of norms specific to sixteenth-century Spain. There's a lot wrong with this kind of reasoning. First, Nord's methodology makes no attempt to place the particular translation in any kind of quantitative or qualitative context. Accepting another researcher's report on the translation's length, she considers the translation norm simply 'other' with respect to 'us'. If some attempt had been made to locate a properly translational context, Nord might have found that Fernández de Madrid's translation was considered an aberration even in sixteenth-century Spain, scarcely representative of any general norm.[4] , Nord has simply re-cited a detail from the level of the translation itself, without saying why any translator would amplify to such a degree (Fernández de Madrid was also omitting passages, in fact using the translational situation as an occasion to preach through a foreign persona). Third, the analyst has not pursued secondary discourses like the preface (fragments are given in Santoyo 1987:49-52) in which the translator shamelessly justifies his work in terms of classical fidelity, with references to Saint Jerome and all, in superficial conformity with certain norms of his day.

---

[4] Referring this particular translation, Russell (1985:53) explicitly states that, in his opinion, "It would be a serious mistake to believe [the translator's] attitude to the Latin text of the *Enchoridion* was typical of the Iberian translators of this period, or of the previous period."

Fourth, one can quite easily build up another kind of context – in fact a network – in which translative expansion does appear to be some kind of norm, most obviously in Erasmus's 1516 Latin version of the New Testament (first link) and in the philological translation strategies in which Erasmus found some inspiration, notably those elaborated by the Italian Lorenzo Valla (see Hermans 1992:107), who just happened to be in the employ of the Crown of Aragon, and so on. From Spain to Holland to Italy to Spain-Italy (the Crown of Aragon extended to Naples). So much for the culture-specific norm! And why would Fernández de Madrid produce a highly conventional preface for a translation that was surely norm-breaking within the immediate Spanish context? Well, it could have something to do with the bringing of critical philology to Spain, the association of philology with Erasmism, the attacks on Erasmus led by Diego López de Zúñiga from 1520, the wider shoring up of the Church and its Inquisition, in short, a long history of tension and change that sounds rather more important than just observing that some kind of norm is 'other'.

Something else is going on here, something we've been putting off for several chapters. When I discussed importance in terms of the researcher's interests being compatible or incompatible with the client's (chapter 2 above), I concluded by saying we would have to find out why translation might have been important in the past. We are now in a position to start answering that question. We have seen how quantitative fluctuations and material networks can indicate sites of disturbance in the past, and we are beginning to see how such sites might be related to debates and conflicts over translation norms, not to mention norms governing questions like what is to be translated and who is authorized to translate. In other words, we are starting to appreciate that the kind of importance located in our present can also be found operating within the object, in the ways that past translators established relations between themselves and with their whole range of clients. The importance of the present is formally the same as that of the past. But how should they actually be related?

As we have seen, one kind of relation, the kind most unfortunately associated with culture-specific norms, is achieved by positing that past importance is 'other'. Fernández de Madrid did not translate the way we do, therefore his entire context was not like ours. This stance, which privileges differences, appears to respect otherness in all its relativist dignity. Yet it often achieves quite the opposite. In Nord, the citation of the exotic detail, the reference to just one exceptionally expansive translation, merely serves to justify the researcher's hypothesis. The past becomes cannon fodder for debates in our present; there is no significant attempt to reach out and understand why historical detail might become more than an odd throw-away example. The positing of culture-specific otherness, quite apart from being logically untenable (how do you know how something really functions in a culture that isn't yours?), becomes an underhand way of making the past speak for our purposes. This facile otherness is all too well served by studies of norms, which objectify and distance the historical object in such a way that the importance manifested in the past seems not to intersect with ours.

An equally misleading procedure, already mentioned, is to assume that what is important for us is automatically important for everyone else as well, to the extent that any feature I can wheedle out of a text is to be considered operative in the past. I can read Lowell's introduction as a poem, Mona Baker can count the frequency of the word 'that' in translations, and it's all important because we say so. Although this is the exact opposite of distancing the past, it gives much the same result: we finish up making the past speak for our own purposes, producing nothing that deserves to be called history. That is why I insist there be some relation to past processes of change, and that there be some indication of how these processes were of importance in the past. If this is not done, we finish up expounding no more than the present.

A third mode of thought, impeccably dialectic, is to deny the radical exteriority of the object but to insist on its substantiality. This means asking how we came to study this particular object in the first place; it means realizing that we (in relation with clients and so on) made the initial move leading to the selection of this object from the entire range of possible historical objects; it means that we already have some subjective engagement with the past even before the formal analysis begins. No matter how much we worry about being the conqueror or the conquered, the invasion has already happened. We are there, involved in the object, players. From this perspective, our selected past norms, no matter how accidentally they seem to catch our attention, are never entirely other. Minimally, they always suggest the possibility of an application in the present, a question about why they should not be applied, or perhaps just a demonstration that there are more things in heaven and earth than our endemic norms suggest (for an exemplary application of such questions to translator training, see Toury 1992). There must be some intellectual projection of ourselves into the past, since it is in this particular direction that we have already invested effort. As a nominal Protestant in Catholic Spain, how can I not be concerned with the way Erasmus was translated into Castilian? How can I not wonder what would have happened if the norms had been a little different, a little less oppositional, perhaps more conducive to Erasmus actually coming to Spain in person rather than in translation? (Cardinal Cisneros invited him to the University of Alcalá in 1511; Erasmus declined.) In the same spirit, one might go through the debates of the past in order to find out why some desired change in the present is difficult to bring about, as Venuti (1995) does when reading English translation history in terms of 'invisibility' versus 'resistance'. You can care about past norms; you can learn from their fate. One way or another, what was important in the past must have some connection with what is important in the present; it must extend our frames of reference and our range of conceivable alternatives. If not, we would have no good reason to do history in the first place. Our work on the object would be either impositional or unimportant.

I now return to the question of norms as such. Do we want to build history on them or not? Let me summarize the aspects that make me less than happy about the way they are currently studied:

- Since norms are constraints, one should be able to say what they are constraining (social tension and debate), but this is overlooked by the dominant emphasis on stability rather than change.
- In keeping with the search for stability, the study of norms has paid little attention to the active contradictions between what is done in translations and what is said about translations.
- There is no reason why translation norms should be culture specific (i.e. from one culture only, and throughout that culture), and yet this would seem to be a frequent assumption.
- The study of norms thus tends to make the object exterior to us, allowing the past to be used for ideologically relativist ends.

If norms can be organized in a way able to avoid or overcome these shortcomings, I would have no reason not to be happy with them. The real problem, though, is that the organization of norms into larger units tends to compound the above problems even further, especially when the larger units are described as systems.

Systems?

I believe that systems theory has had a major positive influence on translation history. In fact, the analysis of norms sometimes becomes a mere sideshow next to the bigger machines at the fair. Systems theory, or at least the mode of thought behind its many versions, can be dated from virtually whenever you like. I like to see it as a product of the *Aufklärung* projection of functional totalities, based on a belief in the meaningfulness of nature grasped as a whole; I like to oppose it to the Humanist attention to detail and historical accuracy. With or without the term, systems informed the development of nineteenth-century political economics, and from there the linguistics of Saussure, recuperated by Lévi-Strauss and his generation, whence structuralist approaches to all sorts of social life. Certainly without the term, systems were part of the thought that opposed nineteenth-century aestheticist poetics to the positivism of Naturalism; they later helped link French aestheticism with Russian Formalism.[5] In the meantime, by other routes, we find talk of systems in virtually all the non-human sciences, from ecology to astronomy, not to mention the quotidian critique involved whenever we talk about virtually any reactionary social establishment as 'the system'. Theorists have to state very exactly what they want the term to mean.

The first and perhaps still the most consistent application of systems theory to translation history is in the work of the Israeli scholar Itamar Even-Zohar, who cites the Russian Formalists as the immediate sources for his 'polysystem' approach.[6] A similar connection with the Russian Formalists would seem to have been applied to translation theory through the work of André Lefevere. Whatever the case, since the mid-1970s translational systems theory has operated in terms of a network linking Tel Aviv, Antwerp, Leuven, Amsterdam and various offshoots (among which, Theo Hermans in London and the late André Lefevere in Texas). Within this frame, it has became an essential part of descriptive translation studies, most saliently through the collective *Manipulation of Literature* volume edited by Hermans in 1985, but also through fruitful links like those with the more pragmatic 'transfer' approach to literary translation developed in Göttingen. Further serious networking is associated with José Lambert, under whose guidance the CETRA series of annual research-training programmes has been organized. This dispersed development has entailed several inconvenient aspects, not the least of which is the possibility that no one is quite sure what the term 'system' means any more, let alone how it should be related to norms, to history, or indeed to translation.[7]

---

[5] "Scratch the Formalist", says Genette (1976:312), "and you'll find a Symbolist."

[6] In talking about 'polysystems', Even-Zohar underlines the fact that the systems he deals with are not homogeneous entities but are always plural and open, in the sense that they are systems of systems, and systems within systems. Since this view of systems is nowadays generally agreed upon, we might drop the term 'polysystem', recognizing that all systems can be plural and open. In any case, researchers since Even-Zohar have shown a clear preference for 'system' over 'polysystem', perhaps due to the discovery of Luhmann as an alternative source of inspiration.

[7] See, for example, the various contradictory contributions to the volume *Histories, Systems, Literary Translations* (ed. Kittel 1992). More generally, note how often definitions of systems become arguments-by-reading-list, referring back to previous articles, previous authors, previous generations. Many people refer explicitly to Even-Zohar, who does indeed take the trouble to explain what he means by 'system' and how his definitions relate to translation. But

One thing, however, seems clear enough: a system is something more than a network. Networks are based on material connections; systems appear to have more to do with the qualities of the relations themselves; they are more abstract, like norms. Systems also seem to be bigger than norms, functioning either as a set of interrelated norms (a 'genre system' for example) or as a set of 'well-formed' or 'grammatically possible' relations of which only some are accorded the status of norms (as in linguistic approaches). Let me also add that systems seem to do rather more than just arrange elements: they mostly have a spark of life, of things happening, as when planets circulate, engines idle, hearts beat or economies function well or badly. Systems, according to this wilfully simplistic conception, enable identities to ride with historical change. As for the rest, I'm not so sure. Whenever someone tells me systems are 'open', I want them to show me where the openings are. Whenever they say systems are 'dynamic', I want someone to point to the spark, the churning contradiction or the decentring motor. Whenever someone says that systems interrelate things, I want to know what kinds of things are in and what kinds of things are out.[8] If I am told systems are series of binary oppositions hanging in a vague spatial metaphor, I want to know what actual causes link up the elements and then don't link with elements beyond the limits. I'll believe once I've seen.

While I await revelation, I suspect that much of translation history can advance quite well without using the word 'system' at all. If you want to talk about cultures, the best word is probably 'cultures'; literatures can be called 'literatures'; and the same for societies, languages and the rest. One of the real dangers of indiscriminate systems theory is that all these different words tend to be put into the same mix, as if each culture were coterminous with a language, a society and a literature, all under the one concept (in this case paradoxically more polysystem than system), such that we no longer have to look seriously at

---

read Even-Zohar closely, ask his texts exactly why one should talk about systems rather than any alternative concept, and the response is a chain of further back-references, this time to the Russian Formalists, notably Tynjanov and Ejxenbaum (his spellings), in the apparent conviction that an understanding of these thinkers will lead to a correct understanding of (literary) systems (see for example Even-Zohar 1990, particularly 29-32). The result is a science that inherits concepts from past illumination, passing authority constantly down the line, quite independently of any current problems that one might want the concepts to solve.

[8] Eco (1976:36-37) sees systems as being syntactic ("a set of signals ruled by internal combinatory laws"), semantic (a set of states or contents thus represented) or receptive ("a set of behavioural responses on the part of the destination"), quite apart from the combinations of all three invested in what he terms 'codes'. Very few definitions of systems account for these diverse possibilities.

the non-corresponding edges.

Not wanting to get lost in any particular section of this labyrinth, my purpose here is merely to put forward a few observations, hopefully raising a few questions that others might like to answer. My real interest, of course, is in levering out the kind of system most suited to interculturality. I want to set the stage for my own particular brand of system, to be presented in the next chapter.

Leaps of faith

First observation: Leaps of faith or intuition are mostly used to get from the narrowly empirical descriptive level (the stuff of distributions, networks and norms) to the level of systems. There is a kind of history that can be built up brick by brick, hypothesis by hypothesis, link by link, and another kind, the kind that talks about systems from page one, that skips over the petty work and just assumes that all the little pieces are really parts of a larger whole. Systems are supposed to be such larger wholes, one way or another. But has anyone carried out a piece-by-piece analysis of an entire system of translations, translation norms, source or target cultures, or anything else strictly pertinent to translation history?[9] True, I have no good reason to doubt that such an undertaking could be completed successfully: grammars and dictionaries do capture something of the systemic nature of natural languages, so something similar could perhaps be done with translations. On the other hand, I have no guarantee that such a description *can* be completed of systems that are not obviously languages (some parts of natural languages are very linguistically systemic). This particularly concerns borderline cases, the identification of non-systemic elements, and the intersystemic borders that are non-coterminous on the various levels. Are these problems really solved by assuming there are wholes into which the details will fit sooner or later? The conceptualization of systems is a noble and justified enterprise, as great as its *Aufklärung* antecedents. However, in terms of meth-

---

[9] Anyone contemplating the exercise should consider the methodological problems broached in such early structuralist works as Rosengren's *Sociological Aspects of the Literary System* (1968), which studies the 'mentions' of foreign writers in Swedish literary reviews (we would have to replace 'mentions' with 'translations'). Rosengren advances formulas for calculating structurally significant co-mentions, relative structuring and relative integration, and does indeed assess the dynamics of the Swedish system in two key periods. Similar statistical procedures might be adapted from the sociolinguistics of variation. The point, though, is that the many calls for an empirical 'descriptive translation studies' have not been accompanied by piece-by-piece analysis, and thus have not felt the need for strong statistical procedures.

odology, there is a big difference between identifying phenomena bit-by-bit and assuming they have a role in systems, all in one go. Each approach should at least act as a check on the other.

The will to system

Second observation: No one is sure if systems actually exist. Here, for example, is Even-Zohar explaining that a system is

> the assumed set of observables supposed to be governed by a network of relations (i.e. for which systemic relations can be hypothesized) (1990:27).

Note the carefully uncommitted verb forms ('assumed', 'supposed to be', 'can be hypothesized') for which no subject is forthcoming. Note also the whispered tautology: a 'system' is a set of things with 'systemic' relations. How are the elements in the system selected? By the relations one believes might exist between them. And how are these relations selected? By the fact that they are 'systemic' and thus able to 'govern' systems. Precisely. Could they do anything else? All of this appears to be happening in the place of the observer. A 'system' would thus be an intellectual model we use to make sense of certain data, without ever being confused with anything actually in the object itself.

These days, most systems theorists would accept that they are presenting no more than explanatory models. I seem to remember Lotman being described as a monist, in the sense that he thinks systems are actually in the object, but I couldn't point a finger at anyone else. For the rest, systems theory is justified not because it is true, but because it provides explanations for many things.

Perhaps surprisingly, I am unwilling to dismiss the monist position out of hand. Why shouldn't a certain systemic nature be operative within the historical object itself? Why shouldn't explanatory systems theories be truer than they know, or perhaps truer than they want to be? I suspect that systems really do exist. My argument here need not depend on power relations that might impose systems from above (although such relations certainly exist). All I really have to point out is that the necessary collectivity of social life produces desires to belong to identifiable social groups, with corresponding constraints on large sets of possible individual actions. Since belonging is a part of social life, it gives rise not to systems in any strong direct sense, but to a certain desire for systems as safeguards of identity and order. This desire can produce systems within the object.

Let's consider a principle commonly attributed to systems of all kinds: 'tout se tient', as Saussure said of natural languages, 'everything holds together', such that a change in one part of the system brings about adjustments throughout the whole of the system. This could even be an objective definition of a system: when there are no more adjustments, there is no more system. Unfortunately, there is little evidence that this principle actually holds in the more complex social systems.[10] In natural languages, to take the prime example, the introduction of foreign lexical or syntactic elements into one remote and arcane discourse – say, translation theory – certainly need not shake up the entire language. In the university where I currently teach, students learn about linguistic systems, Saussure and all, in their first year; then they start studying English grammar and find, in the classic textbook of our moment (Quirk et al. 1972:46), that there are 'closed-system items' (articles, demonstratives, pronouns, prepositions, conjunctions and perhaps interjections), which are indeed reciprocally exclusive and reciprocally defining, and that all the rest (nouns, verbs, adjectives, adverbs) are 'open-class items' for which the basic principles of reciprocity don't hold. Only some parts of language are really systemic in any strong sense of the word.

In literary theory, a systems theorist might hypothesize that the introduction of a new literary genre will change all the relations between existing genres. But is this necessarily so? Does the principle apply beyond a restricted set of 'closed-system items', perhaps sacred texts, a national canon, or what T. S. Eliot approvingly called the "monuments [that] form an ideal order among themselves, which is modified by the introduction of the new (the really new) among them" (1919:294). A lot else can happen in the publishing markets. Many best-sellers are the literary equivalent of 'open-class items'; much that is new is not at all 'really new' in Eliot's traditionalist sense of the term. An unforeseen genre can stimulate and extend a literary market into areas that were previously untouched, creating something new without significantly affecting the previous genres.

---

[10] The biologist Ramón Margalef (1986) nevertheless insists that ecosystems are not like trains, where if one wagon moves all the others have to (as in the ideal Saussurean *langue*). They are more like the systems that control city traffic, allowing each motorist major degrees of liberty and responsibility, imposing obligatory rules as well as some that are not so obligatory (amber lights). The traffic system produces interesting phenomena like waves of cars, traffic jams, fast lanes, accidents and deaths. Each city has its particular road plans, population densities, traditional temperaments and the social authority. In any Australian city, one of the main functions of the traffic system is to slow cars down. In Paris, traffic police spend their lives telling drivers to go faster. Each traffic system is more or less adequate to its purpose; it can cease to be operational when overloaded or lacking in flexibility. More interestingly for the purposes of translation history, traffic systems regulate the movements of both local and outside vehicles. They allow one to drive through a foreign city, with a greater or lesser degree of difficulty.

Other fields of literary activity, especially those that are highly subsidized, are commonly segmented off, forming fields beyond which very few ripples are created: changes in English-language poetry, theatre and opera would no longer be expected to have structural effects on the development of the novel. Even when such segmentation is not at all desired, it can function as a basic mechanism of systemic defence. For example, one might imagine Venuti's generalized call for 'resistant' translators being socially cordoned off as a trick for intellectuals, thus causing virtually no changes beyond an academic coterie.

The catch, though, is that many people do not want to see the practical uses and effects of segmentation. Let's imagine the presence of anglicisms in a small backwater of a natural language like French, perhaps in computer science or something similar. If that were the end of the story, the anglicisms would almost certainly have little effect beyond the limited circles concerned; they would be segmented off, accepted, their foreignness forgotten. And yet the presence of such intruding terms is commonly vilified as a threat to the entire language, *as if* everything really did hold together, *as if* a change in one relation really were going to undermine the whole lot. There are outcries, debates, legislation, adjustments, a whole series of secondary determinations that effectively annul segmentation. Speakers do not look at natural languages through the eyes of grammarians who can patiently distinguish between 'closed-system' and 'open-class' orders. All words and structures are seen as being elements in just the one system. And whether or not the French language actually is just one system, the secondary moves to defend or debate its status do indeed make everything hold together, not gratuitously associating the language with a timeless national identity, forming an ideologically motored system that has little to do with linguistic distinctions. The same could be said for certain canonized genre systems and the like. The introduction of a new literary discourse (or a new television channel, or whatever) may well have no effect on existing genres, but if the guardians of the existing genres *perceive* the new arrival to be a source of potential change for all genres, they will act accordingly, effectively making the new genre a source of change for all existing genres. From this perspective, it doesn't really matter whether there is objectively reciprocal exclusion and reciprocal definition throughout a system. As soon as secondary processes regulate, subsidize or symbolize a series of activities as if they were a system, then those activities have effectively become a system. The items don't hold together; they are held together by people who in some way want to belong together.

Such, at least, is the subjectivized objectivity that interests me: In the humanities, if a system exists, some social group wants it to exist, and they sometimes want it so much that they are going to defend the system against any perceived alteration. At the same time, someone who sets out to attack a series of activities as if they formed a system (much revolutionary theory is similarly systemic) also effectively turns those activities into a system, if only to the extent that the activities attacked are probably going to be defended as such. Conflict will ensue; there will be debates about whether or not a system should be altered; historical researchers will pick up the conflicts and debates, seeing them as issues of importance – which they certainly are – and extrapolating the terms so as to project objective systems as the necessary conditions of the conflict. Where do the systems really come from? Perhaps not from quietly stringing together all the facts. Perhaps historians see systems by picking up traces of various contradictory wills to system. If so, should we be surprised that researchers skip into leaps of faith to reach hypotheses about systems? The same leaps may have already been made within the historical object itself.

I am not against the idea of systems. Whatever the terminology, whatever the mix of substance and illusion, there is something there, in the object, operating as a basic principle of organization that is not dependent on the little pieces. There is more to systems than explanatory hypotheses. I suspect there is also a social will to system. And that desire is eminently human.

Subjectless prose

Systems theory is superficially a kind of prose that does everything possible to suppress a humanized, subjective systematicity. We have already seen part of this suppression in Even-Zohar's description of a system. Here is a further example of much the same thing, taken from Theo Hermans' introduction to the seminal 1985 volume *The Manipulation of Literature*:

> As a theoretical model the polysystem theory appears to provide an
> adequate framework for the systematic study of translated literature.
> (1985:12)

The sentence sounds innocent enough. But let's look at it carefully. Note the verb 'appears to'. Hermans is not making any direct pronouncements on the state of the world; his is a tentative discourse; he moves by exploratory hypotheses that merely offer possible relations; he does not want to tell anyone what to think or what to do. This is science, not politics. But if something 'appears' to have a state or to carry out an action, surely there must be an observer able to perceive the appearance. To whom or for whom does this theory 'appear to provide'? And what about the main verb, 'provide'? Usually someone 'provides' something to someone. Here, an inanimate and abstract object, a theory, 'provides' something all by itself, and to no one in particular. The resulting sentence is entirely devoid of people. Although the verbs would normally imply human activity, here they construct a world where people do nothing: things themselves 'appear', 'provide', 'function', 'account for', 'determine', and a limited range of variants. The verbs belong to a human science without humans.[11] And there are pages and pages of these verbs, books and books.

Now look at the noun phrases in the above sentence. The subject 'polysystem theory' is considered 'as a theoretical model'. Could it be anything else? Can a theory not be a theoretical model? A similar redundancy marks the object of the sentence: this systemic theory leads to ('appears to provide an adequate framework for') something called 'systematic study'. What other kind of study would one expect from a theory of systems? Of course systems theory produces systematic study! There is no real need for all this 'appears to'; no overwhelming requirement to provide 'adequacy' or to act as a 'framework for'. If you presuppose the existence of systems alone, you should finish up with results that are not only systemic (you will find systems) but also, of course, systematic, since the methodological desirability of intersubjectively arranging structured wholes was posited as a value in the first place.

If we try to recuperate the subjects suppressed in these sentences, don't we find researchers who manifest a certain desire for systems, as a question of importance in and of itself? If so, systems theory can surely be seen as a tool used by certain researchers to provide certain results in a certain situation. It has no doubt operated in reaction to the earlier fragmentary approaches of a more docile humanism, just as it sought legitimation for a new discipline, in the heady days when scientific structuralism thought it could explain the world.

Where's the gold?

Since I see translation history as an activity addressing questions of concern to the present, I am not overly interested in aspirations to pure research (cf. Delabastita 1991:152), non-evaluation (cf. Lambert 1989:223-224) or the discovery of abstract laws (cf. D'hulst 1987:17). In short, I'm not much interested in the scholarly cargo that is supposed to fall from metaphors of systemic centres and peripheries. I see little point in producing something whose only

---

[11] Or again, try these sentences from Lefevere: "History is made by people, according to certain constraints that are [...] systemic in nature. / Once a literary system is established *it* tends to try to reach and maintain a 'steady state'..." (1992a:38, italics mine). If history is really made by people, how can the system become the subject of a verb of active intention ("it tends to try to reach")? Surely people collectively try to attain things *through* systems?

value is that it looks like science. There are many other criteria in the world, many things to do. We have noted that systems theory is not very good, for example, at formulating causal hypotheses (it has trouble saying *why* phenomena occurred); nor is it in a comfortable position to put forward many ethical propositions (it doesn't say what phenomena *should not* occur). Yet some of us are profoundly interested in why things happen and why some things should not happen. The gold, for us, lies elsewhere.

I believe there is, or can be, a certain systematic nature in any social object. I am quite prepared to associate that systemic quality with the fact of individual cultures. But I do not believe monocultural systems are necessarily the main determinants on translative processes, nor on the ethics of translation, nor on the possibilities of translations. There is at least one alternative way of looking at these things.

8. Regimes

Despite the shortcomings in some of the ways norms and systems have been applied to translation history, the concepts themselves should be treated with respect. Our task is not to do away with norms and systems but to adapt them to the specific concerns of translation history. What I am looking for is a way to make them appropriate to a conflict perspective that is primarily intercultural, in touch with desires and perceptions, and of current importance. This might be done, I believe, by considering the relative advantages of regime theory.

I first became interested in regimes as a result of contacts with negotiation theorists in 1984. I have been toying and experimenting with the idea ever since, in relative isolation, without close involvement in subsequent developments of the theory and without doing much to hardsell the idea to translation theorists. After more than ten years I am still experimenting; I am not yet in a position to propose any panacea. What I can do, though, is offer a brief explanation of what regimes are and how I have attempted to apply the concept to translation history.

What are regimes?

The concept of regimes was introduced into the study of international politics by John Ruggie in 1975. He defined a regime as "a set of mutual expectations, rules and regulations, plans, organizational and financial commitments, which have been accepted by a group of states" (1975:570). This means that if different countries are going to negotiate or generally do business, their shared regime says how they are going to go about it. A later collective definition describes regimes as

> sets of implicit or explicit principles, norms, rules and decision-making procedures around which actors' expectations converge in a given area of international relations. Principles are beliefs of fact, causation and rectitude. Norms are standards of behaviour defined in terms of rights and obligations. Rules are specific prescriptions or proscriptions for action. Decision-making procedures are prevailing practices for making and implementing collective choice. (cited in Krasner 1983:2)

Within the scope of this definition, studies have been carried out on international regimes currently operative with respect to rivers, lakes and islands, commodity trade, arms negotiations and peace settlements. In all cases, the 'principles, norms, rules and decision-making procedures' do not concern what happens within any one state (or culture, or system) but what happens between such entities when some kind of cooperative relation is to be established in a formal way. More narrowly, we might say that regimes enable negotiators to agree to negotiate.

Regime theory could concern translation history for several reasons. First, although translation is often an important aspect of international relations, theorists have so far done little to conceptualize its specific role within this wider frame. Second, the handful of theorists who relate translation to unequal power relations between cultures, particularly those who do so in postcolonial terms, have remarkably little to say about what translators should actually do with any power they might have in their hands; regime theory can at least posit the goal of establishing cooperation across power differentials. Third, regime theory already has a place for the kind of norms that have attracted attention within translation theory (in fact the general notion of norms could be proposed as a loose blanket covering the 'principles, rules and decision-making procedures' of regimes). Fourth, regimes are already operating in a way similar to systems, at least with respect to their general size (they are bigger than norms), their abstract nature (they are not material networks) and their functional capacity (they enable numerous social relations to be established and transformed). However, there are significant differences between regimes and the kinds of norms and systems we saw in the previous chapter. The specific norms of international regimes belong to quite a different kind of space (they are rigorously not restricted to any one country); regimes are likely to represent and define professional identities rather than anything ensuing from cultural traditions or birthright (they are the stuff of working negotiators, be they Americans, Russians or whatever); they are likely to be more transitory and narrower in function than the norms and systems so far studied in translation history (especially to the extent that a regime need not address issues that have been settled); and they are used to achieve specific aims, to find a kind of gold (which we might call cooperation, crosscultural trust, or understanding).[1] In view of the points made in the previous chapter, these features should be considered serious advantages.

---

[1] Note that my use of the term 'regime' here refers back to its usage within the theory of international negotiations; it does not attempt to cover the related sense of 'regimes of value' in which, for Appadurai (1986:4), "desire and demand, reciprocal sacrifice and power interact to create economic value in specific social situations". Appadurai is certainly useful to the extent that his notion tries to account for "the constant transcendence of cultural boundaries by the flow of commodities" (15). Yet care should be taken with the way Frow (1995:144-45), for example, dissociates regimes of value not only from specific cultural groups but also from specifically intercultural situations, making it difficult to say exactly who might be engaged in such things. Although these senses are certainly related to the notion of regimes developed here, I have sought to restrict regime analysis to the norms operative in intercultural relations. The rest of the world will be explained tomorrow.

Despite the above collective definition, regimes have been seen in at least two different ways. For Puchala and Hopkins, "a regime exists in every substantive issue-area in international relations where there is discernibly patterned behaviour" (1983:63). This is like saying there are norms and systems wherever there is structure. One could thus find out about regimes by analyzing specific issue-areas in international relations, attaching the label 'regime' to anything bearing any kind of pattern. Since literature transfer could be one such area, the insights of Puchala and Hopkins might be slapped onto structured networks for the distribution of literary texts or onto specific translation practices within those networks. All these things could be called regimes or parts of regimes. Yet they might also be isolated misuses of a modish-sounding American term. Let's not rush into this.

Puchala and Hopkins invite us to see regimes almost everywhere in international relations, just as systems theorists tend to see systems everywhere. In fact, another regime theorist, Robert Keohane, has claimed that what Puchala and Hopkins study is indistinguishable from 'international systems' or indeed any norm-regulated behaviour imposed by hegemonic relationships (1984:59n). A more restricted notion of regimes might thus be of interest to anyone wary of the way previous terms have been degraded by indiscriminate use. Keohane's own version attempts to locate regimes as organizational principles that evolve from rational cooperation between sovereign states, without any hegemonic imposition:

> International regimes should not be interpreted as elements of a new international order 'beyond the nation-state.' They should be comprehended chiefly as arrangements motivated by self-interest: as components of systems in which sovereignty remains a constitutive principle.' (1984:63)

Whereas Puchala and Hopkins adopt a basically descriptive approach that seeks to accommodate historical variants, Keohane is interested in the kind of international relationships that should be created in the future.[2] His notion of regimes envisages a world order without hegemony. Yet the interesting part of Keohane's

---

[2] Although now dated, this constructive idealism makes Keohane's arguments about regimes worth pursuing. True, his insights suffer from excursions through rational egoists playing prisoners' dilemmas. True, too, these games conveniently fail to account for the ways their players came to be separated or had their cells defined for them (that is, in our terms, they accept a world of magically divided cultures). Yet extended-play and multiple-player dilemma games do enable the arguments to surface into a more noble light, concluding that cooperation can result between highly unequal parties.

argument is not really the ideal, although we all need ideals. It is the step from non-negotiated rational cooperation (a matter of faith) to regimes as a way of institutionalizing negotiated cooperation. At some point, someone has to enter with a particular will to regime, in the same way as general belonging can give rise to a particular will to system.

These two notions of regimes beg obvious questions about the nature of historical description and its relation to the present. A certain compatibility between the descriptive and idealist concepts should nevertheless follow from what we have said about relating past importance to present importance. Rather than stick the term 'regime' on every kind of patterned behaviour, the idealist approach has the advantage of making history talk about how a regime might be constructed here and now. At the same time, of course, this privileging of the present must be checked by attention to how our current questions were answered by the regimes of the past.

In what follows, I will adopt each of these approaches in succession. First, I will present bottom-up attempts to describe three translation regimes. At the end of the chapter I will briefly discuss a more idealist top-down way of integrating translation into a general view of intercultural regimes.

Starting from debates

When you go ferreting out translation norms, the first thing you have to spot is presumably some regularity. The hunt for regimes, however, or for the kinds of norms and principles that might make up regimes, cannot start from mere regularity. From the very beginning we need a conflict, a disagreement, perhaps a potential dispute, or at least some measure of dissent. We need an underlying conflict so as to locate the points about which two or more sides might have to negotiate. There need not be any actual negotiations in the strict sense of the term, with all parties around a table. Nor should we presuppose any *a priori* conflict between the source and target cultures, since in many cases the source cultures are no longer around anyway. When dragging a concept from one discipline to another, a certain degree of metaphorical play should be allowed for. But we must, from the outset, locate an underlying conflict in relation to which our regime can function as a set of constraints. This means the initial unit of regime analysis should be an oppositional structure. We might generally call this structure a debate.

In practical terms, attention to debates involves looking more at translation theories and criticisms than at the textual or linguistic analysis of translations, since it is on the metatranslational levels that disagreements are most likely to be manifested. Obviously, no one theory or theorizing statement can be taken at face value, since theory is itself understood here as a mode of argumentation, with each act of theorization standing in some kind of opposition to one or more alternative theorizations.[3] If we find a metatranslational statement, we should try to locate the position it was opposing. If we can't locate a clear point of opposition, we should look for causally related critical comments, changes in the actual practice of translations, or variants in the market for translations. In principle, since no one theorizes just to state the obvious, each individual theory or act of theorization should find at least one counterpart somewhere. Each theory should be seen as an element of a wider debate.

An emphasis on past debates might seem to contradict the empiricist location of norms (Toury's preference is for translations, not theories, as points of departure). Yet this is not an arbitrary emphasis. The nature of functional norms is to be invisible except in cases of their transgression, and transgression is mostly the cause of debate. Debates can thus provide some useful shortcuts to the transgressions. Further, since a given textual pattern is often compatible with several aims or modes of reasoning, straight observation of the pattern is not likely to reveal the reasons why it was adopted, defended or attacked.[4] The analysis of theories and criticism, if understood as debates, should reveal the values at stake in the particular historical conjuncture concerned. Thus, although past theories should never become gospels, they can provide very good indications of what kind of norms were important in a particular historical field. For example, it makes sense to work on verse forms at the end of the nineteenth century, when there was considerable public debate about the *vers libre*, but it does not make the same sense to study the *vers libre* in the 1930s, when there was not the same level of debate. In the first case, we might find something like a regime; in the second, we would be more likely to accumulate a lot of data leading nowhere.

That said, the search for conflict can also be well served by the analysis of translations, especially in cases where the need for public theorizing is not

---

[3] I make no distinction between 'theorization' and 'a theory', at least not in the sense that the latter term might be restrictively associated with a systematic rationalist description of an entire field. As Douglas Robinson has had cause to lament (1995:172), the fixation on 'a theory' (or the collective search for one) is a self-serving way of dehistoricizing contemporary translation studies. For me, both terms are subordinate to the notions of 'debate' and 'negotiation' (even the most systematic theories are still engaged in historical debates), which have no reason not to be on the same historical level as the norms of regimes.

[4] As Schleiermacher observed, sophisticated literalism can look like a series of beginner's errors. Similarly, some of Hölderlin's word orderings in his versions of Pindar are strangely close to the style of machine translation outputs of the 1970s. There is no way the two behaviour patterns could be attributed to similar aims or modes of reasoning.

immediately obvious. In suggesting that the study of regimes should start from close attention to debates, I do not want to exclude textual or linguistic translation analysis. My purpose, once again, is to make sure there is some important question to answer prior to wading through all the waters.

A regime for twelfth-century Toledo

Sometimes there are few debates in sight and one has no alternative but to start from basic information about translators and translations. As I entered twelfth-century Hispania I saw no visible translation theory, scarcely a critical comment or preface, not much for regime analysis to grab hold of. Worse, there were so many cultural groups in the ruck that it was hard to see who could be debating with whom. Should one focus on the Muslims, Mozarabs, Jews, Italians, Frenchmen, Englishmen, the few apparently unadulterated Hispanic Christians, or any combination of these groups? To compound the problem, when I questioned my own reasons for studying this particular object – I originally wanted to ask if the Toledan translators were Hispanic or (and?) intercultural – I found that my own debate had been won before it had started: yes, Toledo itself, as a very multi-ethnic frontier town, provided a sufficiently intercultural space for my models to be tested. So what? For the rest, the conflict perspective did not look promising.

It is hard to convey the extent to which a researcher can wander from detail to detail, formulating and reformulating hypotheses, before history begins to make sense. In this case some minor doubts turned out to be more important than I first suspected. A few of them have already been mentioned: the Englishman's account of Toledo, where a translating process is described but no school is mentioned, then the peculiar preface where a non-Latinist translator appears to be writing in Latin. Other things were more immediately signs of debates. When the abbot of Cluny remarks that it cost him 'many prayers and much expense' to have the *Qur'an* translated into Latin, and when the main translators working on the *Qur'an* project describe their participation as a 'digression' from their scientific translations, something was up. The Clunaic church had one set of interests; the translators of protoscience had another. And yet, since much Arabic protoscience was translated for the Toledo cathedral, the two sides obviously learned to work together. Indeed, the more you look at what was going on, the stranger it seems that scientific texts were actually translated for the church, especially since the kind of observational attitudes promoted by these translations would eventually undermine the authority of the same church (a point well made in Lemay 1963).

As soon as I granted the 1142-43 *Qur'an* translation central place in the twelfth-century object, the entire field could be organized in terms of a general opposition between the church and the Latinist translators of science, most of them from other parts of Europe. The procedure was then to consider the various norms of translational behaviour in this light, asking in whose favour they might have functioned. Some norms obviously worked more in the interests of the church; others in the interests of science. But the most interesting features were those that would have been beneficial for both groups and might thus have enabled them to cooperate. These would be the first elements of a regime.

When formulating a regime it is convenient to start from the principles that are most shared and then proceed to those that involve most tension. Ideally, the priority of the first principles will override the tensions of the latter, establishing a more or less coherent hierarchy. My hierarchy for twelfth-century Latin translations of Arabic protoscience is as follows:

1. *The translation of authoritative texts should be literal.* The church believed in literalism because of the sacred status of its own authoritative texts. The translators also found literalism convenient because it meant they could not be held directly responsible for what was said in the texts.
2. *Secondary elaboration may be used.* The abbot of Cluny added a didactic discourse to the *Qur'an* translation he had commissioned. The translators on the side of science were also using secondary strategies, often pedagogic, probably to compensate for the effects of literalism. In both cases the result was a divided discourse legitimizing marked additions to source texts.
3. *Translators should work in teams.* The church was interested in teams because it could put the styli in the hands of its own Latinists. The scientific translators also benefited from teams, first as a distribution of linguistic competence and second as a social format for intellectual debate.
4. *Oral intermediaries may be inferiorized.* The church had little interest in mentioning the role of the Jewish and Mozarab intermediaries who appear to have performed the initial oral phase of the translation process (mostly from Arabic into some kind of Romance). But the Latinist translators, who ostensibly performed the second phase (writing down the oral Romance text in Latin) were not particularly interested in showing subservience to intermediaries either. Most of the Jews and Mozarabs could collect their money and disappear from written history.
5. *Translation was legitimate conquest.* For the abbot of Cluny, translations from Arabic were useful for fighting Islam. For the translators of science, the translations were conquests in the sense of direct appropriation. There was thus room for agreement, but also scope for potential disagreement

about what some translators saw as the inferior status of the Latin target language and culture. The fact that this contradiction did not surface as a conflict – as it would in the fifteenth century – owes much to the way common accord on the principle of literalism blocked any developed debate about the use of eloquent Latin in translations.

6. *Non-Christian texts could be authoritative.* The church could appreciate Islamic science as a counter-authority to Islam. The translators, on the other hand, generally recognized the texts as both authoritative and directly useful. True, they frequently Christianized the texts, making them superficially compatible with the authority of the church. And the church went along with a process that it could hardly have stopped anyway.

These six elements – there could be more, there could be less – were the closest I could come to a regime for twelfth-century protoscientific translations in Hispania. As an experiment, the regime could at least account for a wide range of data, compensating for much absent data and saying something reasonably coherent and passably new. The approach seemed worth pursuing.

A regime for Castilian protohumanism

For my second example we jump ahead several centuries. One of the standing debates among scholars of fifteenth-century Castilian culture is the degree to which it should be termed 'humanist', mostly in the sense of Castilian scholars and translators being interested or uninterested in the linguistic and cultural background of classical texts. To summarize a complex situation, some researchers see fifteenth-century Castile as part of a humanistic pre-Renaissance, since classical works that were edited or translated into Latin in Italy were then translated into Castilian. Other researchers nevertheless insist the Castilians didn't know what was going on, that they didn't really care where the texts came from, and sometimes that the term 'humanist' simply should not be applied to a culture that translates into the vernacular.

The question is culturally important in that it concerns Spain's role in the development of European culture, implicitly posing vexing questions about national belatedness or underdevelopment. A closely related problem is associated with use of the term *humanisme* to describe a Catalan translation culture that developed from the end of the fourteenth century. This second problem involves not just the relationship between Catalan culture and the idea of renaissance (the Catalan term *humanisme* dates from the language's late-nineteenth-century 'renaissance') but also the idea that the Catalans were more advanced than the

Castilians (on all of which, see Badia 1988). The result is a tangled political web in which I have no desire to adopt any particular side. To be honest, these philological debates about categorizing cultures or periods are often a frustrating waste of time. Translation history should be able to cut across the dilemmas. Such, at least, was my reason for seeking a regime in this particular territory.

My initial historical object was a specific translation: Pero Díaz de Toledo's 1455 rendering of Plato's *Phaedo* into Castilian, translated from the Latin version by Leonardo Bruni. I accepted this as a second-hand historical object, analyzed in a very complete way by Nicholas Round (1993). With respect to the above debate, Round basically shows that the Castilian translator made little attempt to understand Plato: Díaz de Toledo would have enmeshed the Greek philosopher in a prehumanist regime whereby literature should do little more than "educate great lay personages in the ethical foundations of right conduct" (Round 1993:107). The translation thus differed from the humanist model on several counts: it was into the vernacular, it gave priority to intelligibility over any source-text eloquence, it expressed little interest in the text's linguistic and cultural background, and it included considerable expansion and some explicitly added didactic material. Round finds these principles to be in accordance with the translation theory expounded by Alonso de Cartagena several decades earlier. As far as the Hispanist is concerned, everything fits into a reasonably coherent system. Plato was translated into Castilian, but he was not translated in a properly humanist way. So Castile did not have a properly humanist system.

If one is looking for a regime, of course, no past theory ever stands by itself. Sure enough, Cartagena's theorization was part of a debate, in fact a major debate that has been seen as marking a watershed in the history of translation theory, initiating the great tradition of the *belles infidèles* (see, for example, Stackelberg 1972:9-10). Alonso de Cartagena, at that time bishop of Burgos, was trading polemics with none other than Leonardo Bruni, the Florentine translator whose version of Plato had served as Díaz de Toledo's source. Here the two sides could not be clearer: Italian humanism, with Bruni in the front line, stood opposed to Cartagena, Díaz de Toledo and whatever was going on in Castile (with Catalan hovering somewhere between the two). Having identified the two sides, my task was to imagine how they might have agreed on some kind of regime.

Care must be taken to establish the network in this case, since there can be no question of just one translation being the only contact between the two sides. Round's study mentions numerous channels of communication between Castile and Italy. There were summits like the Councils of Basle and Florence, which "brought Spanish delegates into direct touch with humanists and their way" (1993:69), just as there were numerous visits of cultured Italians to Castile and

Catalonia (70). Castilian students went to study in Bologna; Naples belong to the crown Aragon.[5] Significantly, Castile was also exporting wool to Florence, a trade that exceeded its purely commercial importance: the humanist translator Bruni was an interested member of the Florentine cloth importers' and merchants' guilds (72) and was thus aware of what was happening in Castile. As for Cartagena, he was from a family of converted Jews who had good connections with the *converso* traders in Burgos, which just happened to be the centre of the politically powerful Castilian wool-export business. Not surprisingly, Bruni and Cartagena patched up their relationship after the minor tiff over translation theory. There were more than theoretical interests at stake.

Within this network, the debate about translation methods can perhaps be reduced to the following elements. In *De interpretatione recta* Bruni privileged target-language eloquence; Cartagena insisted on unadorned source-text fidelity, arguing that eloquence resided in substance instead of style. Although opposing humanist eloquence, Cartagena was not calling for word-for-word literalism. He instead recognized that "each language has its own way of speaking" and that texts should be adapted to these differences except in the case of "doctrines whose value derives from the authority of the person who pronounced them" (in Santoyo 1987:33). This restriction of course harked back to Jerome and would be picked up in about 1450 by a further theorist, Alonso de Madrigal (called 'el Tostado'), who distinguished between word-for-word methods (*interpretacion*) and "exposition, commentary or glosses" (cit. Norton 1984:31-32). In practice, fifteenth-century translators were remarkably free with their 'expositions, commentaries or glosses', basically for reasons that had to do with the relatively uneducated nobles for whom they were working. But this does not properly concern the level of the regime.

If we now look for the shared principles that might have formed a regime – at least in the sense that a Spaniard and a Florentine would have known what they were arguing about – the list is short but not without coherence. In fact, what we find is more like a unified intercultural regime that would have allowed for different ways of translating. Here are what the main principles might have looked like:

1. *Translation should be word-for-word in the case of authoritative sacred texts and sense-for-sense in other cases.* The principle of sacred literalness

---

[5] The network was by no means limited to Italy. Castile was subject to French and Burgundian cultural influences (Round 1993:64); many of the texts translated into Catalan were in fact translated from French versions (Russell 1985:19-20), and there was considerable professional mobility: two Portuguese translators working from Latin into Portuguese could go to work for the Burgundian court as translators from Latin into French (Russell 1985:44).

was of course neither Castilian nor Italian: it came from Jerome and was to dominate a fairly big chunk of European history. Round points out why these terms were of particular importance to fifteenth-century Catholics of all countries: the word-for-word argument had recently been used to distance the Lollard and Hussite heresies (133-134). Thus, although the Renaissance tendency was away from literalism, thought on translation still had to pay lip service to the idea of sacred authoritative texts, not only in Castile but in France and England as well (cf. Russell 1985:19).

2. *There is a natural hierarchy of languages.* As a correlative of the above principle, some languages were accorded more authority than others: first were the languages of revelation, second would have been the current international Latin, and then came the vernaculars, positioned on the lowest rung of authoritative value. There could be no talk of equality between languages. Since the terms of this hierarchy owed much to Isidorus Hispalensis and could be found in Bruni, Cartagena, Pero Díaz and many others, it is a strong candidate for a position in an intercultural translation regime. Bruni and his generation undoubtedly construed the hierarchy in such a way that Latin became the theoretical repository of grammatical perfection, but this does not mean the hierarchy itself did not enjoy wider intercultural status.

3. *Each language has its inherent mode of expression.* Inequality did not leave the lowest rung entirely without value. The vernaculars also had their inherent qualities, their modes of expression, which should be respected and used. This notion of target-language specificity, which could be an undeveloped Sapir-Whorf hypothesis, was not only common to other fifteenth-century theorists like Bessarion and Manetti but could also be traced back to Jerome. It did not necessarily contradict the assumed hierarchy of languages.

4. *Vernaculars can be enriched.* If there was a hierarchy of languages, it followed that the superiority of Latin could be used to improve the lexis and syntax of inferior languages. We thus find extensive Latinization of the Italian and French vernaculars and a "cautious but favourable attitude to neologism and loan words" in Castilian (Round 1993:142,145), whereas earlier translators had used paraphrase instead of bringing in Latinisms. Of course, this principle clearly contradicts the idea that each language has an 'inherent mode of expression', which should suggest that Latinization was not strictly necessary and that translations should first be understood on the level of content.

5. *Vacillation is acceptable.* Traces of this contradiction appear in considerable inconsistency in the Castilian use of Latinisms, particularly with respect to syntax. Yet if, as Round states, it was acceptable to present vacillation

between Latin and vernacular models (1993:156), even to the extent that the vacillation itself might have been "a feature of educated Castilian speech at this time" (157), surely the intercultural contradiction that was producing debate about the status of Latin in Italy was also producing parallel although minor tensions in Castile? That is, the theoretical discussions underlying the choice between Latin and Italian (Bruni actually had a very positive attitude to the vernacular) also had a certain counterpart in Castilian stylistic variants. Although neither phenomenon was a direct mapping of the other, both responded to an intercultural contradiction on the level of a shared regime. This suggests the translator Pero Díaz could well have understood the desire that led Bruni to translate into Latin, since Pero Díaz was himself involved in a different way of manifesting that same desire. The intercultural regime presented a common problem; the two translation cultures developed different ways of solving it.

Castile and Italy were different, but their different ways of translating may well have come from a shared translation regime.

If we compare this fifteenth-century regime with the twelfth-century one outlined above, the points of comparison are enough to suggest the possibility of tracing the transformations by which one regime connected with the other, reformulating and reshuffling norms in accordance with the times. Perhaps the most worrying aspect is that few of the problems or contradictions ever seem to be solved; they tend to be forgotten or they lie dormant for a few centuries. Dissent about eloquent Latin was present in the twelfth century but did not really surface as an issue of importance until the fifteenth. Similarly, the notion of a hierarchy of languages, which should perhaps have disappeared with the triumph of the vernaculars, resurfaces in our own age with respect to the planners of African and Asian languages, eager to defend their native 'modes of expression' but also keen to develop languages of technology. The fifteenth-century regime could be pertinent to more than the fifteenth century; its major contradiction, unleashed whenever 'improvement' becomes an aim, could even be part of all development ideology.

A regime for early twentieth-century anthologies

My third example is quite different. It concerns the early twentieth-century translation anthologies discussed briefly in the above chapter on networks. You may remember that I started with two Spanish anthologies of translated poems. Both texts were in touch with a small network of translation anthologies and, on the wider international scene, a network of non-translational anthologies (the 'Hundred Best' series, published by the British firm Gowans & Gray and including volumes of poems in English, French, Spanish and German). This configuration would appear to give two opposed sides, the international and the national. One might even suppose that some actual negotiating went on before the Spanish translator Maristany started publishing his versions of the international anthologies. Yet the two sides remained very unequal. In fact, it would be fairer to say that the translation anthologies had a parasitic status with respect to the international system producing the non-translational anthologies.

Despite this lopsided relationship, some kind of negotiation frame might still be applied. The various prefaces to the translation anthologies were certainly concerned with establishing their relation with the non-translational anthologies. On the one hand, the translators used the non-translational anthologies as authoritative references for the quality of the poems selected; on the other, they opposed the non-translational work when attempting to justify the decision to present translations rather than originals. Yet such minor give-and-take was about all I could come up with the first time round. A more elaborate methodology was needed. In this case, I attempted to write separate principles for both the non-translational and the translational, the international and the national, hoping that something would turn up when I compared two.

Here are the principles found for the non-translational anthologies (the international 'Gowans & Gray' network):

1. *Only nations with continuous traditions can have anthologies.* This fundamental precept involved a form of reciprocal recognition between the main cultures of European Romanticism, excluding the numerous small nations and regions that were nevertheless developing post-Romantic literatures at the time.
2. *Texts should be selected by authorities within the source culture.* In keeping with the principle of reciprocal recognition, the 'best' texts should arise from within each national culture, in the way that Darwinian natural selection determined the survivors within each milieu.
3. *The anthologizer should be an authoritative source-culture figure external to literary authorship.* The anthologizers were mostly established literary historians and academics, presumably above the ruck of competing literary schools and fashions.
4. *Only dead poets should be included.* If natural selection was to follow its course, it had to be allowed time to do so. This calculated belatedness promoted cultural conservatism, reinforcing the externality of the anthologizer

and usually obliging exclusion of the most challenging or vital contemporary elements.

5. *A natural elite embodies distinctive superiority.* Since the selection was
    in a sense naturally predetermined, the only criterion worth mentioning
    was that of 'the best'.

6. *Anthologies should respond to market criteria.* The Ruskinian limitation to
    100 poems in each volume was not only elitist but also made these 'pocket
    anthologies' financially accessible to a middle-class market aspiring to the
    values of high culture.

7. *The one anthology can supply both national and international markets.*
    The purchase of these volumes as textbooks meant they could find a for-
    eign market without having to pass through translation, particularly in the
    United States. The one condition was presumably that there be nothing to
    damage the refined sensibilities of the young.

In sum, the principles of this highly conservative non-translational regime
would have enabled literature transfers to take place within the specific network
concerned, interrelating various cultures without any need for translators. What
happens when translators do enter such a set of principles? Here is how the
international regime would appear to have been transformed in the hands of
our two Spanish translators, Díez-Canedo and Maristany:

1. *The translator-anthologist can make authorial statements.* Whereas the
    non-translational regime depended on the authority of the source-culture an-
    thologizer as an external guarantor, the Spanish translators tended to disclaim
    any such authority for themselves. Díez-Canedo was involved in group work
    alongside names of far greater stature; Maristany constantly referred back to
    the authority of source-culture anthologies and introduced his translational
    anthologies with his own verse. This positioned the translator-anthologists
    far closer to their actual texts than was the case for the non-translational
    anthologies, allowing them a partly authorial status.

2. *Nationalist and internationalist positions are not absolute.* Whereas the
    non-translational regime was actively nationalist in that it placed partisan-
    ship above crosscultural understanding, the translational anthologizers
    appear to have distanced themselves from much of the authority assumed
    by such a stand. Díez-Canedo translated from French and then from Ger-
    man at the end of the first world war; Maristany was interpreted as neutral
    and then distanced that position by translating from French and English.
    The translators' divisions of the world were far from clear-cut.

3. *Commercial criteria do not have first priority.* If either of these translator-anthologists ever hoped to rival the commercial success of the non-translational anthologies, their market calculations left much to be desired. Not only were their volumes too large for most pockets but they were also rather expensive, being rather longer than the better-controlled non-translational versions. Díez-Canedo was working for a public that had no real need of translations; Maristany had turned his back on the Catalan-speaking bourgeoisie, perhaps the only class and language that might have brought him significant public prestige.

4. *Form should have priority over content.* The non-translational regime had to play all its cards in the moment of selection. But a translational regime necessarily introduces post-selection modifications, deciding which source-text aspects are to have priority. In the case of this particular translation regime, priority was given to criteria of form, ostensibly because of a Parnassian association of poeticity with verse. This criterion also justified the sacrifice of the complex thought and ambivalent syntax of the more difficult poets.

5. *Special attention should be paid to contemporary poets.* Although Maristany respects the 'dead poets' society' principle in the case of his French anthology, his additions are very much oriented toward the poets in favour at the beginning of the twentieth century. Díez-Canedo did not respect the principle at all. The translational regime thus allowed greater risks to be taken in the selection process than did the non-translational regime. This could be because the greater cultural distance diminished the risk of contamination. Yet the principle was also supported by the simplification process allowed by the moment of translation.

In all, this strictly translational regime significantly transformed the non-translational regime, adapting most of the principles to quite new purposes. However, having reached that point, I remember asking myself exactly who was negotiating with whom. I don't suppose the publishers of the non-translational anthologies could have cared less about what two minor translators were doing in Spain. In fact, the only people who would have argued about the translation principles may well have been Díez-Canedo and Maristany themselves. True enough, by the time I had worked down to my fifth principle, the two translators were already in significant disagreement. A potential number six (say, 'the entire anthology should be by the one translator') would have brought them into radical conflict, since Maristany was an individualist attached to the values of a dying aristocracy, whereas Díez-Canedo was a socialist and a socializer, doing all he could to work with other people.[6]

What can be done with these regimes? Quite apart from providing a useful way of tying up loose ends, regime theory could be developed in at least two directions. On the one hand, individual principles like 'improvement of the target language' or 'group translating' might be traced over long historical periods, as I have attempted to do when describing principles of literary transfer such as imaginary relations of brotherhood between writer/translators (1993b) or the assumed sovereignty of cultures (1993c). Alternatively, we could try to follow the step-by-step transformations of entire regimes, hopefully connecting the twelfth century with the fifteenth and the twentieth, and not necessarily limiting our vision to any one target culture. That would be a mammoth project requiring group work. Perhaps it should not be held up by outdated regimes based on individual research like my own.

Translation as a transaction cost

Several further things might be done with regime theory. It could be used to seek or build regimes in the present, going straight for crosscultural understandings, the gold of translation history. Alternatively, on a slightly less idealist level, it could give rise to a speculative history based on the idea of crosscultural cooperation, working top-down rather than bottom-up. Let me close this chapter by outlining one way in which such a speculative project might link translation history with general regime theory.

Imagine that it is in our conjunctural interest to form alliances or relations of cooperation between cultures and that a regime will enable us to do this. According to Keohane (1984:87), the regime will have to perform three functions: establish patterns of liability, ensure a relatively symmetrical distribution of information, and control the transaction costs incurred in the transfer of information. The part that most interests me is the last-mentioned, the costs of having information exchanged, of having people meet, and so on. Obviously, if these transaction costs are very high, few negotiations will take place and the regime will not be effective. Indeed, if the costs are higher than the benefits of coopera-

---

[6] Strangely enough, this precise item, the point of tension where the regime breaks down, recalls one of the principles of our twelfth-century regime, where collaborative work was the norm. Somewhere along the line, the idea of group translating was lost, certainly at some point prior to Etienne Dolet's eminently individualist theorizing of 1540. Yet these things don't disappear entirely. There it was, at the bottom of this minor regime from the early twentieth century. And it is certainly with us again today, in the shared or partitioned work of most professional technical translating/revising.

tion, there should be no negotiations at all. However, if the transaction costs are extremely low, we are likely to form unstable transitory alliances between any number of cultures; none of our relations will develop strong patterns; the regime will fail to build up the relations of trust or predictability required for cooperation. A successful regime must thus establish transaction costs that are not too high and not too low, in the best Aristotelian tradition.

Translation is a transaction cost. If a translator takes too long, requires too much pay or produces work that is too difficult to understand, the regime requiring the translation will fail. Alternatively, if translation were an automatic, mechanical operation tending toward zero cost to and from all languages and cultures, it would be of no consequence at all for the stability of crosscultural relationships. Between these two extremes, translation may structure transaction costs adequate to the formation of regimes.

This idea can be approached from another angle. Where continued translation activity can be observed between a limited set of cultures, you can ask if this activity is in the interests of a regime. You might also ask if the regime involves certain specific principles designed to ensure that the translating keeps within adequate transaction costs. If such principles can be seen as at least partly embodied in historical translation theories, you may have an important way of explaining how the theories come about and in whose interests they could be operative.

Keohane makes one further observation about regimes and relative transaction costs. Although regimes are established to deal with alliances or cooperation in specific issue areas and between specific partners, the life of regime-based institutions can extend beyond the initial function. A clear example would be NATO, which was set up to ensure information flows between the western powers opposing the Warsaw Pact. The transaction costs are apparently so adequate that the NATO regime continues to exist in the absence of the Warsaw Pact. The organization's function obviously cannot be exactly the same as it was during the Cold War. But to replace it with another regime would involve a set of transaction costs much greater than those already in place. So NATO continues.

Similar things can be observed in translation history. For example, the translation of Greek works into Latin via Arabic extended from the twelfth into the thirteenth century. Why? Because a certain regime was set up in Castile for the translation of these works. However, when many of the original Greek texts became available to translators based in Italy or Constantinople, the Castilian regime should logically have disappeared, since the detour via Arabic involved higher transaction costs (linguistic difficulty and textual corruption) than work directly from Greek. And yet the Castilian regime lived on. Exceptional translations like Girardus Cremonensis' *Almagest*, rendered from Arabic, continued to be read and revered despite the existence of direct translations from Greek. Even when the demand for translations from Greek had well and truly shifted to the Italian network, enough elements of the Castilian regime were still in place for Alfonso X to revive translations from Arabic after 1250. Just as NATO lives on, so did the translation activity associated with Toledo.

I mention this aspect to protect regime theory from accusations concerning the kind of subjectivity it presupposes. Although certainly rationalist, a top-down way of applying regime theory can nevertheless explain phenomena that might otherwise appear to be without reason. This is partly because the specific mode of historical thought required by regimes operates at a level relatively independent of any universal human nature (the illusion of natural laws, at least as inherited from eighteenth-century idealism) and relatively undetermined by any culture-specific context (the relativist illusion, still tainted by nineteenth-century nationalism). In its cutting-across of traditional dilemmas, regime theory would seem well suited to the diagonal function of translation itself.

9. Causes

Explanation deals with the central question of translation history: it asks *why* things happened. We can describe curves, networks, norms, regimes and the rest, but none of our findings will be properly historical until we can hypothesize *why* certain translations were carried out in certain ways. To be sure, analyses of norms can say something about how certain things happened as they did, and regimes can even suggest at what level some determinants might be found. Yet these concepts ultimately aim to be consistent only with what we see. To say why things happened, we should be prepared to think in another way as well. Rather than merely 'describe' or 'account for' the surface-level data, historical thought should seek out underlying causes, the motors that drive history along. In the vein of our brief top-down theorizing of regimes, this involves a mode of analysis that is overtly speculative. It posits that there are actual causes at work, some of which function independently of our explanations.

Questions of causation have been dealt with quite badly in contemporary translation theory. In fact, there has been little awareness that causation might actually be at issue. When prescriptive linguistic approaches describe how to 'translate' a source-text unit, the unit is effectively seen as the cause of the translation. In reaction to source-side approaches, more recent theorists assume the dominant cause lies axiomatically on the target side, such that the target system would somehow be the main cause of the translations entering it. Other theories merely pass the buck into unknown territory. For example, some say the dominant cause is the client's instruction to the translator, so that we then have to locate the causes of the client's instructions, and so on. A variant of this evasive strategy is to invest causation in the individual translator's purpose or aim, which once again begs a series of questions leading beyond most disciplinary frames. Similarly, when a wilderness voice claims there is a causal relationship between the material transfer of a text and a translator's subsequent work on that text, the hunt for causes must explain why the text was transferred in the first place. Questions of causation are thus bounced away from strict translation history.

Admittedly, some of the buck-passing theories might be useful in that they point to categories of mediation, in accordance with a model whereby some underlying social determinant is filtered through a series of layers (transfer, client, translator, etc.), becoming subject to transformations before it actually affects any translation. Yet this gives little real joy for as long as the mediatory categories remain uninvestigated in themselves. At present, theorists (myself included) just point to 'instructions', 'purposes' or 'transfer' and let the issue lie there, marginally beyond our domain of presumed expertise. Since this could make the mediatory category look like a complete cause in itself, the result is probably even more misleading than the gung-ho attempts to locate all causes on either the source or target side. Either way, contemporary theory is not shedding much light.

This confusing state of affairs should be reason enough for taking a long second look at the vexed question of causation. In this context, I'm not overly concerned with defending any one camp against the others. What interests me is the idea that everyone might be a bit right. There are so many factors involved in translation that causation is more likely to be diffuse and multiple than focused and unitary. Of course, this also means everyone might be a bit wrong, particularly with respect to currently overlooked aspects like fundamental material causes (the alphabet, paper, the printing press, computers) and the specific agendas of human translators (yes, properly intercultural causes). There is much to be said for casting our net as wide as possible, opening the question of causation to a range of possible responses.

This can only be done if the notion of causation is given some formal organization. With some apologies, I propose to do this by returning to Aristotle, no less, not as a definitive authority but as the author of a useful little checklist comprising four types of cause. The elective inspiration is not entirely accidental. When arguing against the pre-Socratic reduction of causation to primal elements like fire, water and so on, Aristotle was perhaps in much the same situation as ourselves when we argue against the reduction of everything to the primacy of source texts, target systems and so on. His widening vision might show something that contemporary translation theory has forgotten.

Systemic and probabilistic causation

Before this becomes too theoretical, let me give a practical example of why greater attention should be paid to questions of causation. In Schlösser's comments on his 1937 bibliography of German translations from English (discussed in chapter 3 above), the following features are observed and explained in apparently causal ways:

• *There were some fifty editions of Byron translations printed in German in 1900-1905, sticking out from an otherwise smooth curve.*
    Schlösser can find no convincing cause for this (1937:48).

• *About 40% of translations of English literature were by women, whereas only 20% of the authors were women.*
    Schlösser attributes this to the fact that translation is a "predominantly reproductive activity" (146).

•   *German translations of contemporary English authors reach an extreme
low point in 1918 and the years immediately following.*

Schlösser explains that German publishers took time to set up their
international contracts in the aftermath of war, notably because article 299
of the Treaty of Versailles annulled the rights established in all pre-war
international agreements (29).

•   *German editions of English-language texts (i.e. without translation) remained fairly constant throughout the same years.*

Schlösser's explanation is that the publisher Tauchnitz had long
had a policy of publishing modern but well established authors, and
this policy had no reason to be affected by the war (29). The success
of the policy is in turn seen as indication that the readership remained
relatively unchanged over the years (33).

Different kinds of causes are being evoked here. In the case of the anomalous
Byron translations there may be no great underlying causation at work at all.
Several translators were perhaps striving to achieve their individual aims; the
coming together of these aims may have created some kind of *Gestalt* (competi-
tion, tension, synergy, fashion, call it what you will); the reception conditions
were such that all these manuscripts could find publishers. Schlösser can find
no reason for the source (why Byron?), nor any satisfying explanation for the
period (why in 1900-1905?). In such cases we might say the phenomenon
appears to be significantly under-determined, at least until we locate further
information that might enable us to attribute some more substantial causation.
Note, however, that only a causal mode of thought can sense the 'coming
together' and perhaps the need for further information.

In the case of the women translators, Schlösser would have done much better by similarly admitting his ignorance. Why should the reproductive nature of
translation be important? Because many translators are women. And why are
many translators women? Because, we are told, translation is a reproductive
activity. If all translators were men, translation would probably still be a reproductive activity, but this fact would no longer be the pertinent cause or result of
anything. The illusory causality attributed here is no more than presumptiveness,
at least until we have some inkling about why certain translation norms might
have been better suited to women in that particular time and place.

The relation between non-translation and the Treaty of Versailles is obviously stronger than any assumption about women. It also seems stronger than
what might be considered a more logical reason for not translating English authors into German after 1918: having fought and lost a war, wouldn't Germans

have good reason not to be overly enthusiastic about contemporary English literature? Note that the French had relatively little interest in translating contemporary German literature in the years following 1871 (see figure 7 in chapter 5 above). In this particular case, however, we have an indirect way of testing this eminently causal hypothesis. If Germans continued to read *non-translated* English literature without significant change, then surely there was no great rancour that can be attributed to any war. By elimination, the cause of the drop in translations must have been the Treaty of Versailles. Or so it would seem. But can we say why the non-translated English texts were not subject to international agreements in the same way as the translations? Can we assume the readership for non-translated texts was in the same 'Germany' as the readership for translated texts? Were the same social groups involved? If not, how can a hypothesis concerning non-translated texts eliminate any cause in the field of translated texts? More to the point, why should we be looking for just one direct cause – the Treaty of Versailles – rather than a series of compatible causes, including those that might be less than comfortable when contemplated by a German anglicist like Schlösser?

The attribution of causation is a difficult and tenuous affair. Yet translation history can scarcely avoid it. Perhaps in response to these difficulties, more recent empirical studies have sought a controlled approach to causation, so controlled, in fact, that the term rarely rears its ugly head. By refusing to recognize any fundamental distinction between the human and the non-human sciences, the more systemic approaches have been able to follow the general scientific trends of our age. This involves two related principles.

First, systemic empiricism tends to place all causes on the one level. Very different things like translators' preferences, the nature of translation as reproduction, publishing contracts and collective reaction to wartime defeat thus become a series of hypotheses each of which is subject to the same kind of empirical testing. In basic systems theory, causation is an affair of invariable sequences and concomitant variations. For instance, if we find that every nation translates its enemies less after it has been defeated in a war, we might claim an invariable sequence: defeat, then less translations. One might say the first event is a cause of the second. As for concomitant variations, we might observe that every time there is a drop in the number of translations between two countries there is a simultaneous drop in the total trade volume between the same countries. This would suggest a causal relationship between translation and trade.

Yet this kind of thought is very weak in practical terms. For a start, no one can be sure of any causal directionality. Is there less trade because there are less translations, or less translations because there is less trade? In fact, directionality is problematic even in the case of invariable sequences: if we consistently had sequences where there was a drop in translations immediately prior to war (rather than after), would we say the lack of translations caused the war? Or would the translations drop because people thought the war was coming? Nothing in this kind of analysis can specify the actual connections by which A leads to B. If defeat in war does lead to a drop in translations, it must surely be thanks to some kind of group psychological process or cultural strategy, in any event a series of factors C, D and E that our observations have not revealed. Indeed, there is no guarantee that what we observe in A and B (war and translations) are not separate results independently caused by an unobserved factor C (say, economic crisis), so there is no direct causation linking events that nevertheless appear to give invariable sequences or concomitant variations. In the human sciences, you can do all the testing you like but you can rarely be sure you have anything like a pure direct cause, and not just because you yourself may be one of the causes of whatever you observe.

A second consequence of empiricism is based on this uncertainty. Since we can describe effects but we cannot actually know direct causes, the resulting uncertainty of our hypotheses can only really be accommodated by an appeal to probabilistic relations. This involves saying that no possible cause can be eliminated but some are more likely than others. Gideon Toury has written the principle into his basic form for a law: 'if X, then the greater/the lesser the likelihood that Y' (1995:265), to which can be added all kinds of variables concerning conditions and relative probabilities. In some cases this gives 'laws' whose importance is not immediately obvious.[1] In others it enlists a kind of causation that is overtly general and dangerously predictive, suggesting a rationalist human nature that need only be left to itself in order to create a certain kind of future.

Some of these hypotheses are nevertheless genuinely interesting. For example, Toury suggests (if I may be allowed a reformulation) that if culture A considers culture B to be more prestigious than itself, it will tend to tolerate calques and literalist translations ('interference') from that culture (1995:278). This sounds neatly logical, even commonsensical (we imitate people we admire, since it would certainly be irrational to imitate people we did not admire). But is this relation properly causal? If you think about it, surely the people doing the tolerating are more or less the ones who depend on translations for their knowledge of the foreign culture in the first place. If they accord prestige to that culture, the prestige itself may be due to the way those translations are carried out. The

---

[1] For example, Toury posits that "the more the make-up of a text is taken as a factor in the formulation of its translation, the more the target text can be expected to show traces of interference" (1995:276). Yes, but where else could the interference have come from?

calques and literalisms could thus be the cause of the relative prestige, and not the other way around. Or again, why should the relative size of the cultures not play a causal role in such relations? If prestigious cultures tend to be the larger ones (this is no rule, but let's imagine) and if we can hypothesize that the smaller the culture, the higher its ratio of translations to non-translations (as suggested in Chapter 4 above), we might want to develop Toury's law in the following way: 'the smaller the culture, the more it will tend to tolerate calques and literalist translations ('interference') from larger cultures'. And so on. Any number of hypothetical laws can be produced. But nowhere in the chain of reasoning would we get beyond invariable sequences, concomitant variations and their probabilistic riders. We will have all the causes on the same level; we will never be able to isolate a single cause; we will never be sure we have seen all the pertinent causes. Worse, we end up with a potentially end-less string of hypotheses concerning what is likely to happen in one situation or another but no thought able to tell us who or what is responsible for what happens, nor, of course, any ethics about what *should* happen.

I have no desire to deny the value of research into probabilistic and pre-dictive kinds of causation. Before doing anything to change the course of the world, it is obviously good to have as much knowledge as possible about what is likely to result. Yet the past is never an infallible guide to the future, and the ultimate purpose of translation history is not necessarily to provide unidimensional signposts, no matter how many shades of grey they may be painted in. Probabilistic laws should not be confused with the gold. And the gold, the active construction of a future, could be just as well served by a slightly more varied view of causation.

Aristotle

Aristotle distinguished between four causes. According to the standard illustra-tion, in the creation of a statue the marble is the 'material cause', the creation of a beautiful object is the 'final cause', the creation of an object with the defining characteristics of a statue is the 'formal cause', and the sculptor is the 'efficient cause' (*Metaphysics* I,3). The textbooks take us so far. The four categories were used in medieval poetics (Minnis 1988) and have continued to play a certain role in aesthetics. Empirical science, though, has wanted none of this. As we have seen, it has reduced the range of four to just one, without any distinction between what a piece of marble allows, what a creative person does, or what the specific roles of norms and values might be. Nevertheless, if we try to maintain the range of Aristotle's causes and apply them to translation, the result might be something like the following:

- Material or initial cause (*causa materialis*): Everything that precedes the translating and is necessary for its achievement: the (assumed) source text, language, communication technology, and so on.
- Final cause (*causa finalis* or *causa ut*): The purpose justifying the existence of the translation, its *utilitas*, the use that is to be made of it, no matter whether this be a positional function within a target culture or the ideal completion of an action.
- Formal cause (*causa formalis*): The historical norms that allow a translation to be accepted as a translation, no matter who is doing the accepting (the client, the receivers, the translator, other translators).
- Efficient cause (*causa efficiens* or *causa quod*): The translator, be it individual or collective, along with everything specific to the translator's collective position.

The four causes at least give the picture more dimensions than it has from most empiricist perspectives. Of course, there could be more than four, there could be less, depending on how you want to cut the cake. Yet Aristotle should remind us that every translation requires at least these things: a technology for producing texts, an (assumed) source text, a purpose for the completed translation, an idea of what a translation is, and a translator (well, the four have already become five). Take any one of these away, and you have no translation. Since all these causes are necessary, there should be no question of seeing any one factor as 'the cause' of a translation, although there can certainly be debates about which factor or combination of factors is dominant.

The recent history of translation theory has seen a shift away from one narrow kind of initial causes (basically the source texts and language systems of linguistic approaches) to final causes (the systems and receivers on the target side). There has also been some focus on the formal causes embodied in norms, although they have needlessly been mixed up with final causes thanks to blind assumption of their cultural specificity. On the other hand, virtually no attention has been paid to non-linguistic material causes, nor to efficient causes, since recent theories have had precious little room for people.

The following comments will attempt to redress some of this imbalance. I will stress the fundamental importance of material causes by quickly restating the theory of material transfer; I will give a brief critique of the focus on final causes as it affects systems theory and action theory; I will make a few comments on norms and voodoo as formal causes; after which I will claim a properly causal role for translators and their intercultural place, an argument that will be developed more fully in the next chapter.

Transfer as material causation

Any search for the material cause of a translation must certainly look at the
source text, perhaps at the source language, and very probably at the target
language as well, since the target language is also raw material that we can't
do much about, rather like the marble out of which the sculptor creates a
statue. For a linguistic approach to translation, all these factors could be material causes. Yet this doesn't take us much beyond the comparative analysis
of texts. For the rest – and there is a lot else to history – some wider view of
initial causation seems necessary.

Aristotle holds that change occurs in four categories: substance (generation
and destruction), quantity (increase and diminution), quality (alteration) and
place (motion) (*Physics* 200b.33; *Categories* 15a.13). Translation primarily
responds to changes in place, which is the category concerning both object
transfers and subject transfers. A text changes in quality because it moves
through space and time, although there are all kinds of constraints on its relative elasticity and points of semantic rupture. Translation can be seen as a way
of introducing further qualitative change in order to counteract or capitalize
on the change in place. If an Arabic text has become opaque because it has
been moved to a milieu of Latinist readers (the initial cause is the material
movement), translation into Latin will attempt to reduce the opacity resulting
from that movement (a Latin version will be more generally understandable).
Translation is thus both a qualitative change in itself and a response to a change
in place. It presupposes movement on the level of transfer.

Within this limited schema, one change might be said to explain the other.
The text is translated because it has been moved or is going to be moved. Even
if the movement comes chronologically *after* the moment of translation, the
change in quality still presupposes the change of place, and not the other way
round. We might say that, given these two changes, the change concerning
quality is caused by the change concerning place. Or more simply, translation
is caused by material transfer (change of place), making transfer a material or
initial cause no matter what the actual order of events.

Consider a case where material transfer and translation are parts of the one
process. We could say that the Greek *Almagest* was translated into Latin in
1160 because someone moved a source manuscript to Sicily. If the manuscript
had not been moved, it would not have been translated. But few would call
this a satisfying historical cause. One can legitimately demand to know *why*
the manuscript was moved to Sicily. The answer, of course, would be 'so it
could be translated'. It was translated because it was moved, and it was moved

so it could be translated. This doesn't get us very far. A useful distinction may nevertheless be made between the two sides involved. When we say that a text was moved so it could be translated, we are describing the translation as the *final* cause of the movement. And when we say that the text was translated because it was moved, we are really talking about a rather elementary *material* cause, a change that had to happen before the translation could proceed. Texts had to be present before they could be translated. The translation was the final cause of the movement, and the movement was the material cause of the translation.

Material causes sometimes look like the least engaging side of life. They concern necessary but insufficient conditions for translation; they can't tell us very much about what translation actually does; they are certainly the stuff of archaeology, buried in the details of dates and manuscripts. However, if we look at history on the widest time scale, material causes are among the most profound and far-reaching factors one could wish for. For example, the technique for making paper moved westwards from China, reaching Baghdad just prior to the ninth-century 'school of translators' there, then reaching Christian Hispania just prior to the thirteenth-century translations associated with another great 'school', that of Alfonso X. Paper does not produce translations. But its manufacture has certainly assisted in some major changes in translation history.

Material causes can also be important at the much smaller level of the basic links in any kind of transfer network. Consider the links assumed by Vernet (1984) when he boldly suggests that in 1265 lunar eclipses were observed simultaneously and in a coordinated way in China, Egypt and Toledo. To support this argument he has to show that Chinese knowledge passed to the Muslim astronomers who worked under the patronage of Mongols and that it then moved from Egypt to Castile through the exchange of embassies between Alfonso X and the Egyptian Mamluk sultan Baybars (see also Samsó 1987). It is a fascinating hypothesis. Yet even if the material connections can be proved, with the dates in the right order and sufficient periods allowed for the conquest of distance, the argument would still only concern the material causality dealt with by archaeology. One would also have to find efficient and final causes to explain the transfer in properly historical terms. Who wanted these transfers to take place? For what ultimate purpose? The identification of material causes can show the movement was possible; other kinds of causes must show it was probable or in some way humanly reasonable. Material causes aren't everything.

Final causes in theories of systems and actions

The flat causation to be found in system-based approaches is partly offset by

certain action-based theories of translation. It is convenient, though facile, to
date these latter theories from Holz-Mänttäri (1984) and Reiss and Vermeer
(1984), bringing together the propositions that a translation is a teleological
action achieving crosscultural communication (*Handlungstheorie*) and, from
a slightly different perspective, that the dominant factor in a translation is its
purpose (*Skopostheorie*). Whereas systems theory is concerned with translations
as texts occupying positions and carrying out functions by virtue of those positions, action theory looks at the actors involved in the production of translations,
the function of which is determined not by a final position but by a teleology
somehow inscribed in the action itself. Most theories of systems and actions
are superficially convergent to the extent that systems theorists privilege positions in the target system and action theorists see the dominant purpose in terms
of the desired function of the target text. Although the notions of function are
quite different, this roughly shared location could allow the two approaches to
dovetail in some respects: in both cases, causation is somewhere toward the end
of the production process. These are theories of final causes. Both approaches
have their blind spots.

With respect to systems theory, a major fly in the ointment is Toury's forth-
right declaration that "translations are facts of the culture [he previously said
'system'] which hosts them" (1995:24). This must imply that, for the purposes
of the theory – or for as far as the theory makes us see –, the basic cause of
a translation is its position within the target culture. There are at least three
quite obvious problems with this methodological procedure.

First, as Toury recognizes, "translation activities and their products not
only can but do cause changes in the target culture" (1995:27). This amounts
to saying that the target culture, if it is the cause of the translations it receives,
causes changes in itself. Onanistic determination is quite possible, I suppose,
especially if we believe each individual culture is inexorably marching toward
its own self-selected destiny. Yet there is thankfully little else in Toury's theorizing to support such a belief. Cultures are born, live, die or become other
cultures, largely as a result of properly external causes.

Second, if we must accept that "cultures resort to translating precisely as a
major way of filling in gaps" (Toury 1995:27), we would first have to explain
how any target culture can perceive the existence of its gaps without at least referring to a particular source culture that has corresponding non-gaps. This means
some features of the source culture must be necessary for the very formulation
of the translation project, no matter who carries out the translating. So is there
any reason why the source culture should not also have a causal role, at least in
cases where it's still alive and kicking?[2]

Third, there are many situations in which a target culture has translations
sent toward it or even forced upon it, directly or indirectly, as would be the
case of virtually any imperialist or colonialist transcultural relationship one
would care to name. Toury's answer here is that a dominant source-side figure merely "makes the observation that something is 'missing' in the target
culture" (1995:27) and that by virtue of this observation the target culture is
somehow the real cause. This is absurd. If the colonizer had not come along
to point out an alleged gap, there would have been no awareness of the gap
and thus no translation. For several centuries the Spanish Crown made laws
about how translation should be carried out in its colonies, including the ways
translators should be exiled or executed if they did not conform to the rules
(Gargatagli Brusa 1996), and now we have to tell them they weren't really
controlling anything! There are substantial reasons to mistrust this inadvertent
sweetening of crosscultural relationships.[3]

The application of action theory to translation has been strangely productive in its consequences, perhaps even more productive than straight systemic
descriptions. This is because, unlike Toury's empiricism, it quickly leads to a
complexity of competing purposes, a complexity that requires some further level
of conceptual organization, something better than action theory. Let's sneak up

---

[2] A simplistic reading of Toury might suggest that the target culture knows what translations
it needs even before it gets them. And yet the function of a completed translation cannot be
known with any precision until it exists. Indeed, if it *could* be known exactly, there would be
no reason for the translation. This is because translators, especially any that really do have
both feet in the target culture, can ignore not only the exact effects of their work but also
the exact nature of the information they are translating. For example, the twelfth-century
Latinists translating scientific texts from Arabic could not be blamed for misunderstanding
many passages in the source texts. If they had understood them, there would have been
no reason to transfer the knowledge in the first place. The knowledge would have been in
Latin already. More generally, all else being equal, if a target-culture mind were so perfect
as to foresee exactly what changes would ensue from the introduction of new information
into the target culture, then that mind could optimally introduce the information directly,
without recourse to translation.

[3] A similar shortcoming has nothing to do with Toury yet remains reasonably widespread.
When researchers believe that final causes are truly dominant in the form of readership
profiles, they sometimes attempt to define the readership on the basis of textual features
(for example, the choice of a certain register in the translation is assumed to indicate a
certain kind of readership). This procedure is especially prevalent in the medieval field,
where the translation is sometimes the only pertinent information available (for a clear
example, see Cherewatuk 1991). What happens, of course, is that the features of the text
are methodologically attributed to the readership, so the readership automatically becomes
the only plausible cause of the features. Yet no relation is proved, since the hypothesized
relation could not possibly be disproved.

on this phenomenon step-by-step (begging forgiveness once again for putting *Handlungstheorie* and *Skopostheorie* in the same bed: their differences are not really germane to our purposes here).

A translation-to-be has a final cause, a purpose (*Skopos* if you like) in the sense that it will have to carry out a function with respect to specific people in a specific target-side time and place. If this final cause is dominant, it must carry more weight than the kind of initial causes located in or around a source text. As Holz-Mänttari has argued, action theory thus overrides all mechanistic attempts to say 'when X in the source text, then Y in the target text' (1990:71). Whatever the variants, the general theory certainly breaks with the determinism of equivalence-based linguistic research, which was indeed associated with the aspirations of machine translation (by definition mechanistic).[4]

As such, action theory does not say how anyone should translate. It merely states that, whatever happens, the final cause is always dominant. In fact, the principle of target-side dominance can justify both extreme freedom and extreme literalism. For instance, when Pero Díaz de Toledo translated Plato, his purpose was to provide his patron with moral guidance; when Leonardo Bruni translated the same text, his purpose had far more to do with spreading knowledge of classical culture. The two purposes were slightly different, the two translation methods were significantly different (despite the possible existence of a common regime), but the target-side purposes were in each case dominant. That's all the theory is saying. Whatever happens (i.e. with the same certitude as Toury's assumption), the game seems to be played out on the target side.

The problem here is that we don't really know who is playing the game. The purpose of a translation might be determined by the client's instructions, the make-up of the potential readership, or the brilliance of the translator. Different theorists accord different weightings to these factors. A certain evasion of hard thought thus commonly leads to idealist assumptions that markets, clients and translators are in some kind of fundamental agreement, often due to the axiomatic sovereignty of the (never incompetent) translator, who can assess the market correctly and convince the client accordingly. What happens when these three factors are in contradiction with each other? The theorists are not much help: Nord tends to give priority to the client's ('initiator's') instructions (1991a:9); Holz-Mänttari (1984:62ff.) and Vermeer (cf. 1989:68) stress the translator's professional ability to assess the situation; and as for effective market constraints, no one in this camp is particularly interested in things like socially

---

[4] It is difficult to understand why this theory has continued to be associated with extensive machinery for source-text analysis (Snell-Hornby 1988, Nord 1991a), since it is in fact saying that source texts contain no hidden keys. Tradition dies hard.

determined individuals. Of course, if the theorists start looking for conflict rather than axiomatic compatibility, they will perhaps finish up writing something like regime theory.

Action theory nevertheless deserves time and attention to the extent that it might be pointing to the existence of intelligent life somewhere within the translator. On the surface, each hypothetical translation-in-situation has a purpose that the theorist can see and that the competent translator should be able to detect and fulfil. This is one way of making sure all competent translators see the world through the theorists' eyes. But if we take seriously the argument that the purpose of the translation is not mechanistically determined by anything that preceded it, surely the non-mechanistic cause is the translator, perhaps as a competent individual or, more probably, as a figurative extension of the theorist's ideal student. Nevertheless, given assumed compatibility with clients and market factors, the heroic role of translators is ultimately rather reduced: they would carry out actions not because anyone tells them to do so, nor because social conditions demand it, but because they choose to do the right thing for all concerned. Same action, different cause.

Is this significant? In cases where only one action corresponds to the ideal purpose, where the translator must do what the client and the conditions command, the only significance is a minor irony: the translator agrees to submit, since there is nothing else to agree to. If, however, clients and conditions allow more than one viable action, then the translator must assume a causal role and could even have a history. Further, there is no reason to believe that the conditions ensuing from strictly initial or final causes merely fix the limits within which the translator's actions may be viable. If translators always have the choice of non-translation, of refusing the conditions altogether, they must surely be seen as major determinants in their own right.

Equivalence as formal cause

Before getting to efficient causes, though, let me use Aristotle's 'formal cause' to tie up a few loose ends. Remember that in the classical example the sculptor sets out to produce an object with the defining characteristics of a statue, and these defining characteristics are called the formal cause. Similarly, the translator sets out to produce something with the defining characteristics of a translation. Initial and final causes may determine what kind of statue or translation is to be produced, but there is a level on which one can talk about the form – and thus the formal cause – of statues and translations as such.

Formal causes became unpopular in science because they relied on a world of Platonic ideals. They should also be unpopular with anyone vaguely aware that, since all phenomena tend to other phenomena, there are no necessary discontinuities just because our languages possess the word 'statue' or 'translation'. The nominalism occasionally useful for constituting corpora is generally unhelpful when conceptualizing causation. And yet there are still reasons for talking about formal causes with respect to translations.

The first reason is that a lot of theorists are already talking about formal causes, usually disguised as 'equivalence', 'norms', 'conventions' and, for us, 'regimes'. Others touch on formal causes when attributing change to culture-bound things like 'different conceptions of narrative' (Allen 1991, on three versions of a medieval history) or, more simply, 'individual attitudes towards translation' (Pratt 1989:200, referring to work into medieval German and Dutch). Whenever anyone discusses what a translation should be like or was expected to be like in a particular time and place, they are effectively referring to defining features that could have played a causal role in any particular act of translation.

A further and less obvious reason for considering formal causes is that the study of pseudotranslations (most notably by Toury) reveals a great deal of indirect information about the variable characteristics of translations, although little has been done to conceptualize the reason why the revelations are possible. If we now posit that a pseudotranslation results from an active formal cause (the idea of producing a translation) without any corresponding initial cause (there is no source text), the outcome should be expected to reflect with unusual clarity the specific role of formal causes.

A third reason, specifically to ward off charges of bad philosophy, is that we have already defined translation in suitably formal terms. To summarize the arguments presented in chapter 4, what I see as the defining discontinuity of a translation is a feature of the way discourse is received ('this is a translation because the person who says "I" is not the producer of the discourse'). Since we assume at least this discontinuity between translational and non-translational discourse, it is fair to hope there is some form inhabiting anything we activate as translational discourse.

Fourth, to say the same thing in more mainstream terms, the most general level of translational form can be projected as 'equivalence', roughly understood as a translation's capacity to be received as if it were the source text. This 'as if' (*as if* the translation were the source text) indicates a fictional status, a belief, or at least a willing suspension of disbelief on the part of the person doing the receiving. The creation or maintenance of the fiction is, by my definition, one of the aims of a translation.[5] It thus plays a causal role. And what is maintained is a form.

Although the forms of translation vary throughout history and across cultures, although they are constantly fought over through regimes, nothing we recognize as translational communication can function without the belief, no matter how misfounded, that the translation can be received as if it were the source text. If there is no such belief, no such form in operation, the communication might as well be something else, reported speech, commentary or the like. This is voodoo, of course. A translation performs or fails as an ideal translation because people believe it can do so, just like a dollar note performs as an ideal bearer of a certain value. If people stopped believing, we would no longer have any translations, nor many banknotes.

For all these reasons, ideas about what a translation should be or is expected to be must be taken as properly causal elements in the generation of any particular translation.

Translators as efficient causes

The efficient cause of a translation is the individual or collective translator, if only because you need a translator – or the mechanical or illusory extension of one – in order to have a translation. There would seem to be little reason to deny the translator a properly causal role. Yet this is exactly what is done whenever one of the other modes of causation is accorded an exclusive function. If everything is already in the source text, then the translator becomes a mechanical extension of that text; if everything is decided by the target system, then the translator is merely a bearer of functions within that system; if the purpose of the translation is everything, then the translator is merely a person expertly privy to that purpose; and if the world of forms were the end of the story, the translator would be the instrument of fictions, and not the other way around. However, given that none of the above categories can convincingly exclude the others, there are grounds to hope that some kind of active causation can ensue from the translator. People can actually change things.

Since the nature and possibilities of translators as causes will be dealt with

---

[5] This is obviously not the only definition of translation as a form. When Walter Benjamin states quite bluntly that "Übersetzung ist eine Form" (1923:50), he would agree with us that there is a formal discontinuity between translation and non-translation, he would perhaps even concede that some translations maintain the fiction of equivalence, but he would by no means accept that this is a feature of the best translations. Yet Benjamin's evaluations do little to alter the existence of forms; here I am happy enough that he recognizes translation as a form that can bring about certain consequences (notably new readings of the original and a continuation of its 'afterlife'). That is, Benjamin recognizes formal causation.

in the next chapter, let me simply mark their place here, as an opening for questions that might now have a reason to be asked.

Multiple causation

If, as I have suggested, all four (or more) types of causes are necessary before we can have a translation, and if, as I have argued, none of these causes can be accorded any *a priori* dominance that would downgrade the others to the level of inactive necessary conditions, it follows that the kind of causation we find operative in translation history must be plural in its very nature. For every translation that we might want to explain in terms of causation there are at least four possible causes at work, any one of which might be dominant. There can be no guarantee that any one cause can explain all the facts.

This is by no means a new idea. It goes back to theories of multiple histori- cal determinants coming together to produce the ideal moment, the situation where everything is right for the optimal success of an action.[6] The idea has been used to explain why, for example, the 1917 Revolution was Russian, not because of any one cause but because numerous separate causes – the multiple contradictions of capitalism, if you will – just happened to come together in Russia (Althusser 1965:93-116). In a sense, multiple causation means that the truly dominant cause is none other than the moment when all other causes work together. And imperfect actions, the ones we are far more likely to deal with in our research, could be the result of non-ideal moments.

Is this important for translation history? It could be, particularly if we find ourselves plagued by classical bugbears like the untranslatability or relative difficulty of certain texts. We can now answer this kind of question by suppos- ing that, in a given time and place, the causes may not have come together in a highly felicitous way, and yet greater translatability could result in a happier conjuncture in another time or space. In principle, though, the questions we want to answer need not have anything to do with ideologies of perfection. Nor need they deal with the whole range of possible causes. We could simply busy

---

[6] Although this sounds like an astrological principle, I feel happier attaching it to the idea of καιρός, elaborated by Gorgias then Isocrates, according to which improvised oral dis- cussion is superior to written communication because one can react to the ideal moments formed by factors like material location, the people you are talking with, the flexible rules of exchange, and one's own subjective involvement. In short, multiple causation is an es- sential feature of living dialectics. Not by accident, living dialectics have in turn informed our central notion of importance, the debate as an object of historical research, and of course the regime as a form allowing negotiation.

ourselves with the effects of a certain technology, a certain clientele class, the development of a particular regime, or the role of a translator. None of these fields need constantly refer to all the other modes of causation. Yet none of them are sufficient to produce the conclusion that technology A brought about change X, clientele B was responsible for feature Y, and so on. The great lesson of multiple causation is that whenever we have just two facts and we are tempted to see one as the cause of the other, we first have to look around to see what else was happening in history. The chances arc that there was a good deal more than what we dreamt of initially.

10. Translators

I believe human translators have had something to do with the history of translation, although I readily admit it is hard to say exactly what their general role, on an individual or collective level, is or might have been. Since I suspect translators might even have done something important in history, I am interested in elaborating the working hypothesis that they are active effective causes, with their own identity and agenda as a professional group. This broad hypothesis has occasionally paid good dividends in my own research. I concede, however, that it is not productive in all situations; it by no means addresses all the major questions facing translation history; it constantly involves the risk of getting lost in biographical details. I formulate the hypothesis here merely in the hope that, whatever field they are involved in, translation historians might take a little time out to think about translators as people.

Translators, not 'the translator'

I am consciously using the term 'translators', in the plural, so as not to paint myself into the far more abstract term 'the translator', in the singular. My strategy is to encompass and go beyond at least two senses in which one might legitimately talk about 'the translator'.

One kind of 'translator', singular, corresponds to the subjectivity implicit in any translative discourse: a translator is the discursive figure that has produced a translation, and that's about all discourse analysis, and any reader, need know. No matter, on this level, that there could have been two or more human translators working separately or together on the translation. The abstract 'translator' is thus a discursive product of the translation, and not the other way around.

A slightly different kind of 'translator', also technically singular, is the one who is presumed to be competent, who is supposed to abide by the reigning norms, and who is worth paying some kind of standard rate for translating. In this case the figurative subjectivity has a financial, social and perhaps juridical status, as well as a properly professional position to the extent that it might have relations with other professional subjectivities. Since any similarly competent translator might have done much the same job and been paid much the same rates, with variants that are considered professionally insignificant, all competent professionals become the one competent professional. This particular 'translator' is thus a product of the profession, and not the other way around.

Let's not just write off these two abstract senses of 'the translator', which share a basic anonymity. They certainly have their place in translation criticism, sociology and professional ethics. The problem, though, is that neither of these abstract singular entities is likely to create much history, at least not in the sense of becoming an active efficient cause. If translators are to be seen as properly intervening in history, they must somehow wield more power than can a mere discursive subjectivity or an anonymous professional happy to abide by the established norms of the profession. In short, if translators are to have a significant degree of active power, they must somehow be more than what they do or what they are anonymously paid for.

A third kind of translator, by far the least elegant for respectable theorists, is the one that has a material body, in addition to all the above. In fact, the material body, as a mobile biological unit, is all I really need in order to break with the forms of abstract anonymity.

A human body does several things. It consumes resources, it affords pleasures and pains, it interrelates and reproduces, and it moves. This means translators who have bodies must be concerned with getting paid not just for one translation but for providing services throughout their lives, for the continued feeding and care of their bodies, usually by doing more than one translation and very often by doing a lot more than translating. Translators with bodies might also be expected to avoid physical hardship, prison and torture, be it for themselves or for their family and future generations. And translators with bodies tend to be more mobile than any norm, purpose or system. They can get up and go from town to town, culture to culture; if they eat and exercise, they can survive from period to period. Elemental things. None of these aspects are very important from the perspective of the abstract 'translator', singular. Yet they are all extremely pertinent to the way translators can help shape translation history. That's why, when I talk about 'translators', plural, I refer to people with flesh-and-blood bodies. If you prick them, they bleed.

Let's look at some of the differences a body can make.

Translators can do more than translate

The rapid expansion of translator training since the late 1980s has been bolstered by an institutional discourse that posits a social need for specialist translators and interpreters, implicitly people trained to work in this field and no other. The result is widespread belief in what we might call the ideal 'monoprofessionalism' of translators (I take the term as including interpreters). There is some little irony in the fact that the same years have been associated with a wider social discourse on the need to break down labour-market rigidities in all fields and to introduce new modes of non-specialization, usually called 'flexibility'. Tertiary education has had to incorporate training programmes that prepare graduates to adapt to rapid technological progress and to change their professional employment several times in the course of their careers. The relatively new pedagogical idea of the specialist translator would thus seem to contradict the current nature of general employment, unless translation has somehow become the one profession where graduates can now expect to have life-long job security, a possibility that I very much doubt.

The institutional discourse on the monoprofessionalism of translators has occasionally influenced the way translation history has been approached in recent years. Part of this influence might be attributed to the descriptive focus on translations rather than people, so that translators are defined as anyone who has produced a translation, regardless of whatever else they might have done. The more anecdotal versions consequently indulge in extended focus on the few great specialist translators of the past, while relatively little attention is paid to the many other activities by which the vast majority of translators have managed to gain various degrees of power. In some cases, typically encyclopedia articles, translators remain lists of names. The effect is predictable enough: since we are interested in translation we too easily create the illusion that all listed translators were nothing but translators. A certain kind of history is thus seductively professionalizing the past in order to promote a brave new specialized future.

As much as I think this is a misleading way to tackle translation history (and translator training!) I am unable to cite any extensive research that can prove, at least in a general way, how people become translators, how long they work as translators, or how often they combine translation with other remunerated activities. Some fragmentary studies nevertheless suggest that assumptions of long-term mono-employment should be doubted. A list of 434 Brazilian translators since the seventeenth century (Wyler 1995) identifies only nine who had no other profession. A report on twentieth-century literary translation from Arabic into Hebrew (Amit-Kochavi 1996:33) mentions 150 translators, only one of whom is a full-time translator. A study of early twentieth-century British translators from Spanish (Callahan 1993) finds little evidence of translation as a financially necessary full-time activity and concludes that, in this particular field, "most translators appear to be young people who want to do almost anything to penetrate the literary world and to make a living from literary activity" (104). These assessments ring true with respect to my research on *fin de siècle* French literary translators, where there appear to have been very few long-term professionals and the most prominent of them (we will meet one in a moment) were basically writers and journalists who also translated. If nothing else, the few available studies confirm that questions about multiple employment are at least worth asking.[1]

Ideas about the employment of translators can also be gleaned from studies of individual cases, which at least provide ammunition for arguments against the focus on 'great specialist translators'. I have already mentioned examples like Leonardo Bruni's membership of the Florentine cloth importers' and wool merchants' guilds, although it should be added that he also just happened to be Cancelliere of the republic for some seventeen years. I managed to sneak a few similar cases into the volume *Translators through History* (Delisle and Woodsworth 1995); I beg forgiveness for mentioning them again here, with minor corrections: In the English tradition, remember that Chaucer, in addition to translating and writing original works, was a court official with the title of 'Comptroller of the Customs'. William Caxton translated from French and is of course best known as the first printer in England, yet he was for many years a rich and influential wool trader in Bruges, becoming 'Governor of the English Nation of Merchant Adventurers' in the Low Countries and financial advisor to Margaret, duchess of Burgundy. Or again, John Hookham Frere, as a translator of Pulci, helped introduce the *ottava rima* into English in the early nineteenth century, yet he was also a British Under-Secretary of State for Foreign Affairs, a staunch opponent of Jacobinic ideas, and a diplomat whose career came to an ignominious end when he wrongly advised the British army against retreat from the French at La Coruña, Spain. But perhaps the clearest statement of multi-faceted professionalism comes from one of the most influential part-time translators in history:

> Are they doctors? So am I. Are they learned? So am I. Are they preachers? So am I. Are they theologians? So am I. Are they debaters? So am I. Are they philosophers? So am I. Are they dialecticians? So am I. Are they lecturers? So am I. Do they write books? So do I. (Martin Luther, *Sendbrief*, 1530 in Störig 1963:18)

One might regret that many translators are not just translators, or that they are not translators for long. And yet, is it entirely by chance that some of the

---

[1] To be fair, there is also evidence of increasing monoprofessionalism in this field. A 1994 survey of 181 members of the Société Française des Traducteurs found that 25% of the sample combined translating with another professional activity and that for 19.75% translating was a secondary activity (Cancio 1995:14). Note, though, that these were non-literary translators who were by definition monoprofessional enough to become members of the Société Française des Traducteurs; this particular finding cannot be considered representative of all translators. With this caveat in mind, the fact that just under half the sample (47.77%) had been born outside of France could well suggest something more general about the intercultural status of the profession.

greatest translators, those with the most effective power to determine their own translations and to shape many others, were also translators who had numerous other professional activities? If we are interested in how translators, who sometimes seem entirely hemmed in by mighty causes beyond their control, can nevertheless become active causes of translations, the multiple nature of their employment might be a major key. Thanks to their status and competence in other professional activities, some translators gain considerably more social and intellectual power than they would otherwise have as just translators. On a more mundane level, part-time, sporadic or even hobby translating may well be associated with relative financial independence from target-side factors like clients, publishing markets and readerships. If this is so, 'translation as a profession', at least as understood as full-time long-term employment, could paradoxically restrict the ability of translators to challenge power structures. Some translators are active effective causes precisely because they do more than translate.

In the medieval field, assumptions about monoprofessionalism curiously impinge on ideologies of translation assessment. It is common enough to see translation errors and major textual transformations being fobbed off onto intermediary scribes, thus protecting the professional status of the translator. For example Kalinke (1991), dealing with thirteenth-century Norse-Icelandic translations, argues that her translators were accurate but their later redactors were not. On the other hand, C. W. Marx, describing Middle English material, argues more consistently that since "authors, translators and scribes were frequently one and the same" (1991:266-67) it makes little sense to try to single out the work of individual translators. The historical object would become the entire transmission process, warts and all; the work of translators would be strictly inseparable from the labours of all the rewriters who have nudged along the course of history. This debate is of some importance with respect to the way medieval translations should be edited. Kalinke tries to get back to the original translation (1991:48), whereas Marx tries "to account for variation and discrepancy as part of a textual or manuscript history" (1991:256). Note that this issue has little to do with our insistence on the specificity of translational discourse (see chapter 4 above), since the text produced by a copyist can function just as translationally as one penned by a full-fledged translator.[2] What is at stake is rather the philological ideology that creative work should be evaluated as

---

[2] Scribes would thus translate between varieties of early written English: "when they copied manuscripts written in dialects other than their own, they showed little concern for the original spellings, but changed them to accord with their own traditions and preferences. Moreover, if they failed to understand a word in a passage they were copying, they would change it to one they did know." (Leith 1983:38).

the product of an individual, making scholars feel they must isolate and name an individual as translator. Needless to say, this mode of thought should have little place in translation history, not just in view of the multiple employment of translators and the multifarious nature of cross-cultural transmission, but also because the kind of creativity involved in translation itself is by nature profoundly shared, if only with an author.

There is also a crudely financial aspect to multiple employment, an aspect that has proved unexpectedly fecund in my work on twelfth-century Hispania. As might be gathered from various comments in the previous chapters, I am no fan of the 'School of Toledo'. I tend to see the concept as a nationalistic fabrication; I am ideologically inclined to believe there was never any such thing as a school of translators at Toledo. However, when I came to consider the financial status of the protoscientific translators working in the Iberian peninsula at the time, many questions were difficult to answer. What did these men live on? Where did they get the considerable resources they must have required in order to travel, to purchase parchment (and possibly paper), to pay collaborators and to gain access to source-text manuscripts? Could they have made any kind of living as professional full-time translators? On the one occasion that money is explicitly mentioned – the *Qur'an* project discussed in our chapter on regimes – we find the abbot of Cluny making a song and dance about how much he had to pay the translators to do the job, and the main translator, Robertus Ketenensis, then describing the translation as a 'digression' from his true interests in mathematics and astronomy (Kritzeck 1964:62). From these passages it might be inferred that the translator had no extensive means of independent support (he accepted to work for the abbot's gold) and that, although no doubt trained in a monastery like virtually every scholar at that time, he did not normally depend on the church structure (he was a traveller whose interests were in other fields). Interestingly, Robertus's efforts on this particular translation were also rewarded by his appointment as archdeacon at Pamplona in 1143. But he couldn't have stayed there long. He signed a translation in Segovia in 1145 and drew up astronomical tables for London in 1149. Vocational integration into the church structure was obviously not his personal aim. He was a travelling scholar who no doubt took on whatever well-paid jobs were going; yet his path was significantly determined by his own thirst for knowledge.

So how did Robertus make a living? The question concerns not just him, but the entire network of travelling translators with whom he was in contact in the north of Hispania (see chapter 6, figure 12 for the 1140s and 1150s). To cut a long story short, by eliminating alternatives one reaches the hypothesis that these translators transferred what they learned from Arabic not just by translating but also by teaching. This hypothesis has the added advantage of squaring with information on twelfth-century educational practices, agreeing with the one independent account of what was happening at Toledo (Daniel de Merlai's *Philosophia*) and explaining certain signs of tension in the records of the Toledo cathedral (see Hernández 1985). Of course, as a travelling translator-teacher I am quite pleased to think that other translators might have lived in much the same way as myself. Yet my questions led back to the very hypothesis that I had originally hoped to dismantle: I found that there are grounds to suppose some kind of teaching activity was associated with what tradition has called, perhaps with unsuspected correctness, the 'School of Toledo'.

Translators have personal interests

Any understanding of translators as people must seek to explain why they become translators and why they stop working as translators. Good answers to these questions require research into personal backgrounds. Before diving into one or two stories, let me just mention an alternative way of formulating general hypotheses about the matter.

Observing a French-German student group, Jean-René Ladmiral finds that certain bilingual students initially offer their services as translators for the less-bilingual ones. As translators, these better bilinguals seek a position of relative prestige, the power to control and direct exchanges. Yet this power is very temporary. The translators are so busy conveying someone else's words that they sometimes lose the capacity to speak in their own name. They find themselves "stuck in the exhausting and unappreciated role of linguistic mediators, deprived of the chance to say what they want to say themselves. Some eventually protest against this 'exploitation' by refusing to translate" (in Ladmiral and Lipiansky 1989:63-64). Although translating initially looks like an act of power, the translating translator can become relatively powerless. Some people try it for a while then seek to recover their own voices.

This pessimistic view finds some support in history. One need only think of the young would-be writers who "want to do almost anything to penetrate the literary world", as Callahan puts it. On a collective level, the kind of structure outlined by Ladmiral might also help explain the parabolic nature of the translation frequencies observed in chapter 5 above. Could it be that certain social groups become linguistic mediators in search of enhanced status then abandon that role as soon as it is no longer advantageous? People move in and out of translation; the frequency graphs jump up and down. But there are many other causes to be considered.

Some cases are especially complex. In ninth-century Baghdad Hunain ibn Ishaq translated a book on bones for an influential physician named Masawaih. The translation, says Hunain, was carried out in the 'clear speech' that the client demanded. Why should the translator not have had the power to decide such questions alone? Because, it seems, he was not on the same social level as Masawaih, who had earlier refused to teach Hunain medicine: Masawaih had sent the young Hunain away, saying, 'You would do better to carry out the trade of your people [Hunain was Syrian],' that is, to work as a money-changer. This inspired Hunain to gain solid knowledge of Greek and Arabic and to become a translator (Badawi 1968:34). Momentarily denied access to the medical profession, Hunain made a profession of translating.

A more interesting question is this: Given the chance to do something more advantageous (like medicine, perhaps), why would anyone in their right mind want to stay a translator? Historians agree that Hunain returned to medical studies and became a physician (Salama-Carr 1990:26-27). And yet he kept on translating, apparently attaining enough social power to decide how texts should be translated. Why did he bother? The reasons can become as devious as you like. There may be such a thing as a pure love of translating. More often, though, there is some kind of emotional relationship with a particular foreign culture or individual author. Casebooks could be filled with relationships like Chapman with Homer, Jackson Knight with Virgil, or perhaps Baudelaire with Poe. The trouble with this line of investigation is that it frequently becomes entangled in the webs of personal psychology or psychoanalysis. The real question is how far the translation historian should go. In principle, the details of private lives should be pertinent only to the extent that they explain what was done in the field of translation. But the limits of this pertinence are notoriously difficult to perceive.

My illustration here is the case of Henri Albert, a professional intermediary who did more than anyone else to create the French Nietzsche. Albert wrote on Nietzsche from 1893; his first Nietzsche translation was published in book form in 1898; he was in charge of the *Mercure de France* project to publish Nietzsche's complete works (individual volumes of which were selling up to 1200 copies in the two weeks following their release); some of his translations were successful enough to remain in print through to the 1960s. Although active as a literary journalist and occasional author in his own right, Albert saw his life mission as being to make Nietzsche known and appreciated in France. He was a professional translator in a sense that goes beyond merely financial details. Why would anyone dedicate themselves, body and soul, to such a task? Some kind of answer might be found in the biographical details. Allow me to summarize what I have found (in Schaeffer 1962, Schockenhoff 1986, Kintz et al. 1989)... be warned, though, that I shall wilfully take this story further than most want to go:

Henri Albert was only marginally French. He was born in 1868 in Nieder-bronn, Alsace, some three years before the region went to Germany. His full name was Henri-Albert Haug, a Norwegian name for a passably Germanic family, since his grandfather had come from Wurtemburg as an army sergeant with the occupying forces in 1815. Albert grew up in Alsace, becoming a bookseller of some kind in Strasbourg. In 1887, at the age of 19, he went to Paris and worked as a journalist for various periodicals. Most of his work from 1891 was for the *Mercure de France*, where he regularly wrote the 'Lettres allemandes' section, commenting on recent German literature. Although his first translations in the *Mercure* were of Max Stirner (in 1894-95), his commentaries on Nietzsche were constant from January 1893. In December 1894 the *Mercure de France* announced a project to translate and publish the complete works of Nietzsche, the rights to which were negotiated by Albert. Our man became the main translator and editor of the project, in addition to which he published articles and translations of Nietzsche in the *Mercure* through to 1914. Albert was also a two-way intermediary. From 1899 to 1904, the years of his most intensive translating into French, he wrote the 'Französische Briefe' section of the German periodical *Das litterarische Echo*, based in Berlin, and then contributed to *Die Literatur*. In 1902, at the height of this two-way work, he published a collection of his own poems. He also maintained close contacts with Alsace. From 1902 he was the Strasbourg correspondent for the *Journal des Débats*; from 1904 to 1913 he was in charge of sections of the *Messager d'Alsace-Lorraine*, and his publications in this period include *La force française en Alsace* (Paris, 1902), *La langue et la littérature françaises en Alsace* (Paris, 1906), *L'Alsace-Lorraine contre la force allemande* (Paris, 1912) and even, according to the records, *Le problème de la navigation en amont de Strasbourg* (Strasbourg, 1914). He died in Strasbourg in 1921, no doubt with a sense of having navigated home to a French-ruled Alsace.

Although a minor figure in most histories, Albert was an effective professional intermediary, especially to the extent that his opinions on Nietzsche and German literature were cited as authoritative statements in several sectors of the French press. In view of this minor authority, perhaps due to his status as a literary critic more than as a translator, the biographical point of most interest must be Albert's decidedly anti-German preferences. Although a professional intermediary working both ways, he was extremely one-sided in his sympathies, perhaps more French than the French, certainly biased to the point of denying his German-Alsatian origins and even to the extreme of publicly renouncing, in 1897, the substantiality of the Alsatian cause.[3] In promoting Nietzsche, Albert's overall strategy was to deny the Germanness of his source texts, making Nietzsche as anti-German and as pro-French as Albert himself. Since this was perhaps the translator's main contribution to the French Nietzsche, it is certainly pertinent to ask how Albert's anti-German feelings arose, particularly since he himself was of German stock. This is where the plot thickens.

The translator's father, Charles Henri, was a lawyer who became mayor of Niederbronn from 1870 to 1874 – the early years of the German occupation – and was Conseiller Général for Lower Alsace from 1873 to 1886. He died in 1888. We might surmise that he was fairly well integrated into the power structures of the Alsatian *Reichsland*. Yet his sons seem not to have been so well placed. The eldest, Gustave-Émile (born 1861), was a member of the anti-occupation student association Sundgovia. When this association was outlawed in 1887 following a major electoral protest against German rule, Gustave-Émile left for Paris and took French nationality, going on to become president of the French Geological Society in 1902. The second son, Hugo (born 1865) was a member of the same student association, undertaking activities that earned him expulsion from a German-language university in 1887 (perhaps he should have moved to Paris). He went on to become General Secretary of the Strasbourg Chamber of Commerce, helping Albert with his journalistic activities in the region after 1903. The third son, our translator, seems also to have been involved in the banned student association, which would explain why he too left for Paris in 1887. Just for the record, the translator's younger brother, Ernest (born 1871), although no doubt too young to leave in 1887, became a missionary in Gabon from 1895.

We thus have a family dispersed by the events of 1887. The father died the following year. The centred family unit had been taken away by the German occupation. Curiously, of the four brothers, the only one to marry was Hugo, the second brother who was expelled from university but stayed in Alsace. Those who left, including Henri-Albert, remained single.

These details could explain the translator's aversion to German power, which had taken away his family centre. Yet they might also account for a

---

[3] In the 1897 *Mercure* survey of opinions on Alsace-Lorraine, Albert states that "le mouvement en faveur de l'Alsace-Lorraine est un mouvement factice, entretenu en France par les Alsaciens-Lorrains qui y sont fixés et par les personnes ayant besoin de ce tremplin politique" (796-7). As if Albert fitted neither of these descriptions! Further, from the same text, "Voyez l'Allemand à l'étranger: après deux générations il a perdu sa marque; il devient un des représentants les plus typiques de la race où il s'est implanté et qu'il régénère" (797). This could be self-description, self-deception, or an attempt to gain acceptance in the Parisian cultural centre.

certain attraction toward Nietzschean disdain of the family and its values. Indeed, we can see the translator engaged in a denial of his family background: Henri-Albert Haug was born with a Nordic family name and was a product of Germanic occupying forces. To adopt a pseudonym, in this case simply by removing the family name, was to erase the trace of his origins. The translator insisted he was not Germanic, well before he made the same claim for Nietzsche.

Most of this would seem to be marginally pertinent, especially since it explains how a translator of Germanic stock, brought up in very close contact with the German language, could nevertheless be very anti-German.

But what of further details like, for example, the translator's long intimate relationship with the minor French critic and poet Jean de Tinan? Does this have anything to do with translation? In this case, yes. Henri Albert was particularly misogynous in his literary criticism and he gave great prominence to Nietzsche's misogynous traits. He had little time for the women that he saw perturbing Nietzsche's legacy, notably Lou-Andréas Salomé and Nietzsche's sister Lisbeth, with whom he negotiated the translation rights. To this extent, the translator's sexuality may well have had some bearing on the way he translated and presented his author. Yet there is no necessary connection between homosexuality and misogyny. More details would be needed. How far should we excavate for the causes? One might surmise from the biographical facts that the translator (and his brothers) reacted against the father, but what was his relation to his mother? The documents available to me say nothing at all about the matter. A few tons of personal material are probably to be found in the letters Albert sent to his brother Hugo, which are conserved in some archive in Strasbourg. Should I go to Strasbourg and inspect the letters? Need I really find out about the mother? Does the humanization of history require the dredging of private lives? Is it all so important?

Importance should certainly limit my wanderings (at least until I find someone to pay for my jaunt to Strasbourg). It is one thing to try to find out why a particular translator was anti-German and misogynous, yet quite another to explain how these features were not only concretized in his work on Nietzsche but were also accepted by a very significant readership. Only this latter aspect, the properly translational manifestation of desires, can be of true importance for translation history. The personal causes exist, but so do a series of social causes that help shape events. In the case of Henri Albert, it is worth cutting short the psychoanalysis and integrating at least three factors of a more social nature.

First, when Albert took on the project to translate Nietzsche, he was not well accepted by certain conservative or elitist sectors of the Parisian literary milieu. Hughes Rebell (1895) declared that only the aristocrats of French thought

– above all those with a perfect command of French style – should translate an aristocratic philosopher like Nietzsche; Wyzewa (1896:689) derided Albert as "the self-appointed interpreter and faithful apostle of Nietzschéisme", declaring that, despite what Albert said about the matter, the most fervent admirers of Nietzsche were the Germans. As an Alsatian outsider, a possible German or bearer of Germanic French, a relative *parvenu*, and a mere journalist to boot, Albert had to prove he deserved a place in the Parisian literary world. Given this situation, we should not be surprised to find him becoming more French than the French, if only as a means of self-defence.[4]

Second, the prominence given to Nietzsche's misogyny might be due to Albert's leading with his strongest cards, hoping to cash in on the anti-femi-nism associated with the rash of Schopenhauer translations, which had been passing for popular German philosophy since the early 1880s. As for Albert's homosexuality, it was certainly nothing unusual for the society of the aestheti-cist *petites revues* of Paris, where the names that come and go include Proust, Gide and several dozen Des Esseintes look-alikes. Homosexuality could well have helped the social integration of an Alsatian outsider.

Third, the apparent paradox of an anti-German translator coming from an essentially bilingual border region is understandable not only in terms of individual psychology but also on a properly sociolinguistic level. Research by Eugen Weber (1976) suggests that in the late nineteenth century the region of France that had the most developed national consciousness and the correspond-ingly highest percentage of French speakers was precisely the north-east, the area of heaviest settlement by Teutonic Burgundians, Franks, Normans and more recent invaders. The reason for this was not necessarily any perverse psychological compensation for non-French origins. National consciousness in the area was more likely to be a sociolinguistic consequence of the road and water networks that were more extensive in the north-east than anywhere else in France, setting up a logic that might raise questions as far east as a well networked city like Strasbourg.

And so on. For almost every inner causation that one finds in a translator's personal biography there is a wider, social mode of causation that enables or accepts inner factors to leave their mark in the public world of translations.

---

[4] A more complex reason for Albert's one-sidedness is suggested by Schockenhoff (1986:81). There is good evidence that Nietzsche very much wanted to have his works translated into French and was frustrated that this did not happen (the first significant translations were published after Nietzsche lost lucidity). There is much slighter evidence to suggest that Albert thus considered the French responsible for Nietzsche's insanity, and that this guilt motivated him to make amends.

Neither side can properly be understood without the other; private lives should not become black holes.

Translators can move

Thanks to their material bodies, translators can move. And thanks to their knowledge of foreign languages and cultures, they can often move further and more easily than many of those who depend on their translations. This could mean translators are never simply 'in' a culture or a society, not even when they appear more French than the French. It might also mean they can seek power by using networks in at least two ways. They can travel outwards and have their translations move back to the larger urban centres, as was the case of the foreign translators in the frontier towns of twelfth-century Hispania. Alternatively, translators can personally venture into the central cities, mining concentrations of values and become integrated into established power structures, as was the case of the late nineteenth-century Paris that attracted Henri Albert and many other border dwellers. These two opposed models might lead to a few general hypotheses about the ways translators move through networks. Let me briefly explore the models through a few stories:[5]

The Latinist translators in twelfth-century Spain came from many parts of Europe. Their names tell the story: Adelardus de Bada (from Bath), Hermannus Dalmata (Carinthian, probably trained at Chartres), Plato Tiburtinus (from Tivoli, Italy), Robertus Ketenensis (from Chester or Kent), Rudolfus Brugensis (from Bruges), Johannes Hispanensis (from Seville, or Hispania – yes, Hispanic, but quite possibly a Mozarab or a converted Jew), Hugo Sanctallensis (from Santalla, perhaps an unadulterated Hispanic, for want of more precise information) and then perhaps the greatest of them all, Girardus Cremonensis (from Cremona, Italy). All these people were in the Iberian peninsula seeking Islamic knowledge.

Within this twelfth-century network, translators tended to travel outwards, toward frontier towns and cities, then have their translations move back towards the central cities, principally those of the first European universities. However, the central cities quite quickly accumulated enough intellectual capital to attract scholars and translators inwards, becoming places for the intercultural production of knowledge. The role of the frontier points consequently declined; relatively few thirteenth-century translators voyaged outward in search of new values. Their network was already different: instead of a sending periphery and a receiving

---

[5] The following paragraphs have appeared in the volume *Translators through History*, pp. 193, 195-7.

centre, they now worked between a sending centre and a receiving periphery.

To test this broad model, let me now jump ahead to the late nineteenth-century network, no doubt the result of passages and links accumulated over centuries. The centres are not so different: Paris and London are still major places for intellectual production, although we should perhaps sketch in a string of cities like Berlin, Munich and Vienna (see Figure 11 in chapter 6 above). The translators tend to be in the central cities or travelling towards them. Their translations arc moving outward, toward the peripheries that various transla-tors have left. Within this second network, anyone looking for texts tends to travel toward the centre.

Evidence for this pattern is easily gleaned from the 'Notes from Abroad' appearing in numerous periodicals across the globe at the end of the nineteenth century. The authors of the notes, whether published in central cities or along the periphery, were very often translators earning their living from the circu-lation of news, scandal and fashion of one kind or another. But *where* were they when they signed their 'Notes from Abroad'? In the French and British periodicals, they were usually in Paris or London. In the periodicals in Ger-many, Russia or Mexico, they were also often in Paris or London. Established in the centres, they sent their news and translations, frequently done from intermediary versions, toward the peripheries.

Further evidence can be gained through a survey of the different cultures mixed in the centres. The group visiting Mallarmé, to take a cult example, was not just French but comprised writer-translators of the order of Stefan George and Arthur Symons. The foreigners actually writing in French included Wilde, Strindberg, Wyzewa, Milosz, Merrill and Viélé-Griffen, then a series of lesser lights like the Englishman Henry Davray, the Italian Ada Negri, the Netherlander Cyriël Buysse, the Dane Tyge Moeller, the Armenian Archag Tchobanian, and so on into grey obscurity. These people were able to translate both into and from the French repertoire of texts. But the important point is that many of these late-nineteenth-century translators, especially the two-way cases like Henri Albert, were materially located at the centre of the network. Even those who opposed the values of *fin de siècle* Paris tended to do so from within the city: Max Nordau, the Hungarian-born German-speaking critic of modernist decadence, lived in Avenue de Villiers, as reported in certain 'Notes from Abroad' written by the French-speaking Guatemalan translator Enrique Gómez Carrillo, who also lived in Paris, who visited Nordau, and who spoke to him in Spanish, since Nordau's family origins were to be found in the Jews who once traded across the frontiers of medieval Hispania (see Gómez Carrillo 1921, vol. 11:156-160).

Comparing this late-nineteenth-century network with the pattern operative in the twelfth century, we find at least two possible consequences of the ways translators moved.

First, the nineteenth-century translators tended not to seek out texts considered great because of their age. They had no developed sense of stored value. Whereas the twelfth and thirteenth-century travellers worked on religious, philosophical and protoscientific texts that had gained the authority of time, the modernist translators sought values that were new, transitory, and the stuff of lively debate. This is well known. Yet it has an important consequence: Whereas medieval protoscientific translators often paid homage to authoritative writers through various degrees of literalism, the modernist translators were more wont to churn out texts that were quickly produced, quickly read, and often quickly plagiarized. Time was of the essence. A novelist like Zola was published in Spanish in the same year as his works appeared in French. Nor was such speed necessarily hampered by geographical distance. In Sydney, Christopher Brennan wrote a parodic version of Mallarmé's *Un Coup de dés* just a few months after the original was published in Paris in 1897 (see Brennan 1981). As time became a key factor, we should not be surprised to find a few translation norms becoming more liberal.

Second, the foreign values entering the large central cities tended to circulate so fast that they had little time to accumulate around any one work. There was no single great text to translate, neither ancient nor modern. There were of course multicultural debates about the relative virtues of writers like Baudelaire, Rimbaud, Wagner, Nietzsche, Ibsen or Tolstoy, all of whom had moments of discovery and fête in the French periodicals and their peripheral echoes. Yet the discussions came and went very quickly. Greatness was temporized, and with this, levelled out. Few of the central translators approached their sources in excessive awe. Translation thus confirmed its position as just one of several methods for the transmission of knowledge. Hence, perhaps, the significant multiple employment of translators, who were often writers and journalists dabbling in several fields at once.

To sum up an argument that needs much further testing: The relative mobility of translators, coupled with variable directionalities within networks, can affect not only the time frames in which translations are carried out but also the way in which translators find employment.

Translators can go by several names

As a postscript on a tenuously related issue, let me briefly state why translators' names should generally be given in the language in which they are found, particularly in the case of medieval names.

Great confusion can result when Latin names are rendered into a vernacular of some kind. The man I have been calling Robertus Ketenensis is sometimes called Robert of Chester, sometimes Robert of Kent and occasionally Robert de Ketton or Robert de Retines, since the Latin 'Ketenensis' and its variants ('Retinensis', 'Castrensis' etc.) can bloom in any of these forms. By keeping the name in Latin, at least we don't mix up Kent with Chester and the rest. We remain slightly more honest about the limits of our knowledge.

This problem is compounded in the many cases where the identity of the translator is far from sure, particularly when a series of similar-sounding names might refer to one translator or to several. A classic example is the 'Avendauth' studied by d'Alverny (1964), where different names go to different people, although the resulting attributions should be contrasted with the somewhat less convincing detective work of Lemay (1963:649), where the same names are reduced to the one person (Lemay actually equates 'Avendauth' with 'Johannes Hispanensis'). Such labyrinths are impossible to navigate if we are not given exact manuscript names. Worse, the blunt use of vernacular identification can falsely suggest there is no labyrinth at all.

The problem also concerns the way we see networks. When medieval translators wrote their names in Latin, they were not doing so as English-men, Frenchmen, Castilians or whatever nationalized culture we now tend to impose on them. When Clara Foz (1987, 1991) surveys the twelfth and thirteenth-century translators in Spain, her habit of giving vernacular names goes hand-in-hand with her initial division of the translators into two teams – 'Spaniards' versus 'foreigners' – where the Jewish translators, converted or unconverted to Christianity, count as 'Spaniards' (presumably the same would apply to Mozarabs).[6] This might be good for a view of multicultural Spain, football matches, and perhaps even for regime theory, if only we knew why such a grouping could be important. But when we have a translator whom the manuscripts call 'Dominicus archidiaconus' or 'Dominicus Gundisalvi', whom most historians dub 'Gundisalvi' or 'Gundisalinas' – although 'Gundisalvo' for Menéndez Pelayo (1880-81, vol. 1:31) – why should Foz now call him 'Do-mingo González', no doubt in honour of a well-known president of a far more

---

[6] Note that in her 1991 paper Foz makes this same initial division between the home and visiting teams (34), then, in the same paper, introduces a rather more interesting partition between Jews and non-Jews (37), without indicating why this second way of cutting up cultures might be better than the first. That it *is* better is nevertheless a fact to be appreci-ated: the first division is based on unmasticated presuppositions; the second ensues from an analysis of the translation process itself.

recent Spain? Etymology can indeed get us from 'Gundisalvi' to 'González' (Lemay 1963:658). But it's a trip the translator never made. Before we recreate the past entirely in the image of our present, before we eclipse all the distance that might make us think twice, it seems better to keep the translators' names as we find them, as far as possible. Please.

It is a matter of respecting the integrity, both physical and cultural, of past translators.

11. Intercultures

I use the term 'interculture' to refer to beliefs and practices found in intersections or overlaps of cultures, where people combine something of two or more cultures at once. For me, interculturality is not to be confused with the fact that many cultures can be found within the one society or political unit (the term for which is 'multiculturality'), nor with the fact that things can move from one culture to another (which should be referred to as 'crosscultural' transfer). The basic idea of interculturality can be represented graphically as follows, where an interculture is assumed to be operative in the overlap of Culture 1 and Culture 2:

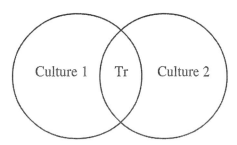

As you can see, I have smuggled a symbolic translator (Tr) into the intercultural space. This is a hypothesis, not a definition. With a little more elaboration it will become an operational fiction, a story that can help us think critically about other stories. For the moment, though, the diagram merely posits that an unspecified number of translators can be seen as members of intercultures or as having some degree of interculturality. The overlap in the middle could perhaps be the Alsatian *Reichsland* of Henri Albert's youth, the twelfth-century Toledo of the Jewish and Mozarab intermediaries, the island of Pharos where 72 rabbis apparently produced the Septuagint, the Central Asian regions where 176 equally legendary monks transmitted the Buddhist sutras from India to China[1],

---

[1] Beyond the legend (given in Ikeda 1986), John Kieschnick of the Academia Sinica informs me that: "The earliest translations of Buddhist texts into Chinese date from the third century. These were carried out in private by one or two monks. Small-scale, private translations were soon replaced by large-scale translation projects supported by the court. These translations [...] involved large gatherings of monks, sometimes numbering in the hundreds. The chief translator, usually a foreign monk, would recite a foreign text and then translate it orally into Chinese, at the same time explaining the meaning of the text. At this time, those in attendance were given the opportunity to ask the chief translator questions. When these questions were resolved, a scribe would then write down the translation" (personal communication, April 1997).

even the Brussels that now houses the world's largest ever translation bureau. Or it may have no geographical basis at all.

If we sharpened up a few definitions, this hypothesis might become testable and even valid to various specifiable degrees. Yet my aim here is just to put forward reasons why it could be important. I want to explain why the hypothesis should be formulated and tested, over and above any generalizable results.

Of course, one reason why interculturality could be important is that theorists and historians constantly overlook it, sometimes to the extent of finding our hypothesis unthinkable. Why should this be so?

Where intercultures are hidden

There is common agreement, among even quite disparate theorists, that translators belong to one culture only, the target culture. As we have seen, this assumption is broadly in keeping with the attribution of dominant causality to target-side factors, in overreaction to the days when all causality was invested in source-side factors. Theory has been switched from one extreme to the other. It is thus difficult to find any generally accepted model that corresponds to the intersection in the above diagram. A brief look at comments from three theorists might explain why.

In a typically fecund aside, André Lefevere refers to translators as remaining "within the boundaries of the culture that is theirs by birth or adoption" (1992a:13). The mention of people actually changing cultures (through 'adoption') is a huge advance on models that assume everyone stays exactly where they were born. But note the conjunction: "birth *or* adoption", apparently one or the other, since there is only one culture in play ("the culture that is theirs"). It follows that boundaries have only two sides; there is no middle ground, no intersection, not even for an intercultural master like Lefevere.[2] Strangely enough, just a few pages on in the same book we find a clear example of operative interculturality: "In eighteenth-century France," says Lefevere, "many potentially subversive works of literature (and philosophy) were routinely said to have been published in Amsterdam and Strassburg, that is, outside of the domain of the power of the literary system" (1992a:22). If we can assume some of these publications actually were produced in places like Amsterdam and Strasbourg, should we still

---

[2] Professor Lefevere died on 27 March 1996, after these lines were written. The many tributes paid to him have since made it very clear to what extent his work was intercultural: Flemish-born and American 'by adoption', he was a poet in English and Dutch, and translated to and from English and Dutch as well as Old High German, Middle High German, modern German and French (my thanks to Theo Hermans for this information).

insist that boundaries only have two sides? A French translation published in Amsterdam both is and is not 'within the boundaries' of French literary culture. Lefevere's notion of system seems not to accommodate this possibility.[3]

Although writing from a significantly different perspective, Lawrence Venuti similarly assumes that translators belong to the target culture. This can be seen in minor slips like his suggestion that translators working into English somehow need to defend their "rights as a British or American citizen" (1995:9). I work into English but I am neither British nor American. Even stranger is Venuti's insistence that translators should remind readers of "the unbridgeable gaps between cultures" (1995:306), as if translators could have knowledge of the 'unbridgeable' without ever having been on the other side, in which case they would of course be in the position of bridges themselves. Venuti's virtues lie elsewhere.

Gideon Toury is like Lefevere and Venuti – and almost everyone else – in that he fails to see intercultures. Yet he does at least try to conceptualize the term, producing a critique that merits a rather longer commentary.

Toury seems to admit the existence of intercultures but he then retreats to more comfortable circles: "in reality there would at best be a series of different 'intercultures', each one pertaining to a particular target culture" (1995:172n). That is, he tries to imagine an intersection but cannot get over the idea that translators belong in target cultures, in the same location as the 'place of trans-lated literature' or even of a culture-specific 'translation culture'.[4] Presumably this means that the overlap area in the above diagram should count twice, once

---

[3] A similar problem could ensue from the *loi Toubon*, which obliges French public firms to honour only contracts written in French. The resulting obligation to translate all deals into French could reportedly increase the costs of some complex international contracting by up to 60% (*The Economist* 1995:69). However, French public firms can avoid the added transaction costs by doing their deals outside of France, thus creating a space that is actually inside the French economic system but beyond French political control.

[4] The term 'translation culture' is used here to render the German term *Übersetzungskultur*, apparently coined in Göttingen to describe the cultural norms governing translations within a target system, on the model of *Eßkultur*, which would describe the way a certain society eats (see Frank 1989). The term has also been used in a slightly different sense to produce expressions like "the great *Übersetzungskultur* of Renaissance Europe", which McClure formulates and describes as "a literary ambience... in which not only specific poems but themes, tropes and verbal constructions are freely transferred from one language to an-other, and cross-linguistic influences are deliberately exchanged in a mutually stimulating inter-relationship" (1991:186). If narrowed down, McClure's ideal could come close to interculturality in a way that the original model of an *Eßkultur* seems not to.

as a part of Culture 1, and again, separately, as a part of Culture 2. In reality, says Toury, there is no such thing as an overlap.

Yet is there any strictly empirical reason for supposing axiomatic belonging to one culture or another ('the culture that is *theirs*')? In Toury's case, the problem could be that acceptance of substantial overlaps would upset numerous other parts of his theory. Most obviously, he would have no firm reason to suppose that translators "operate first and foremost in the interest of the culture into which they are translating" (1995:12); he would have to revise the idea that translators are immediately "persons-in-the-culture" (40); he could not describe norms simply in terms of "translation behaviour within a culture" (56); he would have no reason to elevate the binary choice between source and target to the status of an 'initial norm' that somehow has a purely 'logical' value (56-57), as if there were no ideology involved. In fact, having invested so much in the idea that the world is divided into discrete cultures, Toury naturally finds substantial interculturality "totally unthinkable", declaring that "as long as a (hypothetical) interculture has not crystallized into an autonomous (target!) systemic entity [...] it is necessarily part of an existing (target!) system" (28). Again, is there any empirical evidence for this 'necessity'?

When analyzing empirical evidence of interculturality – a multilingual sign telling passengers on German trains not to misuse the emergency brakes – Toury goes to great lengths to avoid "the ridiculous possibility that it [the sign] is not attributable to any culture", declaring that "there is no escape from regarding the English version as situated in the *German* culture" (29, italics in the text). In his efforts to avoid the 'unthinkable' and escape the 'ridiculous', Toury seems to have come up with the unthinkably ridiculous proposition that as soon as I board a German train (let's say, in Paris) and read a sign in English, I am somehow automatically participating in German culture. To think I wasted all those years studying German – all I had to do was get on a train and read an English sign! What Toury is blind to, of course, is that he and I, along with everyone else in that train compartment travelling all over Europe, could momentarily be conforming to at least some of the norms of an interculture. Although seated, we are not necessarily part of a sedentary host culture.

For a weightier example, consider the case of Moses Mendelssohn, whom Toury (1995:136) shows participating in the translation of Young into both German and Hebrew. Should Mendelssohn be placed in a subculture of German, a subculture of Hebrew, or both at the same time but in different places? True, systems theory could opt seriously for the last-mentioned solution, since its people need be little more than bearers of systemic functions: we could have Mendelssohn change subcultures whenever he changed languages. And yet, if he had a physical body, as most of us admit to, the different languages and the cultures would surely be brought physically together in the one place and time. They would be together in a minimal interculture. Hence the importance I have attached to translators who have bodies. Their material existence gives basic substance to interculturality.

Why should theorists not want to contemplate a substantial interculturality? The question concerns more than Lefevere, Venuti and Toury. It can be traced back at least to Friedrich Schleiermacher, sometimes cited as the first modern translation theorist (cf. George Steiner 1975:237). Schleiermacher went to considerable lengths to ensure that his ideal translators were not cultural hybrids (although his ideal translations might be!); he insisted that translators belonged to one side or the other, and that they should avoid wandering aimlessly "in unerfreulicher Mitte" (1813:63), in what Lefevere translated as "an unpleasant middle ground" (1977:84).[5] Admittedly few modern theorists could be accused of the nationalism that motivated Schleiermacher. Indeed, Lefevere, Venuti and Toury, like most translation theorists, have family or professional pasts that actively cross nations; they would tend to oppose blunt nationalism. But why has no one sought any pleasures from the middle ground?

Note that Schleiermacher's insistence of binary belonging – people should be one side *or* the other – was invested in his formulation of two mutually exclusive translation methods, insisting that the translator work either to domesticate the foreign text or to maintain its foreignness. This fundamental binarism, usually expressed as fidelity to one of two levels, has survived in more recent pairs such as 'formal' versus 'dynamic' (Nida), 'semantic' versus 'communicative' (Newmark), 'anti-illusory' versus 'illusory' (Levý), 'adequate' versus 'acceptable' (Even-Zohar, Toury), 'overt' versus 'covert' (House), 'documental' versus 'instrumental' (Nord), 'resistant' versus 'transparent' (Venuti), and probably a good deal more. On the surface, over and above the many subtle differences between these pairs, it seems translators should look one way or the other, since there is no room for a middle term corresponding to the position of the translators themselves. The way theorists think about cultures maps strangely well onto the way they formulate translation strategies.

When drawing the above intersection for translators, I don't feel like I'm committing any cardinal sin. Yet this simple geometry appears to go against a great and varied tradition of translation theory. Why? Could it be that everyone

---

[5] Note that Lefevere omitted this passage, and indeed almost all Schleiermacher's arguments against interculturality, in his abridged translation of the text (1992b:82). Lefevere understandably did not want to reproduce phrases like Schleiermacher's "Everyone produces original work in their mother tongue only".

has condemned interculturality to a huge collective blind-spot? Has the matter never reached the level of careful reflection? Or is there something in translation itself that promotes a world of discrete cultures?

Translations or translators?

My question is quite practical. Here we have my desk. A French text on the left; a corresponding German text on the right (I follow the directions of cartography). Since translation is supposed to go from one side to the other, I train my eyes to move from one to the other, and back again, since I have no desire to exclude possible reciprocity and exchange. My reading apparently imitates the movements of translation itself. The texts can correspond or deviate, but the very assumption of translation presents me with a series of relations directly between the two. Now, what's in the middle? As long as I just read the texts, the middle is uninteresting table space, an emptiness that my eyes are trained not to see as they move from one side to the other. This, I suggest, is the reason why readers of translations pay scant attention to the middle ground of interculturality. From the perspective of translations, such things are simply not 'observables'.

What might the desktop emptiness represent? A border, certainly, or a frontier space ensuing from a definitional difference: here French, there German, and thus a line somewhere between. My eyes don't see the line; standard translation analysis rarely touches the borders it jumps over. Yet translation surely presupposes and depends on the line that is there, somewhere, between French and German, between France and Germany. After all, if there were no line, would there have been any translating? Better, if there had been no translating, would there have been a line? In this way, we might eventually reach the history of the line, stories about Alsace-Lorraine, perhaps the lost tradition of ninth-century Francia Media, even traces of translators like Henri Albert. This is roughly the way I started to realize something important was happening in the intersections between cultures.

To appreciate the problem, start thinking from the perspective of human translators, bodies and all. If translators are our point of departure, the historical object always involves some kind of intersection. Or, as a more general hypothesis, translators *are* intersections.

A facile logic could be invoked here. On the sociolinguistic level, the translator by definition has more than one language. True, there is usually a hierarchy of competences weighted in favour of a home language. But the existence, to whatever degree, of competence in foreign languages must suggest at least some displacement away from monolingual centres. More generally, translators tend not to share the same linguistic horizon as the people who depend on their translations; they cannot be neatly circumscribed, along with everyone else, in an independent target culture. By definition, then, an approach based on the human translator as a sociolinguistic figure must be shaped by some initial movement toward the middle.

Should red lights start blinking here? Just as the desktop study of translations promotes a world of discrete cultures, the study of sociolinguistic translators tends to a world of axiomatically mixed-up intercultures (even before we delve into the disjunctions of language and culture). We stumble from one set of assumptions to another. This is not a good place to let the matter lie.

Happily, linguistic competence is not everything; interculturality should not be equated with degrees of bilingualism. In fact, such a reduction would make our original hypothesis disastrously unfalsifiable: if all translators approached bilingualism, and if interculturality implied no more than an approach to bilingualism, then all translators would be intercultural by definition, and nothing further need be discovered. But would we want to say, for example, that since Otto von Bismarck knew French – he studied the language from the age of eight, with the help of a Swiss tutor (Mitchell 1971:11) – he was a prime intercultural subject mediating in happy middle grounds? Were all of Henri Albert's Alsatian contemporaries by definition bound by intercultural norms? Were they all translators? This line of thought quickly becomes too powerful for our purposes. Whole social classes and geographical regions could be classified as intercultures, if not every human subject, to one degree or another. Such would be the deconstructionist world of interculturality as primal decentring, with cultures themselves becoming false ideological constructs built on the moving sands of intercultural activity. This is perhaps liberating philosophy. But if we want translation history to solve problems, to envisage a future, perhaps to find some gold, a more concrete notion of interculturality is required.

The task is to define interculturality so that translators can potentially be associated with intersections between cultures, and yet in such a way that our efforts don't dissipate into a world that has nothing but intersections between cultures. I'm not sure I can solve the problem here. The best I can do is indicate several avenues for experimentation.

Strangers and trust

I have sought help from various kinds of sociology. Perhaps not surprisingly, I have encountered something like the kind of critique outlined above. Projects for an ethnography of borderlands are in themselves an undoing of previous

ethnographies of non-borderlands. As Renato Rosaldo puts it, in classical ethnographies "the borders between nations, classes, and cultures were endowed
with a curious kind of hybrid invisibility" (1989:209). This invisibility might
prototypically be that of translation; the recent attention to borderlines as sites
of crosscultural communication might yet provide a stimulating frame for
translation studies. But I'm not sure I know where to go from there. Who are
the individual translators in this border space? How might they be related to
everything else that can happen there?

At one stage I expected orientation from the 'sociology of the stranger', a
more classical line of research that can be dated from Simmel's description
of *der Fremde* in 1908. The strangers of this sociology have tended to be individuals, often immigrants, typically emancipated Jews, people who wander
around the edges of group membership or are somehow momentarily caught
in the passage from one culture to another. They are rarely members of a
substantial intercultural place. Indeed, they are defined in terms of belonging
to properly cultural groups: "The stranger is a member of the group itself,"
says Simmel, "an element whose membership within the group involves being
outside it and confronting it" (1971:144). Among the sociologists who have
followed Simmel we only occasionally find notions of people happy to work
and stay in an intersection. The 'marginal man' or 'cultural hybrid' formulated
by Park – "a man living and sharing intimately in the cultural life and traditions of two distinct peoples" (1928:891) – is generally seen as intending to
join a new culture, without much sense of actively belonging to a place in
between. This vision was certainly justified when sociologists' prime objects
were immigrants in the United States. But the object has changed. More
recent approaches attempt to give the stranger a relatively substantial place,
yet always more one side of the border than the other. Harman, for instance,
sees the modern stranger as "an expert navigator who is 'in between' others",
but in the same breath insists that the stranger is "an inside actor looking out"
(1988:7). The sociological subject stays more one side than the other. Perhaps
this is because to do otherwise would involve questioning the meaning of 'a
society', the nature of societal boundaries, and thus one of the fundamental
units of sociology itself. In fact, the sociology of the stranger relies on a kind
of thought that is very close to the way systems theory has been applied to the
history of translations. It does not seem particularly well suited to a history
of translators, at least not in terms of the intersecting circles sketched above.
There is no reason to believe translators are by definition strangers.

Other kinds of sociology might open more fruitful possibilities. Inspiration
can be sought in the analysis of corporate cultures, workplace psychology, theo-

ries of expertise or professional ethics. This is not the place to pursue all these possibilities.[6] Let me just mention one set of ideas that seems promising.

The sociological theory of 'boundary-maintaining systems' (after Parsons 1953) posits that systems maintain their limits by distinguishing between internal and external relations. In his early development of this theory, Luhmann at one stage remarks that members of a system establish relations that may be internal or external, but that "internal relations merit and are accorded more trust than external ones" (1968:101).[7] That is, the limits of a system are determined not just by on-or-off membership but also by affective relationships, by decisions concerning whom one can trust. The more a situation involves doubt or possible betrayal, the more marked this particular kind of boundary will be. The theory thus identifies an area determined by degrees, without excessive over-determination by ritual ideologies and institutions. The intersection itself need not have fixed boundaries.

These ideas seem particularly suggestive when we remember that translating is a process constantly plagued by doubt and corresponding trust. Not only are translators engaged in relationships of trust with respect to foreign texts[8] but they themselves must constantly seek to be trusted by their clients or receivers. More to the point, since the non-translators who rely on translations have trouble controlling the work of translators in any close way, translators often

---

[6] Some of the possibilities may be pursuing me. As I flick through a slim anthropology textbook I read as an undergraduate, I suddenly find the same intersecting circles as the ones at the head of this chapter. Is that where I got them from? The anthropologist, Edmund Leach (1976:35), explains that the boundary area, which could be the intersection of any two categories, is a place of "special value, taboo", and that "the spatial and temporal markers that actually serve as boundaries are themselves *abnormal, timeless, ambiguous, at the edge, sacred*" (italics in the text). If translators are in the intersection and if, as I have argued, translations are markers of boundaries, one might expect something of the sacred and the taboo to underlie the entire institution of translation and its theorizing. This is a line of thought recently explored by Douglas Robinson (1996). The intersection that is most problematic is somehow over-determined and institutionalized, in the same way as a series of *rites de passage* regulate the anthropological boundary area.

[7] The more recent work by Luhmann is unfortunately less interesting for our current concerns, particularly when he insists on social systems as communication and declares that there is no possible communication between systems, merely 'irritation' (cf. Luhmann 1997:9). No matter how many Luhmannaries might swear by such insight, I see little reason why translation should be categorized as either 'communication' (intrasystemic) or 'irritation' (intersystemic), as if the logic of intersections were impossible to pursue.

[8] Recall that 'initiative trust' is the first moment in George Steiner's 'hermeneutic motion': "All understanding, and the demonstrative statement of understanding which is translation, starts with an act of trust." (1975:296)

have to be trusted because there is no other way of establishing a working relationship with them.

If translators are from an interculture, one might expect them to be mistrusted, at least from the perspective of non-translational 'boundary-maintaining systems'. The institutionalisation of translation would thus impose systems of control and regulation that stress, precisely, the values of fidelity as trustworthiness. When the Egyptians of the Old Kingdom used interpreters from the border regions of the south, they gave the princes of Elephantine – their own foreign-affairs experts – the official title of 'overseers of dragomans' (Kurz 1985:218). Hierarchical control was established; boundaries were maintained. When Jewish and Mozarab translators in medieval Spain were the necessary intermediaries for Arabic texts, the church and the crown placed their own people in positions of overseers: the abbot of Cluny made a Jewish or Mozarab translator work with his own trusted secretary; the archbishop of Toledo had the Spanish scholar Gundisalvi (Foz's 'González') sign texts that were probably translated by Jews (cf. Riet 1972:98*,99*n); Alfonso X put together teams in which Jews and Arabs were ultimately under the guidance of Christians, with himself as the chief guide. Similarly, in our modern field of inquiry, an intercultural subject like Henri Albert would have good reason to be mistrusted by his Parisian contemporaries, as were the Belgian translators of Wagner. In the face of such doubts, Henri Albert would logically react against initial mistrust by looking and sound more Parisian than the Parisians, just as an intercultural product like Alfred Ernst logically adopted the relative literalism that had originally opposed the Parisian and peripheral translators of Wagner.

Interculturality and its negation

A paradox seems able to explain such strategies. Here is the basic hypothesis: Precisely because interculturality implies mistrust and doubt, intercultural translators are ideologically represented and institutionalized in such a way as to dispel mistrust and doubt. The entire discourse on fidelity, which had a certain basis in the translation of sacred texts, was thus dragged across into the secular domain (Copeland 1991). As interculturality became more developed with the rise of urban centres, becoming a phenomenon of the city rather than of geopolitical borderlands, translating was made to look like an affair of sacred bonds. Thus, if translators can be shown to be significantly involved in situations of cultural overlap, the institutionalisation of translation might be expected to cover over all trace of interculturality. This is perhaps why some of our translation theories insist that translators belong to target cultures.

Are these hypotheses falsifiable? If we were saying that all translators are intercultural by definition, especially when they and others say they aren't, we would be in a situation of classical unfalsifiability, reproducing our prejudice regardless of whatever facts we came across. This situation can only be avoided if we oblige ourselves to locate actual evidence of the paradox, on the levels of both practice and theory, and with respect to the relationship between practice and theory. In fact, we must show three things: that particular translators are materially associated with some kind of interculturality, that the institutionalized representation of these translators hides their interculturality, and that there is a causal connection of some kind leading from the first level to the second. Only then might we claim actually to be testing hypotheses, and perhaps even discovering something.

How might we go about answering these questions? Hopefully, I have already set in place a suitable set of methodological tools. On the material level, the reconstruction of networks, especially through the incremental method, should be able to locate cultural intersections in very material terms. Further, it could do this without presupposing that the interculture itself has fixed boundaries, since the networks we have looked at tend to fray at the edges with the links becoming weaker the further we move away from the prime intercultural activity. As for the institutional element, what are regimes if not a model for generating ideologies of translation, including elements that are properly institutional in the sociological sense? When different groups negotiate the norms and procedures deemed pertinent to translation in a certain time and place, they would often seem to be determining the ways in which material interculturality can be eclipsed. Why should they do this? Because, as we have suggested, the causes of translation are multiple and contradictory, such that the material causation of interculturality may conflict with to the more powerful causes ensuing from source-culture and target-culture interests. Hence the extreme importance of bringing out the material and human bases of history. It is there that interculturality is most likely to be found.

Intercultural professions as a social context

I have mentioned the translator's physical body as a material basis for the intersection of different cultures. We can locate hands, mouths and feet that belong to two sides at once. A slightly more developed substantiality concerns the places where translators work, particularly if professional contexts can be seen in social terms, as a question of individual and collective bodies.

Clearly, interculturality does not mean that camps of translators are to be found along the national borders of the world. Interculturality has long ceased to be a direct product of the soil. As we have mentioned, cities, especially the larger cities of our day, are now the privileged places for cultural intersections.

Translators are not the only people likely to be found in the cultural intersections of their urban geometry. They often work for or alongside other intermediaries like diplomats, negotiators, travellers, academics, teachers, journalists, scientists, explorers and traders of all kinds. These people are not necessarily agents of international peace and understanding, but they do work between cultures. The list of intermediaries might also include shadier figures like spies, traffickers of drugs and arms, unscrupulous tourist promoters, experts in ecological dumping, political insurgents, hegemonic colonizers and invading armies. For better or worse, these would all be people who create work for translators. They could also be translators themselves, since many intercultural professions also inhabit bodies that translate.

The actual configuration of pertinent professions would have to be located and described for each case, delving into network links. One might use ready-made networks like the French-German *enquête/Umfrage* of 1895, where a group of French and German (plus a few 'foreign' European) scholars, educationalists, writers, statesmen, military officers, traders and, yes, translators were considered at least intercultural enough to have something authoritative to say on French-German cultural relations. The debate was carried out between these intercultural subjects, not on the level of the French and German cultures as wholes. The main point, though, is that the social context of translators would seem to comprise people who, like translators, are involved in exchanges between different cultures. If this is so, specifically intercultural contexts (the *enquête/Umfrage*) should probably tell us more about translation than can any benignly monocultural context (like a straight sociology of nineteenth-century France or Germany). This is one reason why our networks should start from intersections.

The above is a series of hypotheses, no more than an operative fiction with critical potential. Interculturality should not become a dogmatic view of all history. It should not suggest that monocultures are suddenly irrelevant to translation. Nor should it posit any necessarily stable and continuous object of knowledge, any eternal professionalism or 'intercultural community' reproducing itself generation after generation. I'm not at all sure the idea of community can explain the history of translation, if only because the short-term parabolic nature of translation frequencies would tend to prohibit long-term stability.[9] Translators appear not

---

[9] Note that my use of the term 'community' here differs from what Durišin calls 'interliterary communities', which are basically groups of interrelated national literatures, unrestricted by any intersection. Nonetheless, Durišin does pay special attention to properly intercultural phenomena such as 'the bi- or polyliterariness of certain social groups', 'the dual or multi-

to have the formal reproduction of the diplomatic communities in the large capitals of the world, where professional and social activities are guided by an exceptionally regulated kind of interculturality. Some kind of intercultural community might be nevertheless found among far less structured formations like the foreign writers following the 'moveable feasts' of European Modernism, the international research groups of twentieth-century laboratories, the exchange relationships between Europe's larger translation agencies, or the professionals behind the international networks that bring us multilingual television. Whatever their stability or instability, translators undoubtedly participate in all these groups, just as they create their own intercultural groups. From the foreign translators in twelfth-century Spain through to the exchange students and foreign-language teachers in contemporary translator-training schools, translators have at least hovered around intercultural communities. To say much more, we would need to know more.

An alternative basic link

Let me now make my heuristic use of interculturality a little more formal. Most traditional models of translation take as their minimal link the movement from a source culture to a translator to a target culture, no matter which side the translator is presumed to be on. Their basic link would be rather like the words in the circles at the head of this chapter:

$$\ldots \text{Culture 1, Tr, Culture 2} \ldots$$

Some theorists think a revolution has taken place just because we nowadays look more at target cultures than at sources. But we are actually using the same basic link as the one that privileged source cultures. There has been no radical modification of the traditional analytical geometry. Within this traditional link, conjugations of different types and levels of cultures can happily prolong or restrict the points of departure and arrival, saying how much of one side is shared or not shared with the other, where the translators are, which way they are looking, and so on. But the model does not start from the position of translators; it cannot give priority to interculturality. If, however, the translator's position is considered primary, we can formulate an alternative basic link:

$$\ldots \text{Tr 1, Culture, Tr 2} \ldots$$

domicile of certain writers and certain works', and of course the role of creative translation (see, in particular, Durišin 1989:125-137).

This means that instead of starting and ending with cultures, the basic link pertinent to translation history could start and end with translators.[10] This is what is happening whenever our networks link translators with other translators (Mozarabs, Jews and Latinists in medieval Castile), translation theorists with other translation theorists (Cartagena and Bruni) or even institutional contexts that cross cultural borders (the French and German literary journals of the nineteenth century). This is also what is happening whenever such groups are assumed to be sufficiently in contact with each other to set about forming a translation regime. It follows that the space of a translation regime belongs first and foremost to the intercultural links formed by translators and other intermediaries along and around the limits of the culture in question.

Our reordering of categories also has a useful negative function. We have seen how some researchers (our example was from Nord) compare translators and norms from widely separated contexts and then calmly conclude that, since the translators work differently, their norms are culture-specific. If we stick to our basic link, however, the seven-league jumps become unacceptable. The hermeneutic function of a 'culture', which was once to provide elements for comparison, is now to restrict the translators that can enter into comparison. The norms and regimes we deal with must be associated with the one inter-cultural space, based on the shared substantiality of a specific time and place. If that were not so, we would not be doing history.

What is a culture?

Some readers might be worried that I have speculated about intercultures without ever saying what a culture is. Is this a methodological fault? Not really. It is justifiable to the extent that, in accordance with our revised basic link, intercultures methodologically precede monocultures, just as nomads preceded sedentary cultivation. On the level of procedural logic, too, deconstruction has been around long enough for me not to worry too much about giving primacy to a difference

---

[10] My idea here is calqued on an example explained by Kuhn (1987:12-15). It seems that when Volta produced the first battery, his cell or basic link was the union of two different metals, with wet blotting paper separating the cells. But the modern battery, which works on the same operative principle, has the two metallic poles at the ends of each basic unit, with water in the middle of each cell rather than separating cells. Volta's model corresponded to an electrostatic view; the modern model began as a chemical theory. Although a battery can be thought of in both ways, the concepts allowed by the chemical theory were necessary for the invention's later development. There were two ways of carving up the same basic phenomenon, but one way allowed developments that the other did not.

(although my view of interculturality involves rather more substance than the abstract gramme that triggered Derrida's readings). Since the world began before we entered it, why not start *in media res*, jump-starting from the terms as we find them? We can then draw out the contradictory margins we seek.

A reasoned refusal to give an *a priori* definition of individual cultures might also be seen as a strategic move, not to liquidate the social realities of cultures but in order to find out about them without making too many blind assumptions. There are many reasons to doubt theorists who tell us straight-out what a culture is and who plunge translation analysis into the trivialities of *Landeskunde*, *civilisation* or whatever term is used in English for the study of monocultural backgrounds. To avoid hasty assumptions of monocultures I propose that 'culture' be left undefined, as the area where we have most to discover. More exactly, individual cultures can be defined by negation, not as the sources and targets of texts but as resistance to the movement of texts from one translation to another, from input to output, requiring and distorting the many possible moments of ingoing and outgoing messages. From the perspective of translation history, what was medieval Castilian culture if not some kind of social activity that distorted the movement of texts from Arabic into Latin? Didn't Islamic culture similarly distort movements from Greek? Italian Humanism was a transformational mediation between classical texts and the European vernaculars. And so on. If there were no cultures, there would be no resistance to the free passage of information; messages would remain unchanged. We can thus ask cultures to show their existence by transforming the texts (words, ideas, concepts) that enter through intercultures and leave through intercultures. In this way, a translation history based on interculturality could tell us about cultures, and not the other way round. And the entities that habitually mistrust translators for distorting texts may themselves be seen as the sources of distortions. A pleasing thought.

I am not neutral. It is hard to consecrate individual cultures in a Europe that, for the past five years or so, has seen its southern and eastern flanks pulled apart by claims to national cultural identity. To imagine interculturality, to seek out its seeds in the past, perhaps to plant those seeds for the future, is not to deny the power and appeal of a world divided into individual cultures. It means proposing alternatives. A method that places all translators one side or the other is unable to imagine many alternatives. It will not ask about the relations between translation and the weak intercultural power of European empires, be it the Holy Germanic or the European Union. It will not see intercultures as spaces of non-translation, of alternatives to translation, since translators need not depend on translations. It will not weigh up the benefits of international languages. It will mostly fail to perceive networks, the internet, the intercultural city. It will refuse to envisage a possible world where intercultures may hold more sway than the monocultures they now serve. A method based on interculturality can stir up hornets' nests in all these areas. It could, for example, imagine international cities as places for resolving disputes between sedentary cultures. Jerusalem? Sarajevo? Perhaps Brussels? Beyond cheap causes, to think seriously about interculturality means imagining a different world.

12. Interdisciplinarity

Historians do well to remember that the past is dead. All we really have is the present. Everything else is inscribed material: books and documents, tapes and films, dead words and images. Arguments about the past are not arguments that strictly concern the past, since the past, strictly speaking, can't answer back. Our arguments concern the present; our debates are formulated and carried out between active interests in the here and now.

Because the present deserves priority, we can scarcely be indifferent to the places where we carry out our debates. Our professional locations and networks tend to influence what we say, whom we are talking to, and who is likely to overhear us. It would seem important that we are currently almost all within academic institutions of one kind or another, complete with buildings, salaries, students and power structures. It would also seem important that translation history is not central to any of these structures. Yet does it really matter if our subject finds no firm academic home? Does it matter that we have few specific university courses in translation history, and very few specialized departments of translation studies in which history programmes could safely be housed?

I think not. More exactly, I believe we should carefully distance translation history from the available institutional locations. If our activity can survive being cut up and dispersed in the Holmes map of translation studies, it can outlast the worst efforts of our politician academics. To explain why, I would like to consider briefly the status of comparative literature, the interdisciplinarity of translation studies, and the chances of translation history becoming part of something wider, something called intercultural studies, which could even benefit from having no institutionalized academic structure at all.

Personal reasons for pessimism

Since I can't claim to see the whole of this story, the following account is necessarily based on a potted personal trajectory. In the past fifteen or so years I have worked on translation history within a range of academic locations: two quite different departments of comparative literature, a group for research on the sociology of literature, two translator-training institutes, a centre for research on literary translation, and a fairly straightforward department of English. The people I cite or communicate with are associated with a similar range of academic locations. All these institutional structures allow some kind of translation history to be done. And yet some locations are more welcoming than others, and all impose constraints.

Consider the absence of linguistics in my shortlist of academic institutions. Translation history would appear to have little to do with linguistics in any strict sense, and I have certainly paid little attention to linguistic matters in the course of this book. Linguistics is nevertheless the orientation that dominates the translator-training institutes in Spain, where I currently work. In a not unrelated adventure, at one stage I sought 'prequalification' for the position of *maître de conférences* in France, entering a centralized national system that obliged me to apply in one of ten categories, none of which mentioned transla- tion. Not wanting to limit my chances I applied in two categories: *Linguistique générale* and *Littératures comparées* (yes, plural). To my surprise I was suc- cessful in the first category and unsuccessful in the second, presumably because the word 'translation' in my publications was automatically associated with linguistics and not with a certain French conception of comparative literature. So perhaps we are doing linguistics, whether we like it or not.

Consider, too, the avatars of comparative literature. In France, to stay with the anecdote, one kind of comparative literature is traditionally reduced to parallel studies of authors, the tracing of fortunes and influences, mostly with one side of the binomials located in France. My more generalist approach to translation, with a decidedly sociological focus to boot, could thus be ex- cluded. Another kind of comparative literature nevertheless does what it can to cast its net wider: a *Précis de Littérature comparée* (Brunel and Chevrel 1989) actually includes chapters on 'Translated Literature' and 'Literature and Society'. So is a sociological translation history in or out? Or should we just let the French argue the toss?

The situation is not much clearer in the English-language tradition. As an undergraduate I was enrolled in a programme that was consecutively called 'World Literature and Literary Theory', 'Comparative Literature and Literary Theory', 'Comparative and English Literature', and possibly other things since, but I lost interest long ago. Interestingly, the same programme was associated with an emphasis on semiotics, which was later called 'Linguistics'. As the names might suggest, that particular brand of comparative literature remained open to many comers, integrating the debates of post-structuralism, Althusserian marx- ism, connections with feminism, and the beginnings of postcolonial theory (that was back in the 1970s). Any disciplinary setting for the resulting salad might be described as general literary and cultural theory, mostly forgetting specific restrictions to literature and to methods of comparison. Comparative literature didn't have to be comparative and it didn't have to stick to literature; it was anything we wanted it to be. No one objected to my working on translation;

no one insisted that I work on specifically literary translation.

Let this underscore a further point of perplexity: Since some of our most influential institutional locations have 'literature' in their names, a focus on literary texts has well and truly dominated translation history, sometimes to the point where other forms of translation seem not to exist. I suggest there is no great need to respect this literary focus. I have mostly been able to get away with work on literary translation in courses on technical language, and I've carried out studies of non-literary translation while located in departments of literature. In fact, I make a point of mixing the two, since I see no reason why the division between literary and non-literary texts should have epistemological priority over all other categories of translation.[1] This occasionally upsets people. I have been criticized both for focusing too exclusively on literature and for ignoring literary specificity. The only thing this really upsets is a purely institutional binarism that risks getting in the way of translation history.

In general, then, I suggest translation history can expect to find little adequate structuring in linguistics, comparative literature or narrowly literary studies. These institutional locations should be seen as clients for our research, with all the distancing and negotiating that such a relationship implies. Translation history need not be identified with any one academic institution; it can be sold to several.

A lacking discipline

If we haven't quite said good-bye to comparative literature, perhaps we should have. Susan Bassnett has openly stated what many of us have felt for years: "comparative literature as a discipline has had its day" (1993:161). This is nothing to write home about. The end has come as a stagnation rather than a crisis. On the one hand, as noted, comparative-literature programmes like the one I went through as an undergraduate abandoned the strict comparing of literatures

---

[1] In refusing to pay homage to axiomatic literariness, I perhaps reflect a lesson from Jakobson, who could find literary value in utterances like 'I like Ike'. Too much literary theory can sometimes debase the institution of literature. I thereby oppose André Lefevere's strange arguments against an independent translation studies, which he once regarded as "most unlikely to make the distinction between literary and non-literary, or technical translation" (1991:131, see also Lefevere 1981:46). For me, the refusal to make an *a priori* distinction would be a very good reason for seeking an independent translation studies. Note that just one year after he argued against an independent translation studies, Lefevere co-authored a text declaring that "the growth of translation studies as a separate discipline is a success story of the 1980s" (Bassnett and Lefevere 1992:xi).

long ago. On the other, more traditional departments like the American one I spent a year at have been relatively unable to respond to the fancy theorizing being done in rival departments like French and occasionally German or English. Either way, comparative literature has produced few ideas or models adequate to the way the planetary configuration of cultures has changed over the past twenty or so years. The textbooks still give us one national literature here, another there, and some kind of jumping between the two (or three, or four – the geometry remains the same).

What should replace comparative literature? I suppose Susan Bassnett could be attributed with two replies. The first might be Warwick University's doctoral programme in 'Translation Studies, Comparative Literary Theory, Comparative Literature, British Cultural Studies, Modern British Studies and Post-Colonial Studies'.[2] Has anything been left out? I'm sure everyone can do what they want; some can even do translation history. Whatever else this magnificent title might represent, it is not a disciplinary location.

Bassnett has a second answer, more formal and even visionary. She has proposed that comparative literature become a subcategory of a wider field called 'translation studies' (in Lefevere and Bassnett 1990:12, and elsewhere), among other reasons because, apparently, "a great many of the problems that the Comparative Literature people could not solve were being solved by those working in Translation Studies" (1991:18). The proposal, purportedly based on Barthes' positioning of linguistics as a subcategory of semiotics[3], could be valuable as provocation. But I don't really understand it. Exactly *what* problems has translation studies solved that comparative literature couldn't (apart from the problem

---

[2] "In recent years, doctoral research has included a study of eighteenth century Shakespeare translations into Italian, an investigation into constructions of Egypt by French and English travellers between 1790 and 1850, a study of the theory and practice of African literary translation, a comparative analysis of Arab feminist writings, a study of representations of Turkey in twentieth century detective fiction in English, a comparative study of English and French renaissance women's writing, an analysis of post-modernist theories of translation, a history of English translation of Malay verse, a study of the process of 'Englishing' the Bible, an investigation of the study of translation and reception of selected Brazilian literary texts, a study of the problems of translating theatre texts and many others" (Bassnett 1994:35)

[3] I must have misunderstood Bassnett's claim here. Saussure originally posited that "linguistics is only a part of the general science of semiology" (1916:16). Barthes (1967) almost reversed this relationship by viewing semiology (or semiotics) as a *translinguistique*, a science that was supposed to examine all sign systems with reference to linguistic laws (see also Eco 1977:30). In effect, Barthes was restoring linguistics to its position of dominance, a move that, as far as I know, he did not later reverse. As for the originality of Bassnett's proposal, note that Kloepfer had previously claimed that "a theory of translation practically encompasses the study of literature" (1981:36).

of trying to look new and attract students)? And what should be done with all the bits of comparative literature that were busy comparing non-translational texts? Should they be in or out of the new translation studies?

Here lies the rub. Bassnett's formal proposal can only make sense if the distinction between translation and non-translation is dissolved. This could also make the result compatible with the Warwick menu in translation studies and everything else. Of course, the distinction between translation and non-translation has repeatedly been attacked in several ways: through Lefevere's superordinate 'rewriting' (cf. 1992a), through appeals to generalized intertextuality, and by rejecting exclusive definitions of translation as if they were no more than opinionated prescriptions. If you believe there are no such things as non-translations, Bassnett's proposal must seem a great step forward. You might even agree that "the growth of translation studies as a separate discipline is a success story of the 1980s" (Bassnett and Lefevere 1992:xi). On the other hand, if you believe, like me – and others, for example Frank (1992:371) – that non-translations do exist and can be described as such, this wonderful success story of the 1980s is more likely to reflect a lack of discipline, a disintegration of translation studies, and even a piece of swift intellectual opportunism.

The underlying change has been the massive expansion of translator-training programmes since the late-1980s, which has provided fertile ground for academic jobs and publications in translation studies. If comparative literature has to seek new territory, then translation studies is a potentially lucrative prize. Hence, perhaps, Bassnett's interest in a merger. But she has not been alone. At least four other strategies have been formulated as ways of reaching the desired union:

• Various historians working within German-language reception aesthetics have long seen translation as one among many forms of literary reception. True, translations received little attention in Jauss's most influential texts (1970, 1977) and were more or less sidelined in Grimm's 'reception history' handbook (1977), yet they were granted full status as a 'reception form' in Stackelberg (1972) and have steadily gained in importance through the many publications of the Göttingen Centre for Research in Literary Translation (Sonderforschungsbereich 309).[4] Although this general strategy is not at all

---

[4] See the *Göttinger Beiträge zur Internationalen Übersetzungsforschung* (Erich Schmidt Verlag, Berlin), ten sizeable volumes of which have appeared at the date of writing. The relative success of literary translation studies in Germany must also be seen in the light of *Interkulturelle Germanistik*, the aim of which is basically to study the reception of German language and literature outside of Germany.

oppositional (translation studies and literary studies are considered complementary activities), the interest is certainly on forms of translation that
are closest to critical commentary or inspired reworking.
*   Rolf Kloepfer (1981) espoused a parallel form of complementarity when envisaging literary experts happily helping translators to understand literary texts,
as if translators were unable to find out about literature by themselves.
*   Theo Hermans (1985), among others, chose instead to protest against the
way traditional literary scholars looked down on translations (he didn't
mention translators). Translation studies could thus enter as something
radically new, oppositional, and even scientific in its insistence on non-
evaluation. Yet no one screamed too loudly, perhaps thanks to the influence
of *Rezeptionsästhetik*. Literary scholars just started doing translation studies,
sometimes calling the shift a 'cultural turn'.
*   A fourth kind of strategy can be found in Lawrence Venuti, who takes up
cudgels not in defence of translated texts but on behalf of translators as a social group. Translators, it seems, form an oppressed profession. Since part of
the blame for their situation can be traced back to traditional ways of thinking
about translation, Venuti proposes a magnanimous 'intervention' by theorists
of marxism, postcolonialism, deconstruction, psychoanalysis and feminism
(1992:1, 6), a mix strangely reminiscent of my undergraduate comparative
literature. Nothing suggests translators ever called for an intervention of
this kind. But that's surely beside the point. Like the descriptivists' strategy,
the belligerent decrying of exploitation has upset remarkably few people. It
remains grist to the mill of an expanding academic research industry.

Cultural Studies?

Lists like the Warwick doctoral menu and Venuti's ideal alliance are increasingly brought under the superordinate 'Cultural Studies', which could become
a general location for activities like translation history. I have nothing against
this label; it might name a broad interdiscipline enabling all kinds of wonderful exchanges to take place. Yet I don't see it as a future paradise. And I
suggest its relative success is due more to its slippery polysemy than to any
disciplinary virtues.

'Cultural Studies' could mean the analysis of popular culture or mass culture,
as in the Britain of the 1960s and 1970s. It could mean the Marxist analysis of
class culture and its fragments, in the tradition of Raymond Williams. It could
also mean the positivistic study of particular national cultural traits and customs,
perhaps of the kind that national institutions (like the British Council) like to

sponsor. Or it could mean the generalist critical readings of a Homi Bhabha, or the more technical schemata of semiotics. It could just be a convenient name used to bring together groups that have little in common except cultural discontent. Or is it a similarly convenient way of building a university macro-department in such a way as to minimize discontent? Then again, it might be a way of thinking about the information-managing intellectuals who now have real social power but don't know what to do with it. And more.

Thanks to these possible meanings, the term 'Cultural Studies' perhaps deserves a degree of institutional success: everyone can find something positive in the term. Yet it cannot yet promise any measure of disciplinary or interdisciplinary orientation. Although some kind of Cultural Studies is perhaps the best that translation history can currently expect from a university structure, at least on the condition that the resulting openness not be confused with intellectual strength, at the end of the day translation history might as well be done anywhere else, just as it might as well be sold to whoever will exchange its research for salaries, promotions or prestige.

Academic institutions are our clients, nothing more and nothing less. The material basis for this view is not hard to find: as I sit in my university office and work the internet, my translation history is developed firstly through exchanges with interested people in similar offices all over the world, and only secondly through the way I discuss it with the academics materially located next door. In situations where, as in Spain, research budgets are determined above department level, specialized university bricks-and-mortar can no longer pretend to provide a home.

Intercultural Studies

If the institutional structures are best left to our politician academics, this does not mean our actual work should be without intellectual orientation of one kind or another. As I have tried to indicate in this book, translation history can and should have its own questions, its own methods, even its own ideas about what is or is not translation history. Many other disciplines can be brought to bear on translation history; we are, in this sense, inextricably involved in an interdiscipline, which is no doubt why our work can be done in almost any cranny of the humanities. Yet the core of translation history, like the core of translation itself, involves certain constraints and could even aspire to a certain future development.

I want to suggest, without militancy, that translation history could eventually become something even wider, yet not quite so wide as to be nowhere at all.

The desire to go beyond translation is a normal consequence of interdisciplinarity. So many glorious ideas can now be brought to bear on this one quite narrow object that the ideas probably deserve better. And so we set about explaining a slightly bigger world. This can be done in at least two ways. On the one hand, as is currently happening, the concept of translation itself can be expanded until it fits the object we want to explain, which could be virtually anything at all. On the other, properly translational phenomena can be identified then related to whatever contingent fields call for a similar conceptual approach. This second approach would be the path of intercultural studies. It maintains an exclusive definition of translation and seeks to trace the relations affecting other aspects of intercultures. It remains focused on a geometry of intersections.

I refrain from presenting any map of intercultural studies, as if I had set foot on promised land. One might nevertheless imagine several routes leading from translation studies: one passing through work on material transfer, another weaving through regimes, and others making sense of complex causation or a sociology of mediators. Whatever bridges are crossed along the way, the result should be a more complete picture of the way intercultures operate, and thus, hopefully, a more important account of cultures. For example, in order properly to explain the translations between French and German at the end of the nineteenth century, I would have to know about the pertinent institutionalization of translation, the life of the literary and generalist periodicals, the politics of Alsace-Lorraine, the alliances of Bismarckian and post-Bismarckian Europe, the secret negotiations between France and Germany, the strategic use of colonial interests, relative military strengths, the economics of coal production, the international bankers in Strasbourg, trade statistics, immigration statistics, relations between the left-wing political parties, and much else. This project would ideally be done by specialists working in informal contact with each other, although an inquiring individual could probably manage most of it if sufficiently motivated. Of course, by the time anyone has covered all these aspects, they will have explained much more than a few translations. The work on translations will have become part of the overall study of a particular interculture; translation history will have become part of intercultural studies.

This does not mean fitting everything into intercultural studies. Nor does it involve finding interculturality everywhere. When a scholar like Nicholas Round (1993) sets about comparing Castilian culture with Italian culture in order to explain a fifteenth-century translation, there is a real sense in which he is doing his job as a Hispanist, and doing it very well too. People are trained to study cultures and to compare them with others; cultural boundaries are their professional frontiers as scholars, and we should have no complaint about this. We can make use of their research; we become readers of their texts, especially of their footnotes, looking for marginal details that might become elements of a different story. Intercultural studies nevertheless requires its own intellectual frame, wide with respect to the range of activities it can look at, yet quite narrow in that it excludes everything considered specific or central to one culture or another. Given this fundamental difference, there should be no pretence that any discipline is bigger or better than another. There should be no hierarchy of big fish swallowing up little ones, nor vice versa. The kind of interdisciplinarity appropriate to intercultural studies simply involves doing something different, alongside and in cooperation with others.

As chance would have it, intercultural studies could encompass just about everything I want to do in translation history, and quite a bit more. On the theoretical level, its development would require new attention to the meaning of cultural boundaries and the categories of belonging. On the practical level, a sense of interculturality could be developed from what should happen sooner or later in most translator-training programmes, where translators will have to be taught to do much more than just translate. Indeed, if seen as professional communicators working in intercultural spaces, translators themselves could provide the key to a relatively uninstitutionalized research area, tapping translation studies as a lucrative institutional market and solving some of our historical problems along the way. Translation history might help form the intercultures of the future.

References

Allen, Ros (1991) 'Long is Ever. The Cassibellaunus Episode in Three Versions of the 'Brut'', in Roger Ellis (ed) *Translation in the Middle Ages* (= *New Comparison* 12), Colchester: University of Essex, 71-88.

Althusser, Louis (1965) *Pour Marx,* Paris: François Maspero.

Altick, R. D. (1962) 'The Sociology of Authorship. The Social Origins, Education, and Occupations of 1,100 British Writers, 1800-1935', *Bulletin of the New York Public Library* 66: 389-404.

Alvar, Carlos and Angel Gómez Moreno (1987) 'Traducciones francesas en el siglo XV: El caso del "Arbol de batallas" de Honoré Bouvet', in Julio-César Santoyo et al. (eds) *Fidus Interpres. Actas de las Primeras Jornadas Nacionales de Historia de la Traducción,* 2 vols, León: Universidad de León, vol 1: 31-37.

Alverny, Marie-Thérèse d' (1964) 'Avendauth?', *Homenaje a Millás-Vallicrosa,* 2 vols, Barcelona: Consejo Superior de Investigaciones Científicas, vol. 1: 19-43.

Amit-Kochavi, Hannah (1996) 'Israeli Arabic Literature in Hebrew Translation. Initiation, Dissemination and Reception', *The Translator* 2/1: 27-44.

Appadurai, Arjun (1986) 'Introduction: Commodities and the Politics of Value', in Arjun Appadurai (ed) *The Social Life of Things: Commodities in Cultural Perspective,* Cambridge: Cambridge University Press, 3-63.

Arrojo, Rosemary (1993) *Tradução, Desconstrução e Psicanálise,* Rio de Janeiro: Imago.

Attali, Jacques (1991) *1492,* Paris: Fayard.

Badawi, Adburrahman (1968) *La Transmission de la philosophie grecque au monde arabe,* second edition, Paris: Vrin, 1987.

Badia, Lola (1988) *De Bernat Metge a Joan Roís de Corella. Estudis sobre la cultura literària de la tardor medieval catalana,* Barcelona: Quaderns Crema.

Baker, Mona (1993) 'Corpus Linguistics and Translation Studies. Implications and Applications', in Mona Baker, Gill Francis and Elena Tognini-Bonelli (eds) *Text and Technology. In Honour of John Sinclair,* Amsterdam & Philadelphia: John Benjamins, 233-250.

------ (1995) 'Corpora in Translation Studies: an overview and some suggestions for future research', *Target* 7/2: 223-243.

Balakian, Anna (ed) (1982) *The Symbolist Movement in the Literature of European Languages,* Budapest: Akadémiai Kiadó.

Ballard, Michel (1992) *De Cicéron à Benjamin. Traducteurs, traductions, réflexions*, Lille: Presses Universitaires de Lille.

Ballesteros Beretta, Antonio (1984) *Alfonso X el Sabio,* Barelona: El Albir.

Barthes, Roland (1967) *Elements of Semiology,* trans. A. Lavers and C. Smith, London: Cape (Original: 'Éléments de sémiologie', *Communications* 4, 1964).

Bassnett, Susan (1991a) *Translation Studies,* revised edition, London & New York: Routledge.

------ (1991b) 'Translation and Ideology', *Koinè* 1/2: 7-32.

------ (1993) *Comparative Literature. A Critical Introduction*, Oxford & Cambridge MA: Blackwell.

------ (1994) 'Translation Studies at Warwick – The Intercultural Approach', *In Other Words* 3: 35-37.

Bassnett, Susan and André Lefevere (1992) 'General editors' preface', in André Lefevere (ed) *Translation, History, Culture. A Sourcebook*, London & New York: Routledge.

Beer, Jeanette (1989) 'Introduction', in Jeanette Beer (ed) *Medieval Translators and their Craft*, Kalamazoo MI: Medieval Institute Publications, Western Michigan University.

Benjamin, Walter (1923) 'Die Aufgabe des Übersetzers', reprinted in *Illuminationen. Ausgewählte Schriften*, Frankfurt/Main: Suhrkamp, 1977, 50-62.

Berman, Antoine (1984) *L'épreuve de l'étranger. Culture et traduction dans l'Allemagne romantique*, Paris: Gallimard.

Bihl, Liselotte and Karl Epting (1987) *Bibliographie französischer Übersetzungen aus dem Deutschen 1487-1944. Bibliographie de traductions françaises d'auteurs de langue allemande*, 2 vols, Tübingen: Max Niemeyer.

Blum-Kulka, Shoshana (1986) 'Shifts of Cohesion and Coherence in Translation', in Juliane House and Shoshana Blum-Kulka (eds) *Interlingual and Intercultural Communication. Discourse and Cognition in Translation and Second Language Acquisition Studies*, Tübingen: Gunter Narr, 17-35.

Bourdieu, Pierre (1980) 'Une science qui dérange', interview with Pierre Thuillier in *La Recherche* 112; reprinted in *Questions de sociologie*, Paris: Minuit, 19-36.

Bragt, Katrin van (1989) 'Corpus bibliographique et analyse des traductions. Un programme d'analyse par ordinateur', *Revue de Littérature comparée* 1989/2: 171-178.

------ (1996) *Bibliographie des traductions françaises (1810-1840). Répertoires par disciplines,* avec la collaboration de Lieven D'hulst et José Lambert, Leuven: Leuven University Press.

Brennan, Christopher (1981) *Prose-Verse-Poster-Algebraic-Symbolico-Riddle-Musico-Poematicographoscope. Pocket Musico-Poematicographoscope* (written 1897), facsimile edition, Sydney: Hale & Iremonger.

Brook, Leslie C. (1991) 'The Translator and his Reader: Jean de Meun and the Abelard-Heloise Correspondence', in Roger Ellis (ed) *The Medieval Translator II*, London: Centre for Medieval Studies, Queen Mary and Westfield College, University of London, 99-122.

Brunel, Pierre and Yves Chevrel (eds) (1989) *Précis de Littérature comparée*, Paris: Presses Universitaires de France.

Callahan, David (1993) 'Material Conditions for Reception. Spanish Literature in England 1920-1940', *New Comparison* 15: 100-109.

Caminade, Monique and Anthony Pym (1995) *Les Formations en traduction et interprétation. Essai de recensement mondial* (= special issue of *Traduire*), Paris: Société Française des Traducteurs.

Cancio, Carmelo (1995) 'Être traducteur en France en 1994. Bilan', *Traduire* 165: 4-27.

Cary, Edmond (1963) *Les grands traducteurs français*, Geneva: Georg.

Cherewatuk, Karen (1991) 'The Middle English *Floris and Blauncheflur*, Another Merchant's Tale', in Roger Ellis (ed) *Translation in the Middle Ages* (= *New Comparison* 12), Colchester: University of Essex, 34-70.

Chesterman, Andrew (1994) 'From "Is" to "Ought": Laws, Norms and Strategies in Translation Studies', *Target* 5/1: 1-20.

Clagett, Marshall (1953) 'The Medieval Latin Translations from the Arabic of the Elements of Euclid with Special Emphasis on the Versions of Adelard of Bath', *Isis* 44: 27-28, 38-42.

Comes, Mercè, Roser Puig and Julio Samsó (eds) (1987) *De Astronomia Alphonsi Regis. Actas del simposio sobre astronomía alfonsí celebrado en Berkeley (agosto 1985) y otros trabajos sobre el mismo tema,* Barcelona: Universidad de Barcelona, Instituto 'Millás Vallicrosa' de Historia de la ciencia árabe.

Copeland, Rita (1991) *Rhetoric, Hermeneutics and Translation in the Middle Ages. Academic Traditions and Vernacular Texts*, Cambridge, New York, Port Chester, Melbourne, Sydney: Cambridge University Press.

Coste, Didier (1988) 'Pour une histoire littéraire négative', in Anthony Pym (ed) *L'Internationalité littéraire*, Paris & Barcelona: Noesis, 30-41.

Delabastita, Dirk (1991) 'A False Opposition in Translation Studies: Theoretical versus/and Historical Approaches', *Target* 3/2: 137-152.

Delisle, Jean and Judith Woodsworth (eds) (1995) *Translators through History*, Amsterdam & Philadelphia: John Benjamins/UNESCO.

D=hulst, Lieven (1987) *L'Évolution de la poésie en France (1780-1830). Introduction à une analyse des interférences systémiques*, Leuven: Leuven University Press.

------ (1990) *Cent ans de théorie française de la traduction: de Batteux à Littré (1748-1847),* Lille: Presses Universitaires de Lille.

Dottin, Mireille (1983) *S comme Salomé. Salomé dans le texte et l'image de 1870 à 1914*, Université de Toulouse - le Mirail.

Dujardin, Edouard (1931) *Le Monologue intérieur,* Paris: Messein.

Duméril, Edmond (1934) *Lieds et ballades germaniques traduits en vers français. Essai de bibliographie critique*, Paris: Champion, Reprint: Geneva: Slatkine, 1977.

Durišin, Dionýz (1989) *Theory of Interliterary Process,* Bratislava: Veda, Slovak Academy of Sciences.

Durling, Nancy Vine (1989) 'Translation and Innovation in the *Roman de Brut*', in Jeanette Beer (ed) *Medieval Translators and their Craft,* Kalamazoo: Medieval Institute Publications, Western Michigan University, 9-39.

Eco, Umberto (1977) *A Theory of Semiotics*, London & Basingstoke: Macmillan.

Economist, The (1995) 'What's the French for cock-up?', *The Economist* 336/7927: 69; translated as 'Chère, si chère loi Toubon', *Courrier international* 252: 5.

Eliot, T. S. (1919) 'Tradition and the Individual Talent', in D. J. Enright and Ernst de Chickera (eds) *English Critical Texts*, London: Oxford University Press, 1962, 293-301.

Even-Zohar, Itamar (1981) 'Translation Theory Today: A Call for Transfer Theory', *Poetics Today* 2/4: 1-7.

------ (1990) 'Translation and Transfer', *Poetics Today* 11/1 (= special issue on Polysystem Studies): 73-78.

Foz, Clara (1987) 'El concepto de Escuela de Traductores de Toledo', in Julio-César Santoyo et al. (eds) *Fidus Interpres. Actas de las Primeras Jornadas Nacionales de Historia de la Traducción*, 2 vols, León: Universidad de León, vol. 1: 24-30.

------ (1991) 'Pratique de la traduction en Espagne au Moyen Age: les travaux tolédans', in Roger Ellis (ed) *The Medieval Translator II*, London: Centre for Medieval Studies, Queen Mary and Westfield College, University of London, 29-43.

Frank, Armin Paul (1989) 'Translation as System and *Übersetzungskultur*, On Histories and Systems in the Study of Literary Translation', *New Comparison* 8: 85-98.

------ (1992) 'Towards a Cultural History of Literary Translation. "Histories," "Systems," and Other Forms of Synthesizing Research', in Harald Kittel (ed) *Geschichte, System, literarische Übersetzung / Histories, Systems, Literary Translations*, Berlin: Erich Schmidt, 369-387.

Frank, Armin Paul and Helga Essmann (1900) 'Translation Anthologies: A Paradigmatic Medium of International Literary Transfer', *Amerikastudien / American Studies* 35/1: 21-34.

Fromm, Hans (1950-53) *Bibliographie deutscher Übersetzungen aus dem Französischen 1700-1948*, 6 vols, Baden-Baden: Verlag für Kunst und Wissenschaft.

Frow, John (1995) *Cultural Studies and Cultural Value*, Oxford: Oxford University Press.

García Yebra, Valentín (1983) *En torno a la traducción. Teoría. Crítica. Historia*, Segunda edición corregida y aumentada, Madrid: Gredos, 1989.

Gargatagli Brusa, Ana (1996) 'La traducción de América', in Miquel Edo Julià (ed) *I congrès internacional sobre traducció. Actes*, 2 vols, Bellaterra: Departament de Traducció i d'Interpretació, Universitat Autònoma de Barcelona, vol. 2: 727-742.

Genette, Gérard (1976) *Mimologiques. Voyage en Cratylie*, Paris: Seuil.

------ (1978) *Seuils*, Paris: Seuil.

Gómez Carrillo, Enrique (1921) *Obras Completas,* Madrid: Mundo Latino.

Grimm, Gunter (1977) *Rezeptionsgeschichte. Grundlegung einer Theorie,* Munich: Wilhelm Fink.

Gutt, Ernst-August (1991) *Translation and Relevance. Cognition and Context,* Oxford: Basil Blackwell.

Harman, Lesley D. (1988) *The Modern Stranger. On Language and Membership,* Berlin, New York, Amsterdam: Mouton de Gruyter.

Haskins, Charles Homer (1924) *Studies in the History of Medieval Science,* Cambridge MA: Harvard University Press.

------ (1929) *Studies in Medieval Culture,* reprint, New York: Frederick Ungar, 1965.

Hausmann, Frank-Rutger (1992) *Bibliographie der deutschen Übersetzungen aus dem Italienischen von den Anfängen bis 1730,* 2 vols, Tübingen: Niemeyer.

Hermans, Theo (1985) 'Introduction. Translation Studies and a New Paradigm', in Theo Hermans (ed) *The Manipulation of Literature. Studies in Literary Translation,* London & Sydney: Croom Helm, 7-15.

------ (1991) 'Translational Norms and Correct Translations', in Kitty M. van Leuven-Zwart and Ton Naaijkens (eds) *Translation Studies. The State of the Art,* Amsterdam & Atlanta GA: Rodopi, 155-169.

------ (1992) 'Renaissance Translation between Literalism and Imitation', in Harald Kittel (ed) *Geschichte, System, literarische Übersetzung / Histories, Systems, Literary Translations,* Berlin: Erich Schmidt, 95-116.

Hernández, Francisco J. (ed) (1985) *Los cartularios de Toledo. Catálogo documental,* Madrid: Fundación Ramón Areces.

Holmes, James S (1972) 'The Name and Nature of Translation Studies'; expanded version in *Translated! Papers on Literary Translation and Translation Studies,* Amsterdam: Rodopi, 1988, 66-80.

Holz-Mänttäri, Justa (1984) *Translatorisches Handeln. Theorie und Methode,* Helsinki: Academia Scientiarum Fennica.

------ (1990) 'Funktionskonstanz – eine Fiktion?', in Heidemarie Salevsky (ed) *Übersetzungswissenschaft und Sprachmittlerausbildung. Akten der I. Internationalen Konferenz,* 2 vols, Berlin: Humboldt-Universität zu Berlin, vol. 1: 66-74.

Horguelin, Paul (1981) *Anthologie de la manière de traduire. Domaine français,* Monreal: Linguatech.

Hosington, Brenda (1991) 'Partonopeu de Blois and its Fifteenth-Century English Translation: a Medieval Translator at Work', in Roger Ellis (ed) *The Medieval Translator II,* London: Centre for Medieval Studies, Queen Mary and Westfield College, University of London, 231-252.

Ikeda, Daisaku (1986) *The Flower of Chinese Buddhism,* New York: Weatherhill.

Jauss, Hans Robert (1970) *Literaturgeschichte als Provokation,* Frankfurt/Main: Suhrkamp.

------ (1977) *Ästhetische Erfahrung und literarische Hermeneutik I*, Munich: Wilhelm Fink.

Jacquart, Danielle (1989) 'Remarques préliminaires à une étude comparée des traductions médicales de Gérard de Crémone', in Geneviève Contamine (ed) *Traduction et traducteurs au Moyen Âge*, Paris: CNRS, 109-118.

Jourdain, Amable (1873) *Recherches critiques sur l'âge et l'origine des traductions latines d'Aristote. Nouvelle édition revue et augmentée par Charles Jourdain,* Paris: Joubert (first edition 1819).

Jurt, Joseph, Martin Ebel and Ursula Erzgräber (1989) *Französischsprachige Gegenwartsliteratur 1918-1986/87. Eine bibliographische Bestandsaufnahme der Originaltexte und der deutschen Übersetzungen*, Tübingen: Max Niemeyer Verlag.

Kalinke, Marianne E. (1991) 'Translator or Redactor? The Problem of Old Norse-Icelandic "Translations" of Old French Literature', in Roger Ellis (ed) *Translation in the Middle Ages* (= *New Comparison* 12), Colchester: University of Essex, 34-53.

Kelly, Louis G. (1979) *The True Interpreter. A History of Translation Theory and Practice in the West*, Oxford: Basil Blackwell.

Keohane, Robert O. (1984) *After Hegemony. Cooperation and Discord in the World Political Economy,* Princeton NJ: Princeton University Press.

Kintz, Jean-Pierre et al. (eds) (1989) *Nouveau dictionnaire de biographie alsacienne*, vol. 15, Strasbourg: Fédération des Sociétés d'Histoire et d'Archéologie d'Alsace.

Kittel, Harald (ed) *Geschichte, System, literarische Übersetzung / Histories, Systems, Literary Translations*, Berlin: Erich Schmidt.

Kloepfer, Rolf (1967) *Die Theorie der literarischen Übersetzung: Romanisch-deutscher Sprachbereich,* Munich: Wilhelm Fink.

------ (1981) 'Intra- and Intercultural Translation', *Poetics Today* 2/4: 29-38.

Krasner, Stephen D. (ed) (1983) *International Regimes*, Ithica: Cornell University Press.

Kritzeck, James (1964) *Peter the Venerable and Islam*, Princeton: Princeton University Press.

Kuhn, Thomas S. (1987) 'What Are Scientific Revolutions?', in Lorenz Krüger et al. (eds) *The Probabilistic Revolution,* 2 vols; vol. 1 *Ideas in History*, Cambridge MA & London: MIT Press, 7-22.

Kurz, Ingrid (1985) 'The Rock Tombs of the Princes of Elephantine. Earliest references to interpretation in Pharaonic Egypt', *Babel* 31/4: 213-218.

Ladmiral, Jean-René and Edmond Marc Lipiansky (1989) *La communication interculturelle*, Paris: Armand Colin.

Lambert, José (1988) 'Twenty Years of Research on Literary Translation at the Katholieke Universiteit Leuven', in Harald Kittel (ed) *Die literarische Übersetzung: Stand und Perspektiven ihrer Erforschung*, Berlin: Erich Schmidt, 122-138.

------ (1989) 'La traduction, les langues et la communication de masse. Les am-biguïtés du discours international', *Target* 1/2: 215-237.

------ (1991a) 'Shifts, Oppositions and Goals in Translation Studies: Towards a Genealogy of Concepts', in Kitty van Leuven-Zwart and Ton Naaijkens (eds) *Translation Studies: The State of the Art*, Amsterdam & Atlanta GA: Rodopi, 25-37.

------ (1991b) 'In Quest of Literary World Maps', in Harald Kittel and Armin Paul Frank (eds) *Interculturality and the Historical Study of Literary Translations*, Berlin: Erich Schmidt, 133-143.

Lambert, José, Lieven D'hulst and Katrin van Bragt (1985) 'Translated Literature in France, 1800-1850', in Theo Hermans (ed) *The Manipulation of Literature: Studies in Literary Translation,* London & Sydney: Croom Helm, 149-163.

Laurenson, D. F. (1969) 'A Sociological Study of Authorship', *British Journal of Sociology* 20: 311-325.

Leach, Edmund (1976) *Culture and Communication. The Logic by which Symbols are Connected,* Cambridge, London, New York, Melbourne: Cambridge University Press.

Lefevere, André (1977) *Translating Literature: The German Tradition from Luther to Rosenzweig*, Assen: Van Gorcum.

------ (1981) 'On "Literary" and "Translation"', *Poetics Today* 2/4: 39-50.

------ (1991) 'Translation and Comparative Literature: The Search for the Center', *TTR* 4/1: 129-144.

------ (1992a) *Translation, Rewriting, and the Manipulation of Literary Fame,* London & New York: Routledge.

------ (ed) (1992b) *Translation, History, Culture. A Sourcebook*, London and New York: Routledge.

Lefevere, André and Susan Bassnett (1990) 'Introduction: Proust's Grandmother and the Thousand and One Nights – The "Cultural Turn" in Translation Studies', in Susan Bassnett and André Lefevere (eds) *Translation, History and Culture*, London: Pinter, 1-13.

Leith, Dick (1983) *A Social History of English*, London: Routledge & Kegan Paul.

Lemay, Richard (1963) 'Dans l'Espagne du XIIe siècle. Les traductions de l'arabe au latin', *Annales Economies, Sociétés, Civilisations* 18/4: 639-665.

Lowell, Robert (1958) *Imitations,* eighth printing, New York: Farrar, Straus and Giroux, 1969.

Luhmann, Niklas (1968) *Vertrauen. Ein Mechanismus der Reduktion sozialer Komplexität,* 3. durchgesehene Auflage, Stuttgart: Ferdidand Enke, 1989.

------ (1997) *Die Kunst der Gesellschaft*, Frankfurt/Main: Suhrkamp.

McClure, J. Derrick (1991) 'Translation and Transcreation in the Castalian Period', *Studies in Scottish Literature* 26: 185-198.

McVaugh, Michael (1974) 'Gerard of Cremona. A List of Translations made from Arabic into Latin in the Twelfth Century', in Edward Grant (ed) *A Source Book in Medieval Science*, Cambridge MA: Harvard University Press, 35-38.

Makdisi, George (1990) *The Rise of Humanism in Classical Islam and the Chris-tian West*, Edinburgh: The University Press.

Margalef, Ramón (1986) 'Variacions sobre el tema de la selecció natural. Ex-ploració, selecció i decisió en sistems complexos de poca energia', in Jorge Wagensberg (ed) *Procès a l'atzar*, Barcelona: Tusquets, 121-139.

Marx, C. W. (1991) 'Problems of Editing a Translation: Anglo-Norman to Middle English', in Roger Ellis (ed) *The Medieval Translator II*, London: Centre for Medieval Studies, Queen Mary and Westfield College, University of London, 253-267.

Menéndez Pelayo, Marcelino (1880-81) *Historia de los heterodoxos españoles*, 3 vols, Madrid: Librería Católica de San José.

Menéndez Pidal, Gonzalo (1951) 'Cómo trabajaron las escuelas alfonsíes', *Nueva Revista de Filología Hispánica* 5/4: 363-380.

Mercure de France / Neue Deutsche Rundschau (1895) 'Une enquête franco-allemande' / 'Die deutsch-französische Annäherung. Eine Umfrage bei Deutschen und Franzosen', *Mercure de France* 14/64: 1-65; 14/65: 235-236, *Neue Deutsche Rundschau* 6/1: 286-312, 412-413.

Mercure de France (1897) 'L'Alsace-Lorraine et l'état actuel des esprits', *Mercure de France* 24/96: 641-814.

Milton, John (1993) *O poder da tradução*, São Paulo: Ars Poetica.

Minnis, A. J. (1988) *Medieval Theory of Authorship. Scholastic literary attitudes in the later Middle Ages,* Aldershot: Scolar Press (first edition 1984).

Mitchell, Allan (1971) *Bismarck and the French Nation, 1848-1890*, New York: Pegasus.

Morgan, Bayard Quincy (1922) *Bibliography of German Literature in English Translation*, second edition, Stanford University Press, 1938.

Mounin, Georges (1965) *Teoria e storia della traduzione,* Turin: Einaudi.

Nord, Christiane (1991a) *Text Analysis in Translation. Theory, Method, and Di-dactic Application of a Model for Translation-Oriented Text Analysis*, trans. Christiane Nord and Penelope Sparrow, Amsterdam & Atlanta GA: Rodopi.

------ (1991b) 'Scopos, Loyalty, and Translational Conventions', *Target* 3/1: 91-109.

Nordau, Max (1892-93) *Entartung,* 2 vols, Berlin: Carl Dunder.

Norton, Glyn P. (1984) *The Ideology and Language of Translation in Renaissance France and Their Humanist Antecedents*, Geneva: Droz.

Paes, José Paulo (1990) *Tradução. A ponte necessária. Aspectos e problemas da arte de traduzir*, São Paulo: Atica.

Park, Robert E. (1928) 'Human Migration and the Marginal Man', *American Journal of Sociology* 33/8: 881-893.

Parsons, Talcott (1953) 'Some Comments on the State of the General Theory of Action', *American Sociological Review* 18: 618-631.

Pascua Febles, Isabel and Ana Luisa Peñate Soares (1991) *Introducción a los estudios de traducción*, Las Palmas de Gran Canaria: Corona.

Ponton, Rémy (1973) 'Programme esthétique et accumulation de capital symbolique. L'exemple du Parnasse', *Revue française de sociologie* 14: 202-220.

Poulle, Emmanuel (1987) 'Les Tables Alphonsines sont-elles d'Alphonse X?', in Mercè Comes et al. (eds) *De Astronomia Alphonsi Regis*, Barcelona: Universidad de Barcelona, Instituto Millás Vallicrosa de Historia de la ciencia árabe, 51-69.

Pound, Ezra (1920) 'Our Tetrarchal Précieuse (A Divagation from Jules Laforgue)', in *Instigations*, New York: Bori and Liverright, 253-263.

Pratt, Karen (1989) 'Direct Speech - A Key to the German Adaptor's Art?', in Jeanette Beer (ed) *Medieval Translators and their Craft*, Kalamazoo: Medieval Institute Publications, Western Michigan University, 213-246.

Proctor, Evelyn S. (1951) *Alfonso X of Castile. Patron of Literature and Learning*, Oxford: Clarendon Press.

Puchala, Donald J. and Raymond F. Hopkins (1983) 'International regimes: lessons from inductive analysis', in Stephen D. Krasner (ed) *International Regimes*, Ithica: Cornell University Press, 61-92.

Pym, Anthony (1992a) *Translation and Text Transfer. An Essay on the Principles of Intercultural Communication*, Frankfurt/Main, Berlin, Bern, New York, Paris, Vienna: Peter Lang.

------ (1992b) 'Shortcomings in the historiography of translation', *Babel* 38/4: 221-235.

------ (1992c) 'The Relations between Translation and Material Text Transfer', *Target* 4/2: 171-189.

------ (1993a) *Epistemological Problems in Translation and its Teaching*, Calaceit: Caminade.

------ (1993b) 'The Historical Failure of Brotherhood in International Cultural Regimes', *History of European Ideas* 16/1-3: 120-130.

------ (1993c) 'The Problem of Sovereignty in Regimes of European Literature Transfer', *New Comparison* 15: 137-146.

------ (1995a) 'Schleiermacher and the Problem of *Blendlinge*', *Translation and Literature* 4/1: 5-30.

------ (1995b) 'European Translation Studies, *une science qui dérange*, and Why Equivalence Needn't Be a Dirty Word', *TTR* 8/1: 153-176.

------ (1995c) 'Resistant Translation Strategies in Robert Lowell's *Imitations* and Ezra Pound's *Cantos*', in Christine Pagnoulle and Ian Mason (eds) *Cross-Words. Issues and Debates in Literary and Non-Literary Translating*, Liège: L3, 159-171.

Quandt, Regina (1987-88) *Schwedische Literatur in deutscher Übersetzung. 1830-1980*, ed. Fritz Paul and Heinz-Georg Halbe, 7 vols, Göttingen: Vandenhoeck & Ruprecht.

Quine, Willard Van Orman (1960) 'Translation and Meaning', chapter of *Word and Object*, Cambridge MA: MIT Press, 26-79.

Quirk, Randolph, Sidney Greenbaum, Geoffrey Leech, Jan Svartnik (1972) *A Grammar of Contemporary English*, London: Longman.

Rebell, Hughes (1895) 'Sur une traduction collective des œuvres de Nietzsche', *Mercure de France* 13: 98-102.

Reiss, Katharina and Hans J. Vermeer (1984) *Grundlegung einer allgemeinen Translationstheorie,* Tübingen: Niemeyer.

Rener, Frederick M. (1989) *Interpretatio. Language and Translation from Cicero to Tytler*, Amsterdam & Atlanta GA: Rodopi.

Richards, I. A. (1924) *Principles of Literary Criticism*, London: Kegan, Paul, Trench, Trubner.

Riet, Simone van (ed) (1972) *Avicenna Latinus. Liber de Anima seu Sextus de Naturalibus*, édition critique de la traduction latine médiévale, 2 vols, Louvain: Peeters.

Robinson, Douglas (1995) 'Theorizing Translation in a Woman's Voice. Subverting the Rhetoric of Patronage, Courtly Love and Morality', *The Translator* 1/2: 153-175.

------ (1996) *Translation and Taboo*, North Illinois University Press.

------ (1997) *Western Translation Theory from Herodotus to Nietzsche*, Manchester: St Jerome.

Romaine, Suzanne (1982) *Socio-Historical Linguistics: Its Status and Methodology*, Cambridge: Cambridge University Press.

Rosaldo, Renato (1989) *Culture and Truth: The Remaking of Social Analysis*, Boston: Beacon Press.

Rosengren, Karl Erik (1968) *Sociological Aspects of the Literary System*, Stockholm: Natur och Kultur.

Round, Nicholas (1993) '*Libro Llamado Fedrón', Plato's 'Phaedo' translated by Pero Díaz de Toledo,* London: Tamesis.

Ruggie, John G. (1975) 'International Responses to Technology: Concepts and Trends', *International Organization* 29/3: 557-584.

Russell, Peter (1985) *Traducciones y traductores en la península ibérica (1400-1550),* Bellaterra: Universitat Autònoma de Barcelona.

Salama-Carr, Myriam (1990) *La Traduction à l'époque abbaside. L'école de Hunayn Ibn Ishaq et son importance pour la traduction*, Paris: Didier Érudition.

Samsó, Julio (1987) 'Alfonso X and Arabic Astronomy', in Mercè Comes et al. (eds) *De Astronomia Alphonsi Regis,* Barcelona: Universidad de Barcelona, Instituto Millás Vallicrosa de Historia de la ciencia árabe, 23-38.

Santoyo, Julio-César (1987) *Teoría y crítica de la traducción: Antología*, Bellaterra: Universitat Autònoma de Barcelona.

Saussure, Ferdinand de (1916) *Cours de linguistique générale*, ed. Charles Bally and Albert Sechehaye; trans. Wade Baskin *Course in General Linguistics*, Glasgow: Fontana Collins, 1974.

Schaeffer, Louis Edouard (1962) 'Écrivains alsaciens médiateurs entre la pensée allemande et la pensée française: Henri Albert et Nietzsche, Schuré et Wagner', *Les Lettres en Alsace* 8: 363-368.

Schiff, Mario (1905) *La Bibliothèque du Marquis de Santillane*, Paris: Bouillon.

Schlawe, Fritz (1961) *Literarische Zeitschriften. Teil 1. 1885-1910*, Stuttgart: Metzler.

Schleiermacher, Friedrich (1813) 'Ueber die verschiedenen Methoden des Uebersezens', reprinted in Hans Joachim Störig (ed) *Das Problem des Übersetzens*, Darmstadt: Wissenschaftliche Buchgesellschaft, 1963, 38-70.

Schlösser, Anselm (1937) *Die englische Literatur in Deutschland von 1895 bis 1934*, Jena: Verlag der Frommannschen Buchhandlung Walter Biedermann.

Schockenhoff, Andreas (1986) *Henri Albert und das Deutschlandbild des Mercure de France 1890-1905*, Frankfurt/Main: Lang.

Séguinot, Candace (1988) 'Pragmatics and the Explicitation Hypothesis', *TTR* 1/2: 106-113.

Simmel, Georg (1971) 'The Stranger', trans. Robert Park and Ernest Burgess in Donald N. Levine (ed) *On Individuality and Social Forms*, Chicago: University of Chicago Press, 143-149 (original in *Soziologie*, Berlin 1908).

Snell-Hornby, Mary (1988) *Translation Studies. An Integrated Approach*, Amsterdam & Philadelphia: John Benjamins.

------ (1991) 'Translation Studies – Art, Science or Utopia?', in Kitty M. van Leuven-Zwart and Ton Naaijkens (eds) *Translation Studies: The State of the Art*, Amsterdam & Atlanta GA: Rodopi, 13-23.

Stackelberg, Jürgen von (1972) *Literarische Rezeptionsformen. Übersetzung, Supplement, Parodie*, Frankfurt/Main: Athenäum.

Steiner, George (1975) *After Babel. Aspects of Language and Translation*, London, Oxford, New York: Oxford University Press.

Steiner, T. R. (1975) *English Translation Theory, 1650 – 1800*, Assen: Van Gorcum.

Steinschneider, Moritz (1904-05) *Die europäischen Übersetzungen aus dem Arabischen bis Mitte des 17. Jahrhunderts*, reprint, Graz: Akademische Druck- u. Verlagsanstalt, 1956.

Störig, Hans Joachim (ed) (1963) *Das Problem des Übersetzens*, Darmstadt: Wissenschaftliche Buchgesellschaft.

St-Pierre, Paul (1993) 'Translation as a Discourse of History', *TTR* 6/3: 61-82.

Sudhoff, Karl (ed) (1917) 'Daniels von Morley *Liber de naturis inferiorum et superiorum*, nach der Handschrift Cod. Arundel 377 des Britischen Museums zum Abdruck gebracht', *Archiv für die Geschichte der Naturwissenschaften und der Technik* 8/3: 1-40.

Tarde, Gabriel (1895) *La logique sociale*, Paris: Alcan.

Thorndike, Lynn (1923) *A History of Magic and Experimental Science during the First Thirteen Centuries of our Era*, vols 1-2, London: Macmillan.

Toury, Gideon (1980) *In Search of a Theory of Translation*, Tel Aviv: The Porter Institute for Poetics and Semiotics.

------ (1985) 'A Rationale for Descriptive Translation Studies', in Theo Hermans (ed) *The Manipulation of Literature: Studies in Literary Translation,* London & Sydney: Croom Helm, 16-41.

------ (1991) 'What are Descriptive Studies into Translation Likely to Yield apart from Isolated Descriptions?', in Kitty M. van Leuven-Zwart and Ton Naaijkens eds *Translation Studies: The State of the Art*, Amsterdam & Atlanta GA: Rodopi, 179-192.

------ (1992) '"Everything has its Price": An Alternative to Normative Conditioning in Translator Training', *Interface* 6/2: 60-72.

------ (1995) *Descriptive Translation Studies and beyond*, Amsterdam & Philadelphia: Benjamins.

Van Hoof, Henri (1986) *Petite histoire de la traduction en Occident,* Louvain-La-Neuve: Cabay.

------ (1991) *Histoire de la traduction en Occident. France, Grande-Bretagne, Allemagne, Russie, Pays-Bas,* Louvain-La-Neuve: Duculot.

Vaucaire, Maurice (1907) 'Salomé à travers l'art et la littérature', *La Nouvelle Revue* 46/2: 145-152.

Venuti, Lawrence (1992) 'Introduction', in Lawrence Venuti (ed) *Rethinking Translation. Discourse, Subjectivity, Ideology*, London & New York: Routledge, 1-17.

------ (1995) *The Translator's Invisibility. A History of Translation*, London & New York: Routledge.

Vermeer, Hans J. (1989) *Skopos und Translationsauftrag*, Heidelberg: Institut für Übersetzen und Dolmetschen.

------ (1992) *Skizzen zu einer Geschichte der Translation,* vols 1-2, Frankfurt/Main: Verlag für Interkulturelle Kommunikation.

------ (1996) *Das Übersetzen im Mittelalter (13. und 14. Jahrhundert)*, 2 vols, Heidelberg: TEXTconTEXT.

Vernet, Juan (1978) *La cultura hispanoárabe en Oriente y Occidente,* Barcelona: Ariel.

------ (1984) 'Alfonso X y la astronomía', *Boletín de la Real Academia de la Historia* 181: 349-370.

Weber, Eugen (1976) *Peasants into Frenchmen. The Modernization of Rural France, 1870-1914*, Stanford: Stanford University Press.

Wyler, Lia (1993) 'Public Perception of Translation in Brazil', Paper presented to the 13th FIT World Congress, Brighton.

------ (1995) *A tradução no Brasil. Oficio invisível de incorporar o outro*, Dissertation, Rio de Janeiro: Universidade Federal do Rio de Janeiro, Centro de Filosofia e Ciências Humanas, Escola de Comunicação.

Wyzewa, Théodore de (1896) 'La Jeunesse de Frédéric Nietzsche', *Revue des Deux-Mondes* (4ème période) 133: 688-699.

Index of Names & Topics